IMAGES
of America

TRI VALLEY

COBLESKILL TO COLLIERSVILLE

I0812873

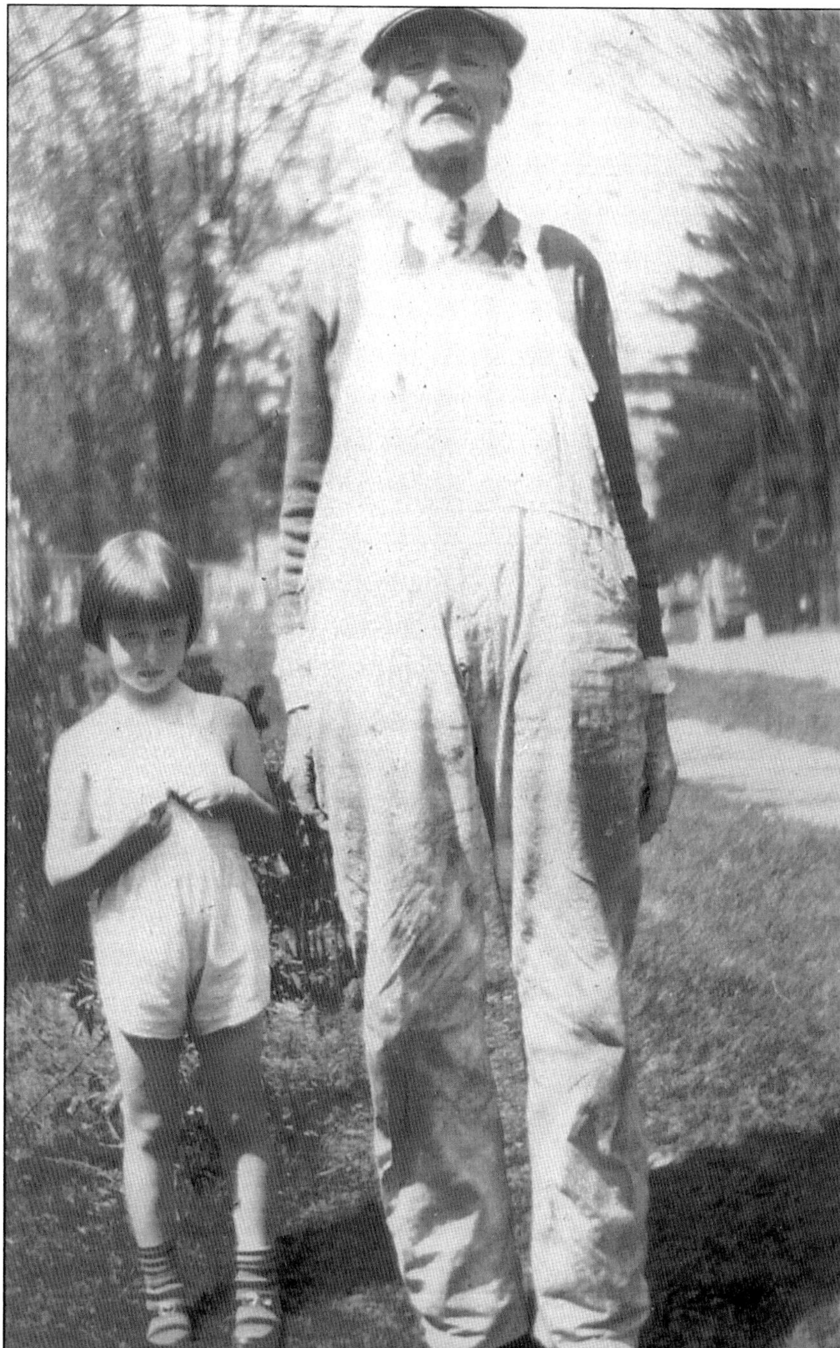

IN MEMORY. I would like to dedicate this book to the memory of my grandfather Franklin M. Wright, who was killed on August 2, 1937, when he was struck by a southbound train. My grandfather, who was deaf, did not hear the frantic blasts of the train's whistle. A paperhanger and painter by trade, he also played the snare drum in the Worcester Band. His obituary said, "He was a man of the highest character, an honored and respected citizen, and a man whose friends are numbered in legions." (The author is shown with her grandfather c. 1936.)

IMAGES
of America

TRI VALLEY

COBLESKILL TO COLLIERSVILLE

Marilyn E. Dufresne

ARCADIA
PUBLISHING

Copyright © 2001 by Marilyn E. Dufresne
ISBN 978-0-7385-0932-7

Published by Arcadia Publishing
Charleston, South Carolina

Printed in the United States of America

Library of Congress Catalog Card Number: 2001091710

For all general information contact Arcadia Publishing at:
Telephone 843-853-2070
Fax 843-853-0044
E-Mail sales@arcadiapublishing.com

Visit us on the Internet at www.arcadiapublishing.com

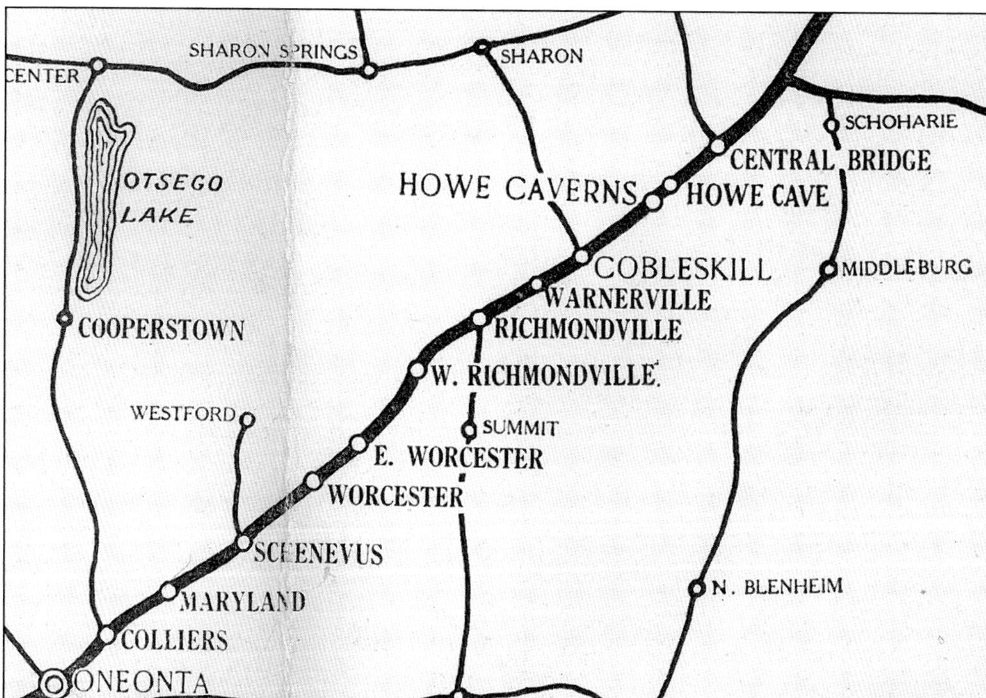

The Tri Valley Area. This map details the New York State area covered in this book. Route 7 through the valley is also known as the Schohanna Trail.

Contents

Acknowledgments

My appreciation goes to all the individuals who helped with research on this book: Jo-ann Corsall, director Marie Bruni, and Fran Green of the New York State Room at the Huntington Memorial Library in Oneonta, and the New York State Library in Cooperstown. Thanks to the following individuals for the loan of their postcards: Dick Mostar of Cobleskill, Ernest and Esther Banks of Richmondville, Ruth All and Sidney Chase of Worcester, and the Worcester Historical Society. Thanks to my brother Willard, who recalled local events that might otherwise have been forgotten.

Thanks to my daughter and son-in-law, Debbie and Mike Woods, for their advice, encouragement, and proofreading assistance. Also, thanks to my husband, Charles, for putting up with me the last few months.

INTRODUCTION

The Tri Valley area is located along New York State Route 7 from Oneonta, the City of the Hills, through Otsego County up Cobleskill way. Winding streams meandering through rolling hills and green valleys eventually join the Susquehanna River.

Peaceful as it might seem, hardships were many for the early settlers in the 1800s. They could not take part in the hustle and bustle of the outside world.

A farmer from the Tri Valley area might have to spend three days traveling along dirt roads to take produce, perhaps a load of cabbage, to an Albany market for sale. In the days before market day, provisions would be packed and produce gathered. The farmer was kept busy in the barn, packing a bundle of hay and binding it with straw rope to keep it from falling out of the wagon. His nights on the road were spent sleeping under the wagon. For maximum cash return, buying food for himself and the horses was not even contemplated. All of this would change with the advent of the railroad.

Rail service from Albany to Binghamton, once a dream, came to pass in 1865 with completion of the Albany & Susquehanna Railroad. Farmers in the Tri Valley could now ship by rail their produce and goods, including eggs, cabbage, potatoes, hops, milk, and flagstone for city sidewalks.

A whole new world became available to country folks. Towns and cities grew. Employment opportunities with the railroad were many, and farmers invested in bigger herds because larger quantities of milk, butter, and cheese could reach a city market.

By 1880, the Delaware & Hudson Canal Company had purchased the Albany & Susquehanna Railroad. The railroad, now operating as the Delaware & Hudson, began to grow as more freight was shipped and as more passengers visited relatives far away, shopped in the city, or attended a country fair. People were dependent on rail service.

Oneonta became an important hub in the Delaware & Hudson expansion. The roundhouse, station, and rail yards were known nationwide. Little stations sprung up all along the tracks in Maryland, Schenevus, Worcester, East Worcester, Richmondville, Cobleskill, Central Bridge, and other thriving small towns.

Almost a century later, in 1965, the last passenger train steamed through the Tri Valley area. The decline in carloads between 1967 and 1974 resulted in a deal between the Delaware & Hudson Canal Company and the Norfolk and Western Railroad, which served as a holding company. Guilford Transportation Inc. purchased the Delaware & Hudson in 1984. By 1988, Guilford had put the railroad into bankruptcy. Canadian Pacific Rail, anxious to acquire routes to East Coast ports in the United States, purchased the bankrupt Delaware & Hudson in 1991. Some small-town stations were torn down. Some found new life as restaurants and storage facilities. Others remained vacant, thus closing a chapter in railroad history.

Diesel freight trains still travel the rails through the Tri Valley area, but the days of passenger service have disappeared, gone like those great billows of smoke that once rose from majestic steam engines making their way through green hills.

Bibliography

A Bicentennial History of the Town of Worcester. Fort Orange Press, 1997.

Bullard, Sandra Martin. *Hop Time.* Cooperstown, New York: Barton-Butler Graphics, 1998.

Fielder, Dorothy Scott. *A Pictorial History of the Town of Maryland.* The Town of Maryland Historical Society, 1990.

Noyes, Marion F. *A History of Schoharie County.* 1957.

Shaughnessy, Jim. *Delaware & Hudson.* Howell-North Books, 1967.

Thurber, Walter A. *The Great Bear Light and Power Company.* Oneonta, New York: Village Printer.

The Sloughters' History of Schoharie County. Schoharie County Historical Society, 1994.

Otsego Stories. The Storytelling Center of Oneonta, 1995.

Files and Resources

Worcester Historical Society.

New York State Historical Library, Cooperstown, New York.

Cobleskill Public Library.

New York State Room of Huntington Memorial Library, Oneonta, New York.

The *Worcester Times* microfilm.

One

Cobleskill and Surrounding Area

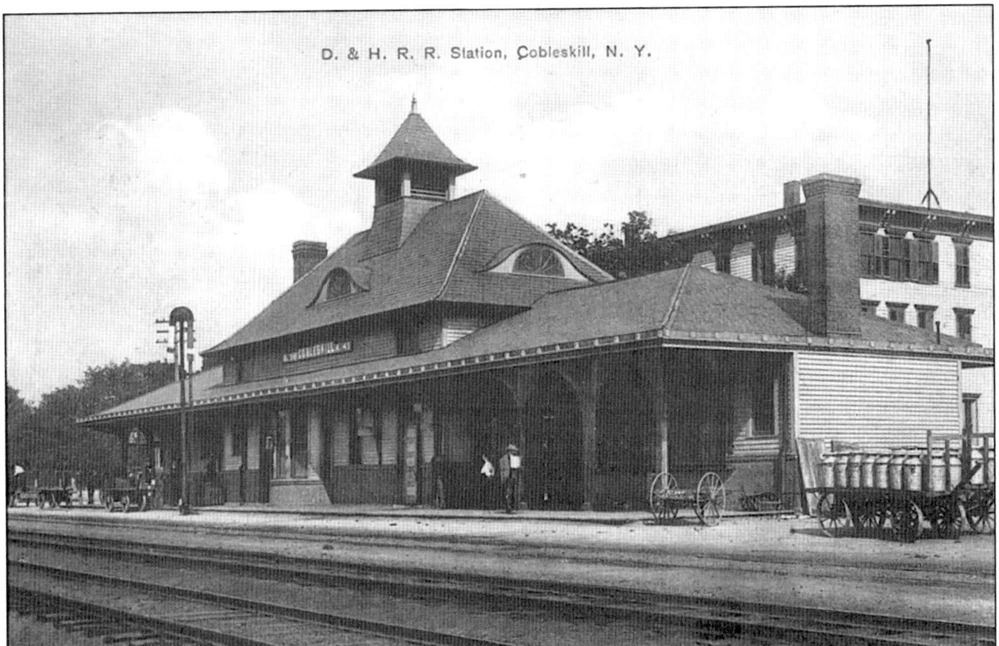

Delaware & Hudson Railroad Station, Cobleskill. Local farmer Monroe Shafer opposed the coming of the railroad and "hoped he would die before he ever saw a train rolling across his farm." He got his wish, passing away the day before the first train arrived in the village. The railroad became a great stimulus to the village of Cobleskill, which, within 10 years, became the most populous village in Schoharie County.

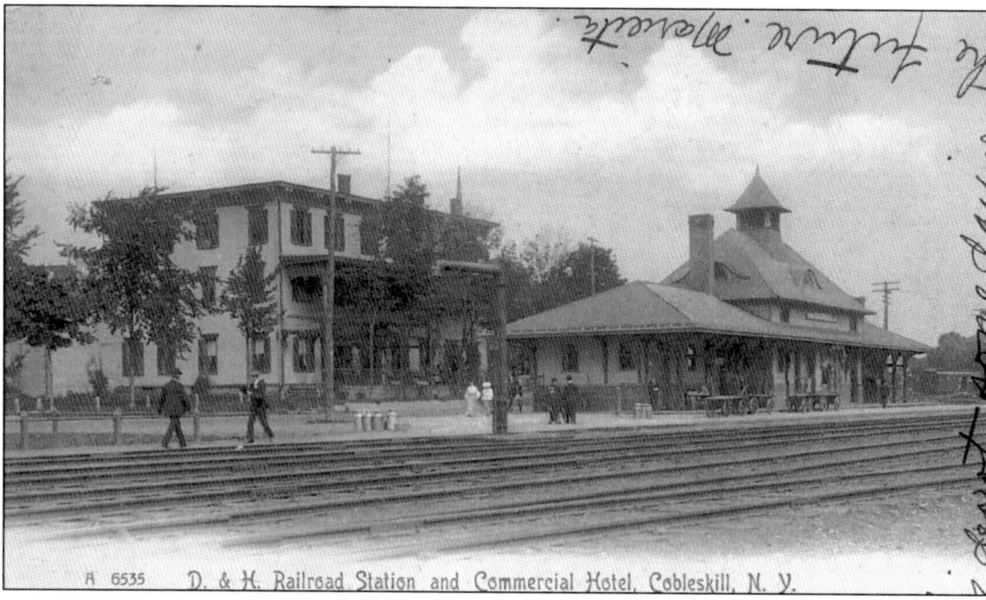

COBLESKILL STATION AND COMMERCIAL HOTEL. This 1906 postcard shows the proximity of the train station to the hotel that was available to disembarking passengers just across the street. Jacob H. Mann, senior editor of the *Cobleskill Index,* had a custom of waking early each morning and walking up the tracks to get breakfast at the hotel restaurant. He was killed instantly on Wednesday, September 7, 1932, when hit by a train. The hotel is no longer there, and the station has served as a unique dining area for several years.

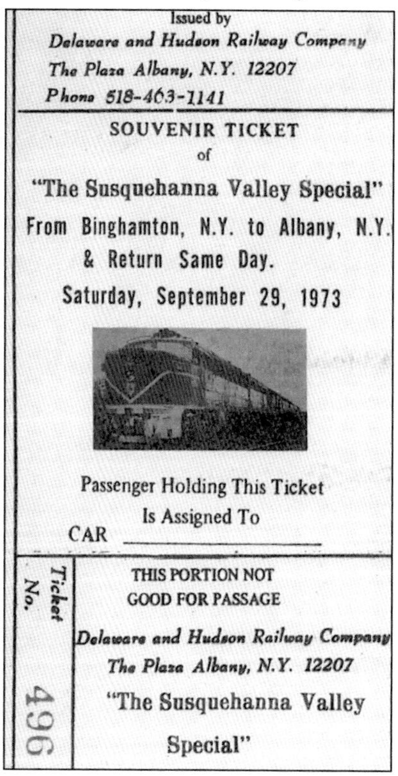

Issued by
Delaware and Hudson Railway Company
The Plaza Albany, N.Y. 12207
Phone 518-463-1141

SOUVENIR TICKET
of
"The Susquehanna Valley Special"
From Binghamton, N.Y. to Albany, N.Y.
& Return Same Day.
Saturday, September 29, 1973

Passenger Holding This Ticket
Is Assigned To
CAR ______________

Ticket No. 496

THIS PORTION NOT
GOOD FOR PASSAGE
Delaware and Hudson Railway Company
The Plaza Albany, N.Y. 12207
"The Susquehanna Valley
Special"

A SOUVENIR TICKET. On Saturday, September 29, 1973, the Delaware & Hudson issued special tickets for "the Susquehanna Valley Special." The train trip, which traveled the same route as in earlier days, was from Binghamton to Albany.

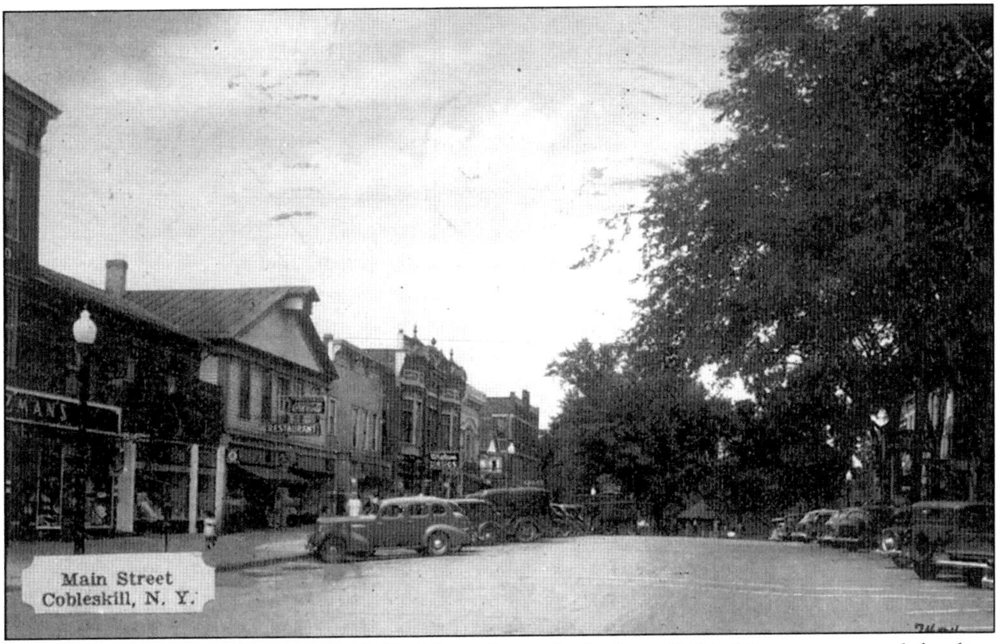

Main Street. This is how Cobleskill's Main Street looked in 1944. Vintage automobiles line the street, and the popular Empire restaurant (now located several miles out of town) can be seen. The building at the far left, Weitzman's clothing store, was destroyed several years ago by arson.

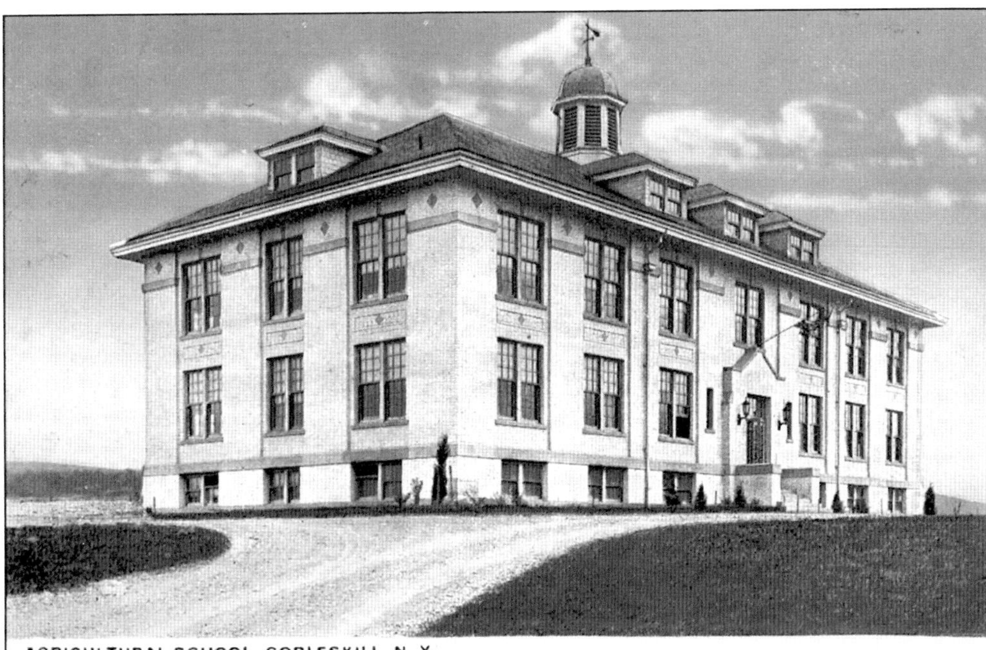

The Agricultural School. This 1919 postcard shows the old agricultural school. What was one building in the early 1900s has now multiplied into a large campus called State University of New York (SUNY) at Cobleskill.

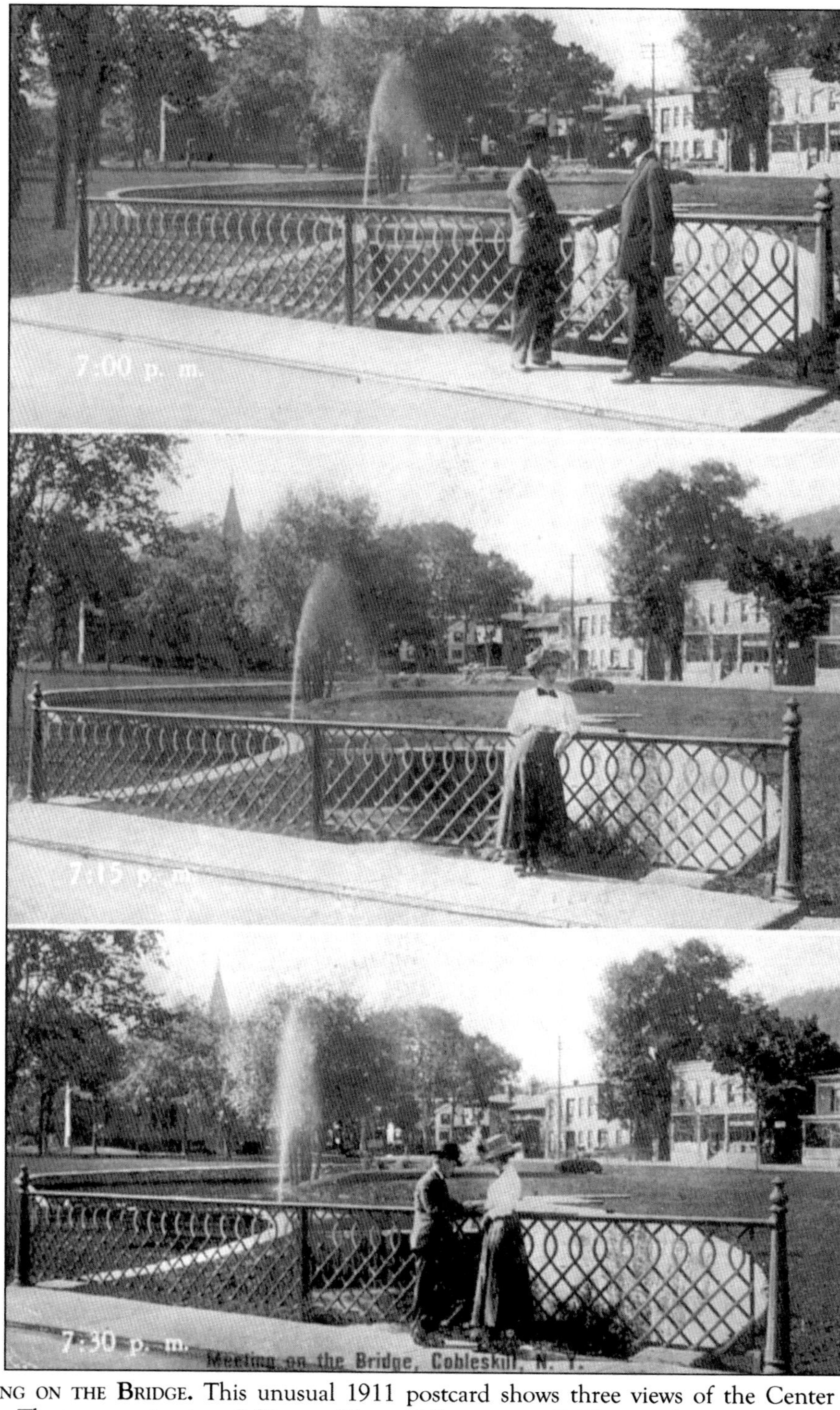

Meeting on the Bridge. This unusual 1911 postcard shows three views of the Center Park Bridge. The top meeting is at 7:00 p.m. The middle scene, at 7:15 p.m., shows a young woman waiting. At 7:30 p.m., one of the men returns to meet the woman. It is fun to imagine what the connections were between these three people.

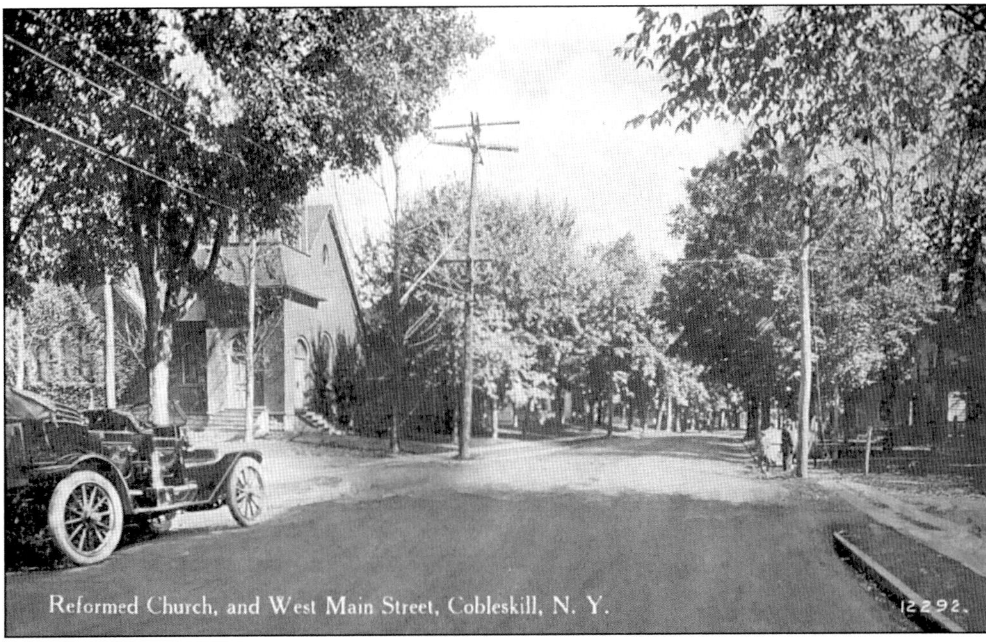

THE REFORMED CHURCH AND WEST MAIN STREET. This tree-lined portion of Main Street offers a view of Cobleskill in the early 1920s. The church originated in 1886 and is now a Masonic Temple. Note the touring car with the large tires and wooden-spoked wheels. There were not many cars on the roads during that period. Leland Hodge was the first person in the village to own a car. He traveled by train to Binghamton to pick up the new vehicle and drive home. When the weather turned bad, he abandoned the car in Otego and returned home by train.

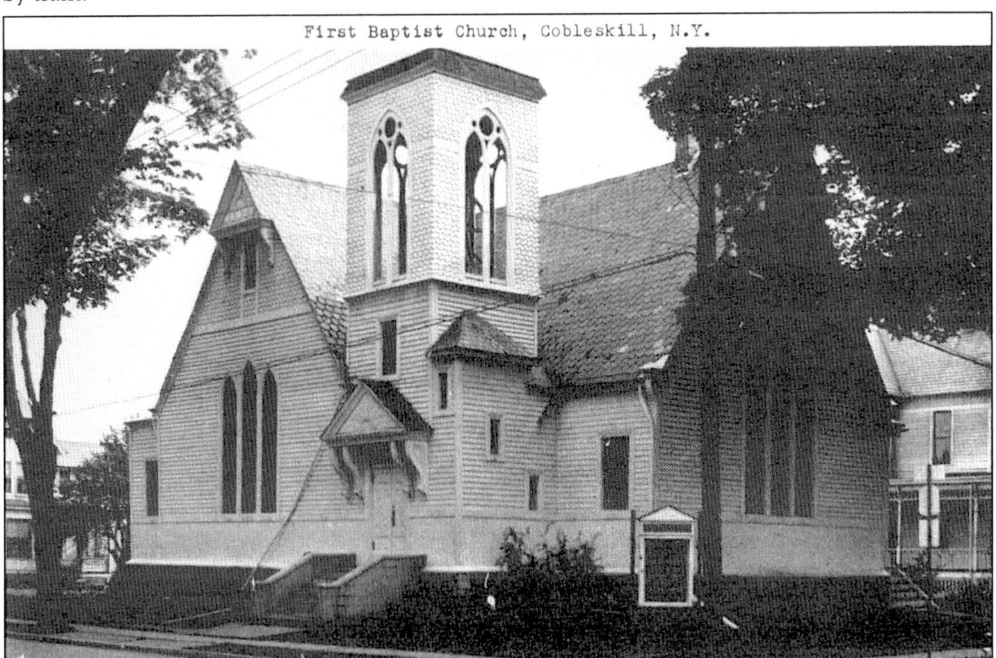

THE FIRST BAPTIST CHURCH. This church still stands at its original location on Main Street.

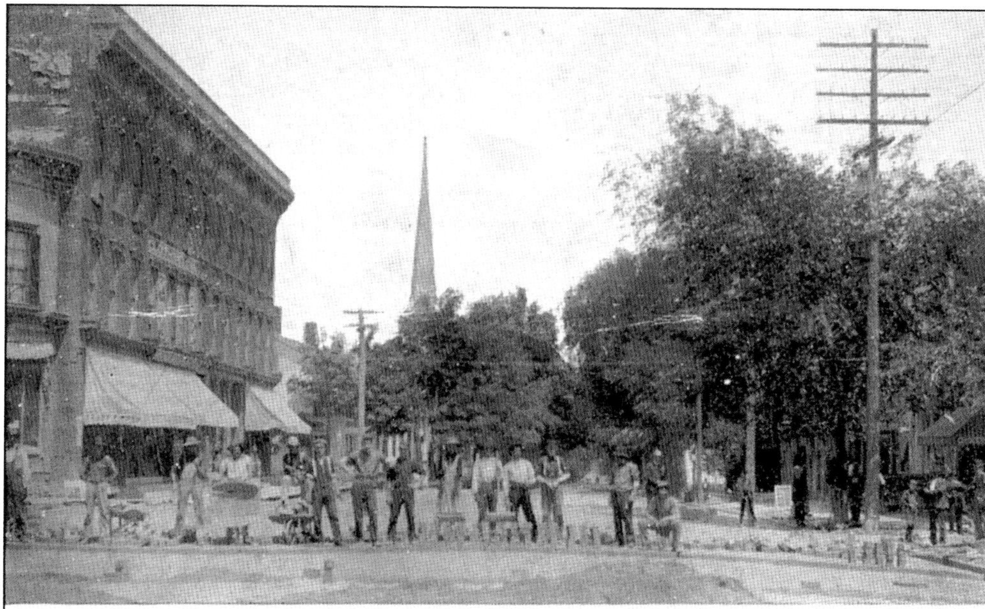

Main Street, Cobleskill, N. Y. Brick work built by T. E. Miller.

Brick Work on Main Street. T.E. Miller and his crew work on the road; the workers seem to be lining Main Street with bricks, probably upgrading the street from a dirt road. In 1903, five townspeople owned cars, which could have prompted the demand for better streets.

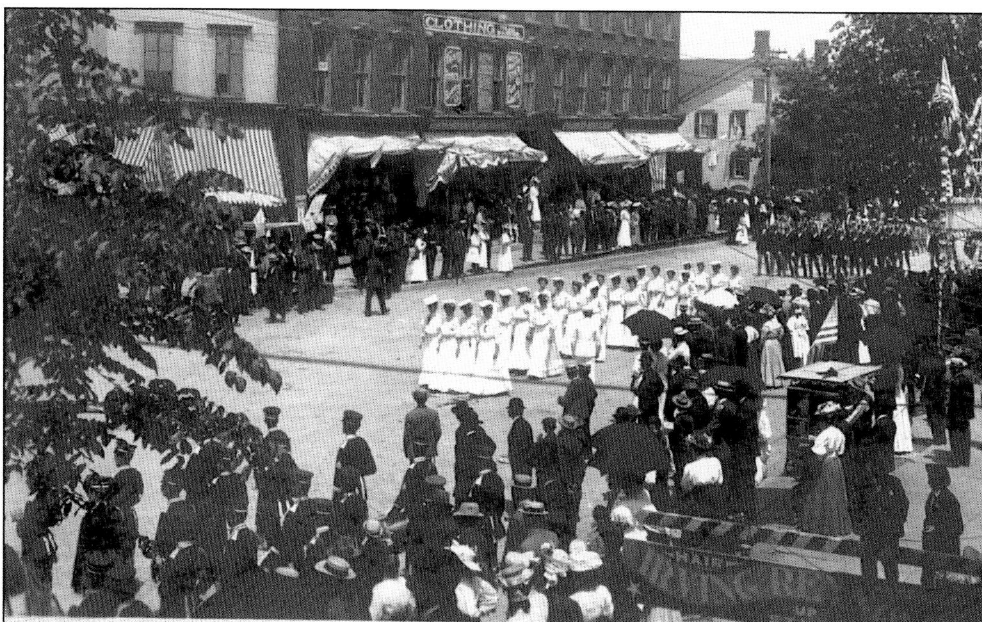

Worcester Girls, July 4th, at Cobleskill.

A Fourth of July Celebration. Everyone loves a parade. Girls from Worcester, dressed in white gowns and fancy hats, take part in the Fourth of July celebration on Cobleskill's Main Street c. 1930.

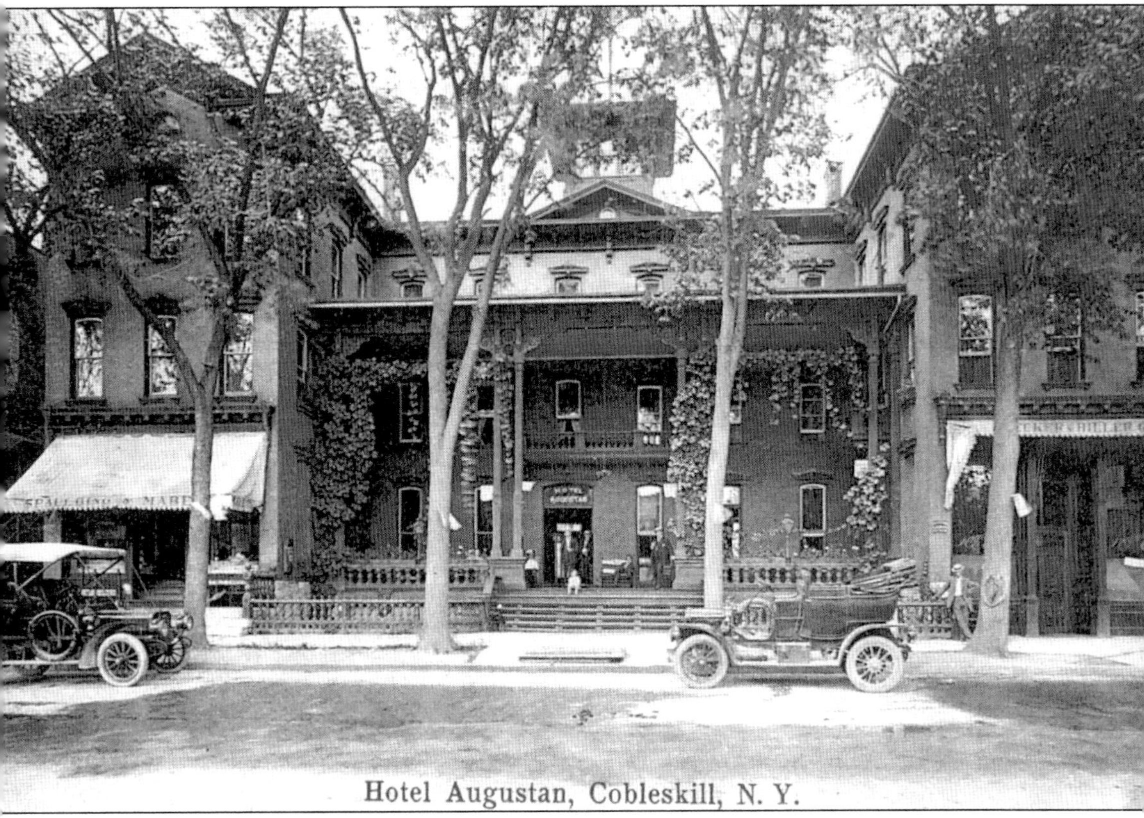

THE HOTEL AUGUSTAN. In 1867, Augustus C. Smith repaired a house built in 1815 by Lambert Lawyer, a wealthy elderly man. The building was in ashes in 1873 and, in 1875, Smith built the brick Hotel Augustan on the grounds occupied by the old building, plus some land to the east as far as School Street. Smith was an energetic executive who anticipated that there would be rapid growth in the village once the railroad arrived. Note the old cars in this early photograph of the hotel, which is now a furniture store and showroom.

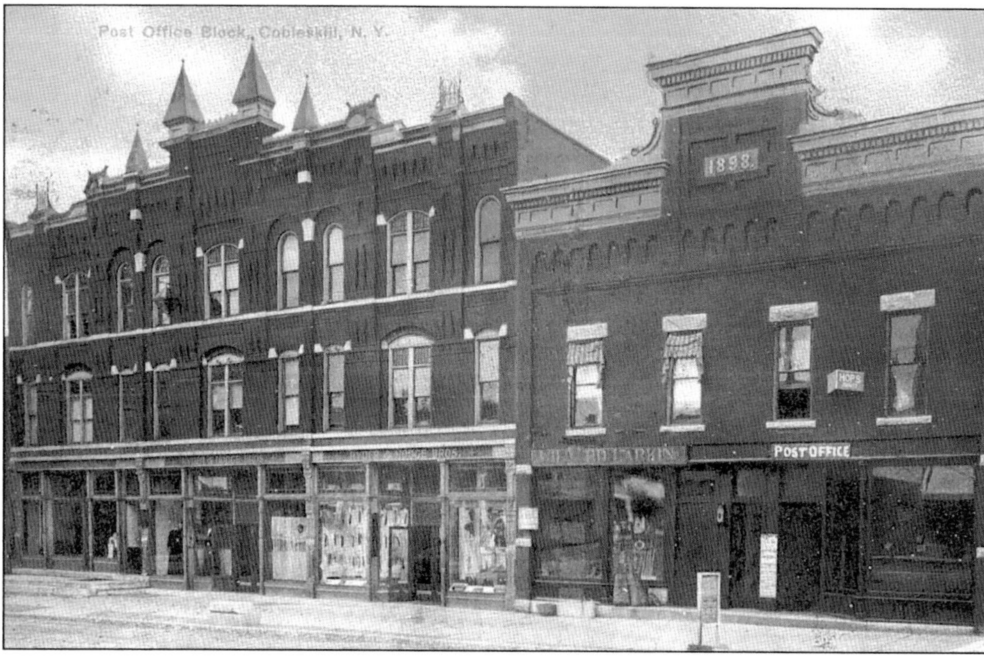

THE POST OFFICE BLOCK. This 1898 brick block on Main Street was once home to the local post office. For many years, a five-and-dime store was located on the left side of the building. The message on the reverse of the card, written in 1909 by 13-year-old Leah Wade, states that she had to stand up all the way on the train from Richmondville to Cobleskill—a trip of about five miles. The card, addressed to Leah's mother in Richmondville, also states that she and her sister "will be careful because we know you will worry."

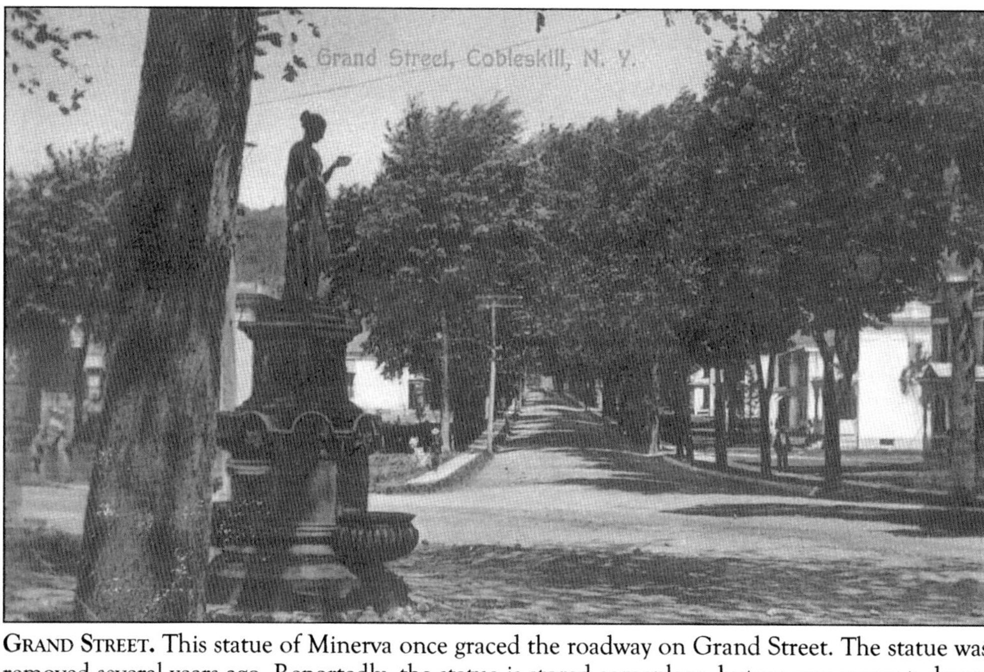

GRAND STREET. This statue of Minerva once graced the roadway on Grand Street. The statue was removed several years ago. Reportedly, the statue is stored someplace, but no one seems to know where.

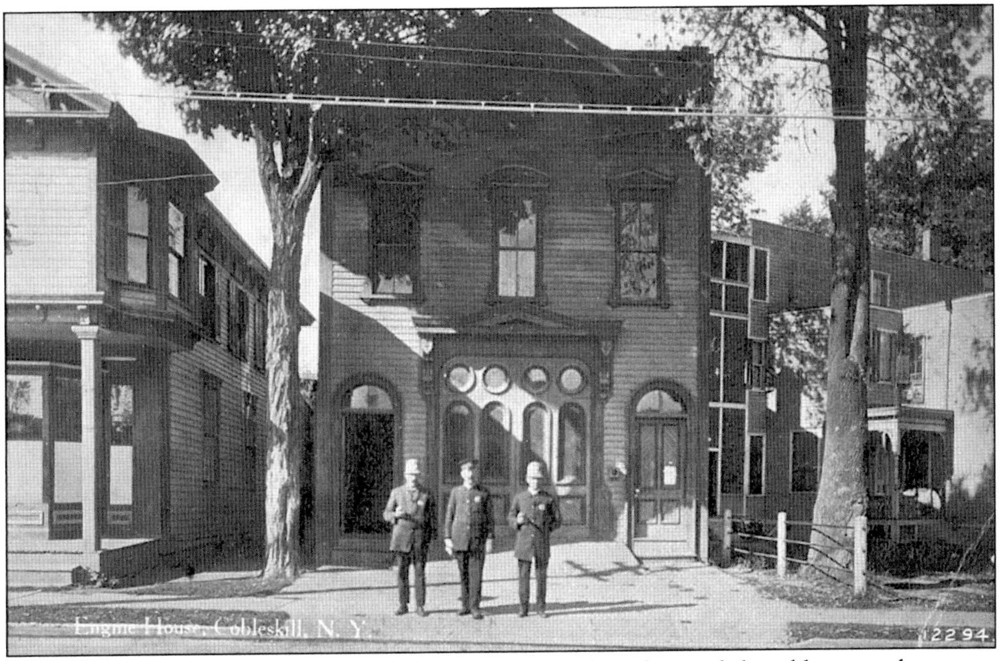

THE ENGINE HOUSE. Three uniformed firefighters stand in front of the old engine house on Main Street. The two-story building, across from the park, probably had a meeting room upstairs. Downstairs there would be room for a one-horse ladder truck and possibly a steam pumper. The building, now a beauty salon, is a good example of early-1900s architecture.

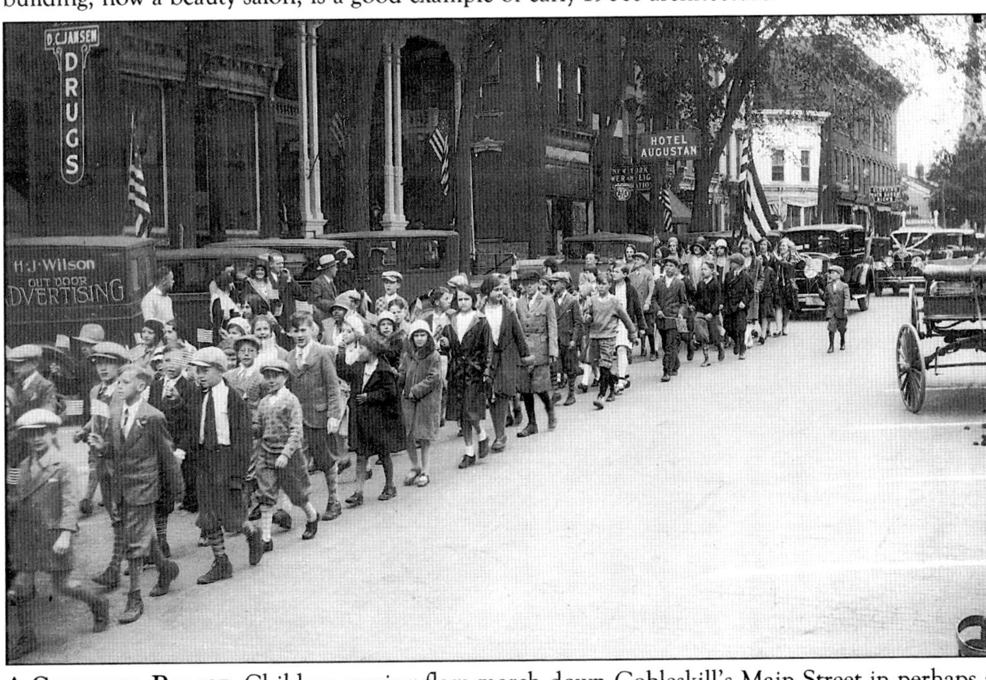

A COBLESKILL PARADE. Children waving flags march down Cobleskill's Main Street in perhaps a Fourth of July parade or in association with an event at the fairgrounds. Knickers and caps on the boys and cotton stockings or ankle socks on the girls are very different from the unisex blue jeans of today. More flags and decorated cars complete the parade.

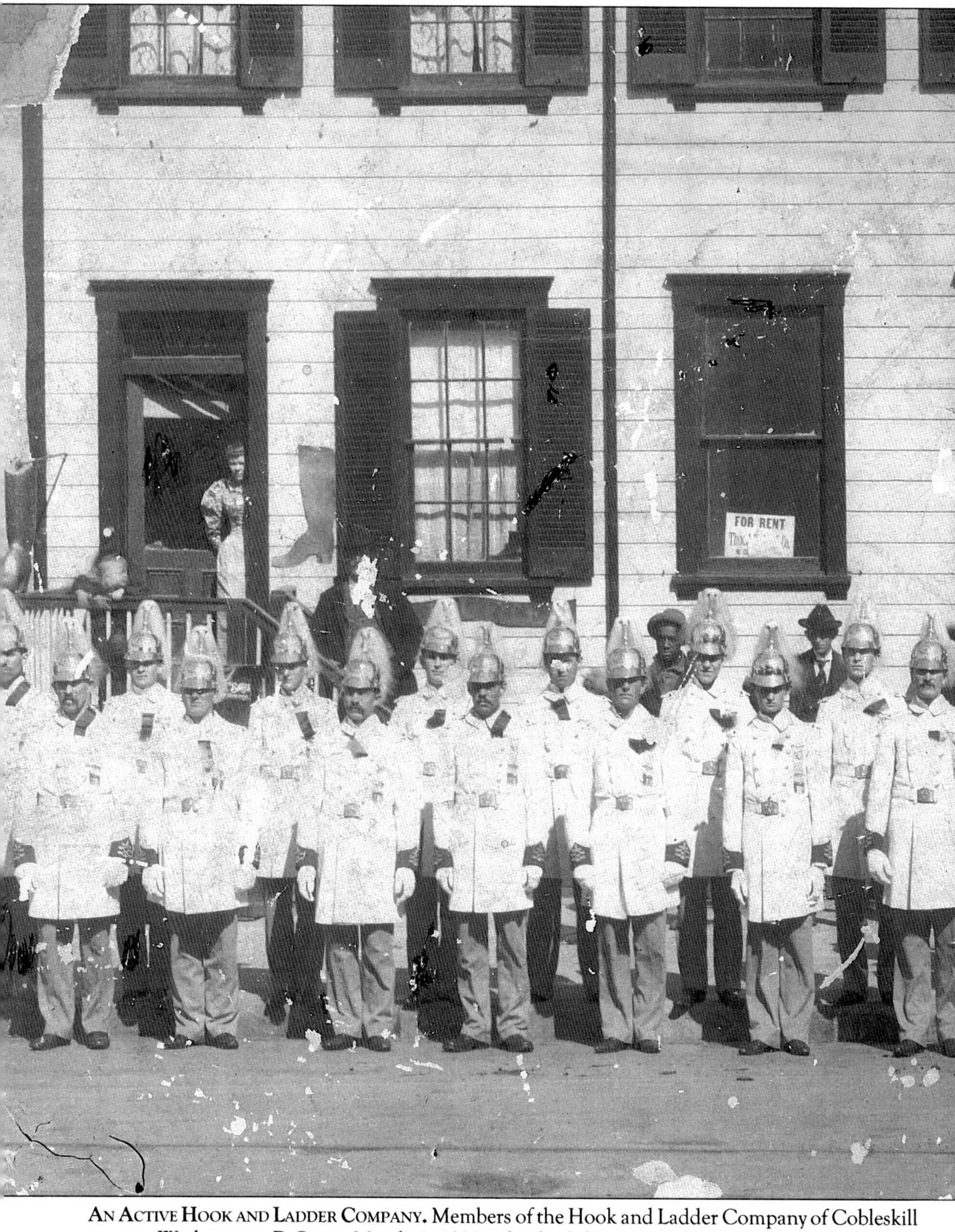

An Active Hook and Ladder Company. Members of the Hook and Ladder Company of Cobleskill were in Washington, D.C., on March 4, 1897. The firefighters took the train from Cobleskill to Washington to march in the inaugural parade. This photograph was taken on 13th Street in the nation's capital. Republican William McKinley served as president from 1897 to 1901, when he

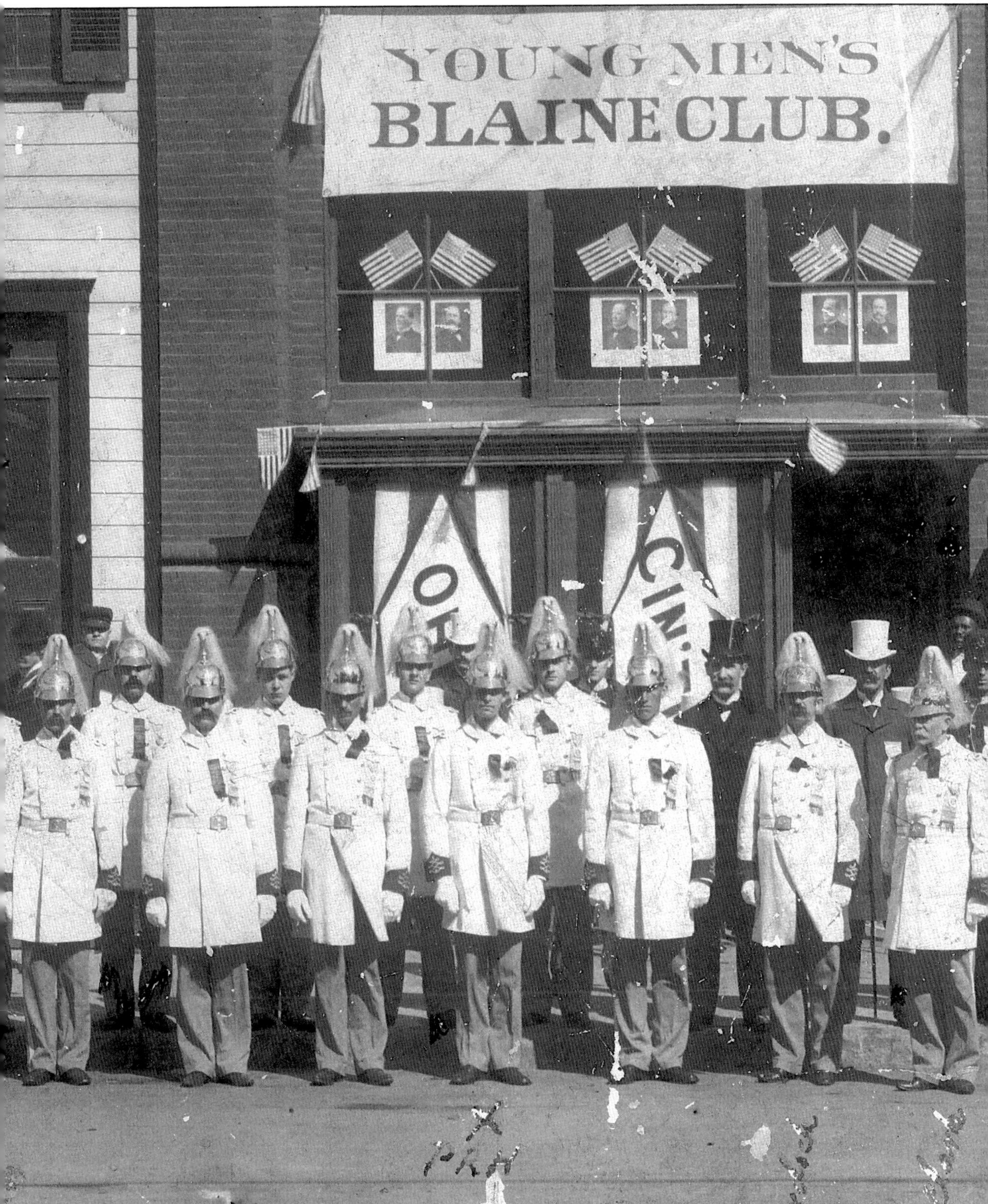

was assassinated. The 11th man from the left is Porter R. Hadsell, who later became chief of the Worcester Fire Department. The 13th man from the left is Reverend Murdock. At the far right is the "Captain of the Clave."

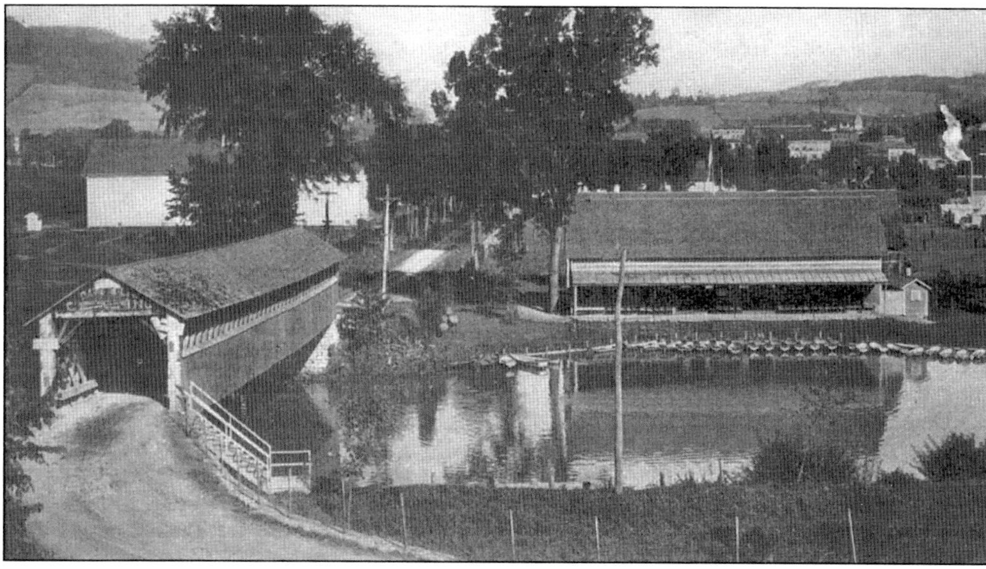

Barner Bridge and Boathouse. This single-span covered bridge and boathouse were once located on Cobleskill Creek, adjacent to the fairground. This creek caused flooding to the fairground in September 1938. A total of 3.75 inches of rain fell in 24 hours. The bridge was put out of commission in 1914 when a support was snapped by a large truck with 35 passengers on the way to the Cobleskill Fair. Traffic had to be rerouted to Warnerville. An iron bridge replaced the covered span. Later, the boathouse was moved to the fair's western entrance and enlarged; it is now part of the fair's office.

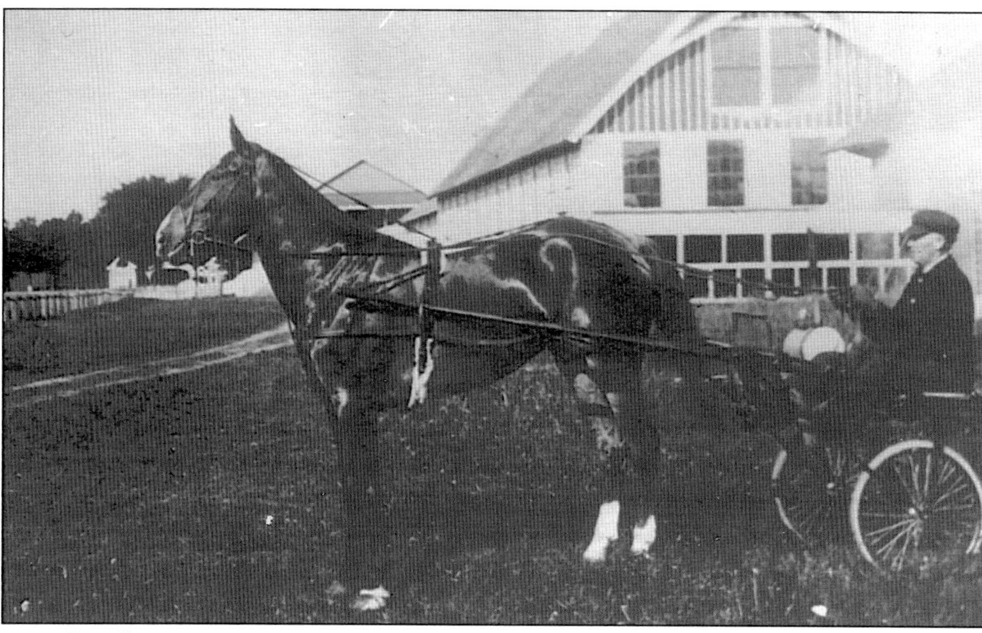

Elias "Lite" Rickard and His Trotter. The Cobleskill Fair brought out the best in horse racing. Worcester's Elias "Lite" Rickard and his trotter took part in the sulky races year after year. Cobleskill is only about 17 miles from Worcester, so many racing fans from that town attended the event.

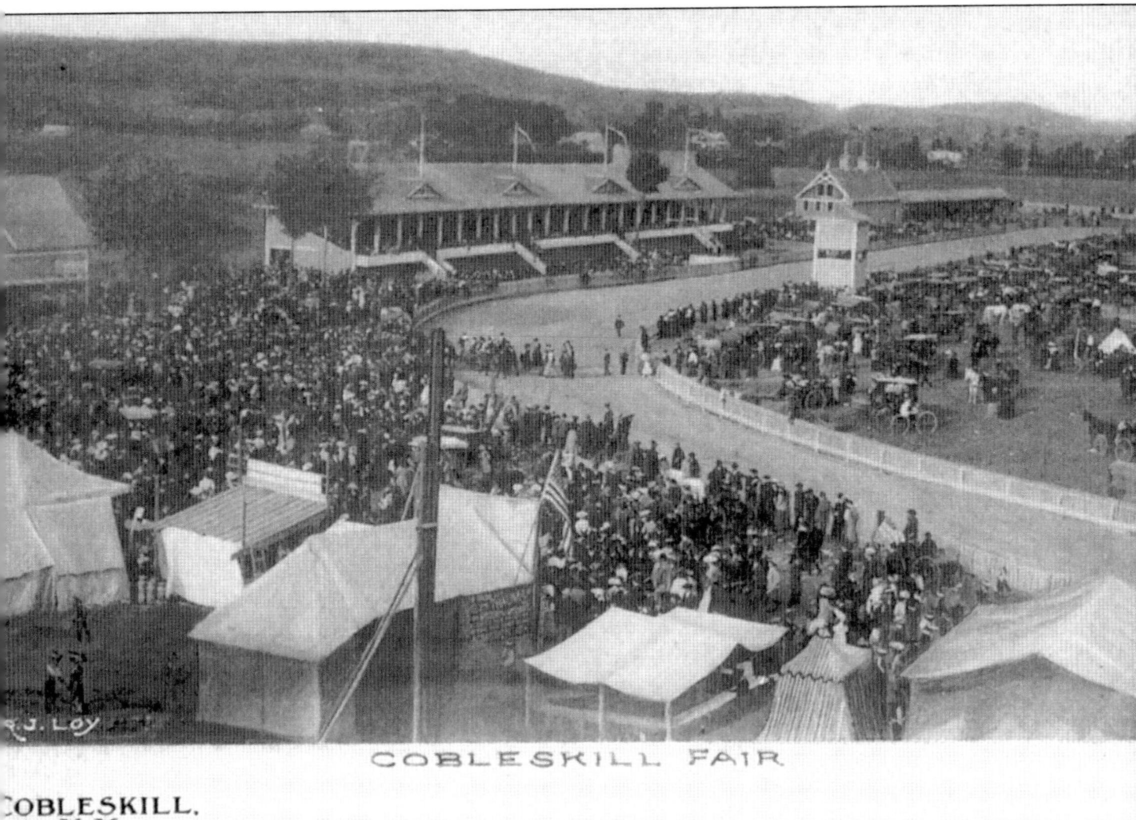

The Cobleskill Fair. The famous Cobleskill Fair began in 1876 when a group of public-spirited men formed an agricultural society. The first stock show and fair took place from September 20 to 22, 1876, and was a resounding success. Farmers and their wives brought horses, stock, produce, and household articles to exhibit. During the presidential campaign of 1900, William Jennings Bryan, one of the greatest orators of his time, spoke to an overflow crowd at the fairground. After speaking, he departed on a special train. The first automobile to be seen in Cobleskill chugged onto the fairground in September 1901. In 1938, following a three-day rain, Cobleskill Creek crested its banks and flooded the fairground, in some places to a depth of three feet. Officials ordered the grounds cleared of livestock and people. Pride is reflected in the design of the exhibition buildings, fashioned after the Centennial of Independence for the colonies in Philadelphia in the late 1800s. Fancy woodwork, wooden roof crests, gingerbread arches, and whimsical window frames highlight the buildings of this fair, which is more than 100 years old. The fair was not only a time to express pride in the harvest but also a time for celebration before winter set in.

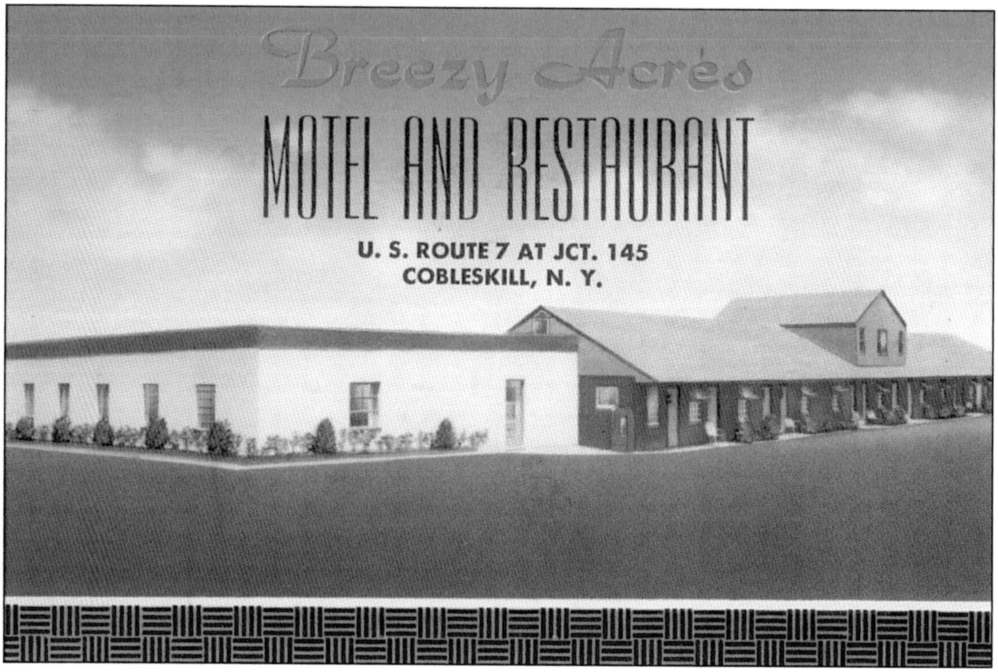

Breezy Acres. Once located three miles east of Cobleskill, this motel and restaurant was torn down in the 1970s when the land was sold to New York State as Interstate 88 was in the planning stages. The motel had 22 units and 8 cabins and was popular since it was near the famous tourist attraction Howe Caverns.

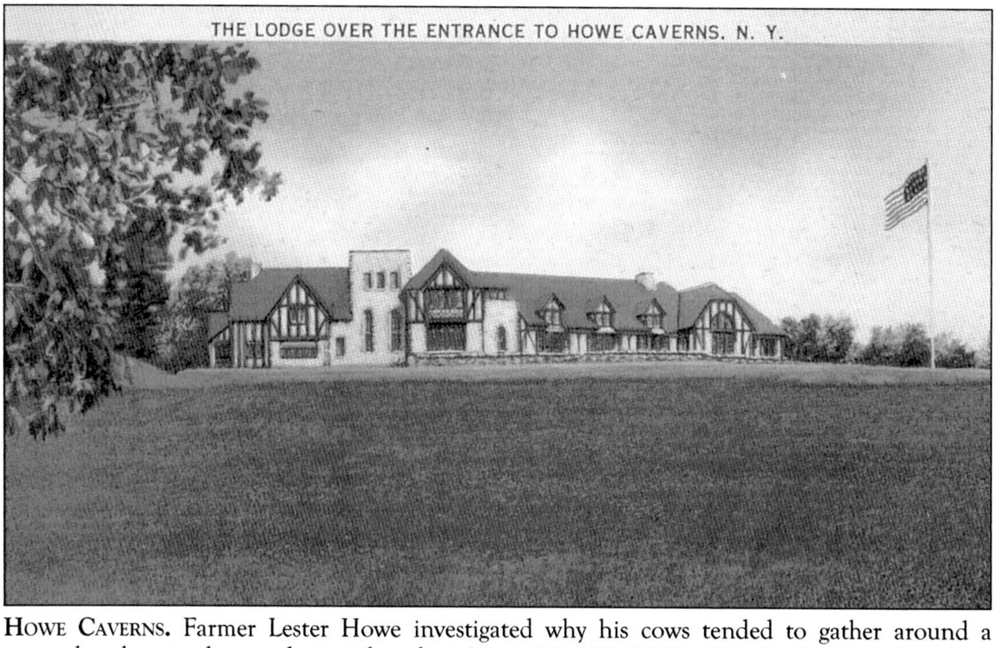

Howe Caverns. Farmer Lester Howe investigated why his cows tended to gather around a particular place in the meadow on hot days. It was May 22, 1842, when he discovered cool air coming from a cave, which was soon known as Howe Caverns. The present lodge, located just east of Cobleskill, was inspired by the old manor houses of England. Howe Caverns, one of the most spectacular natural wonders in the Northeast, attracts about 200,000 tourists a year.

The Pool of Siloam. This is an interesting example of erosion in the form of circular arches, with the pool below perfectly reflecting nature's vaulted ceilings. This is also the entrance to Cathedral Archway, which is in Howe Caverns. This postcard is from the 1930s.

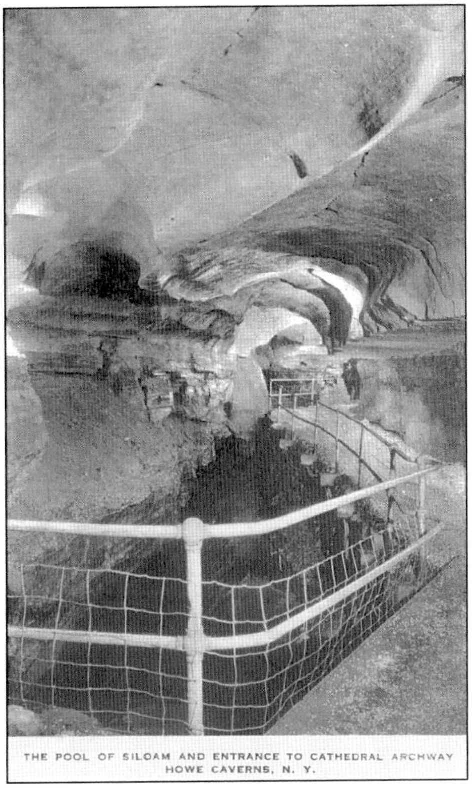

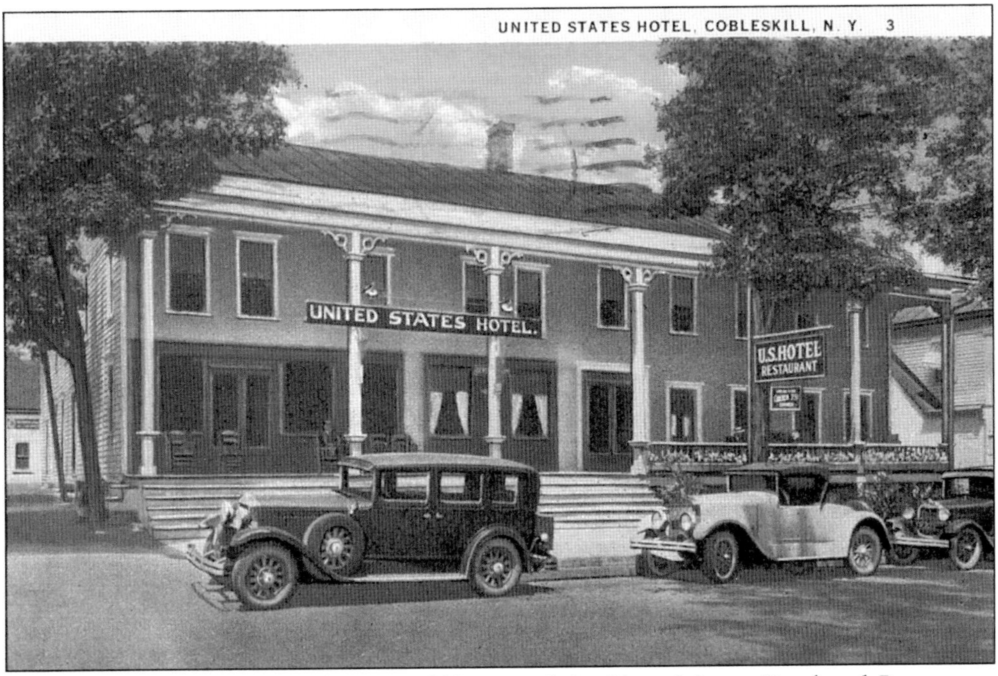

The United States Hotel. This is a 1937 view of the United States Hotel and Restaurant, on Main Street in Cobleskill. The building has housed many different businesses, including Lamberts, Partyland, and Schoharie County Arts Council.

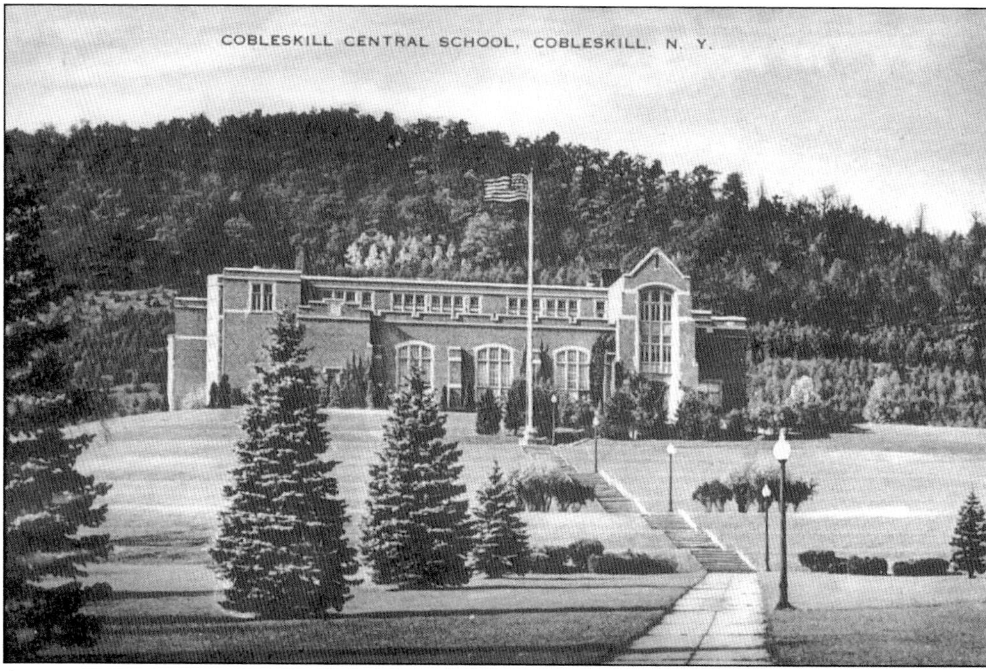

COBLESKILL CENTRAL SCHOOL. Once the central school for Cobleskill, this building is now the middle school for students in Cobleskill and Richmondville. A consolidated district for the two schools was formed several years ago and is located between Richmondville and Cobleskill.

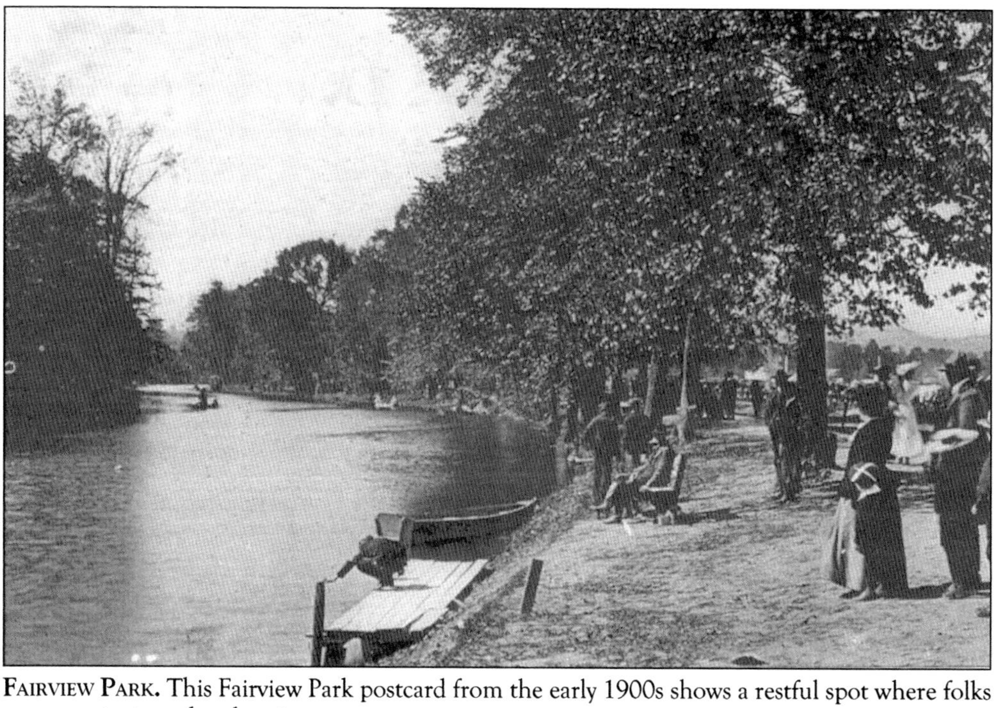

FAIRVIEW PARK. This Fairview Park postcard from the early 1900s shows a restful spot where folks came to picnic and go boating.

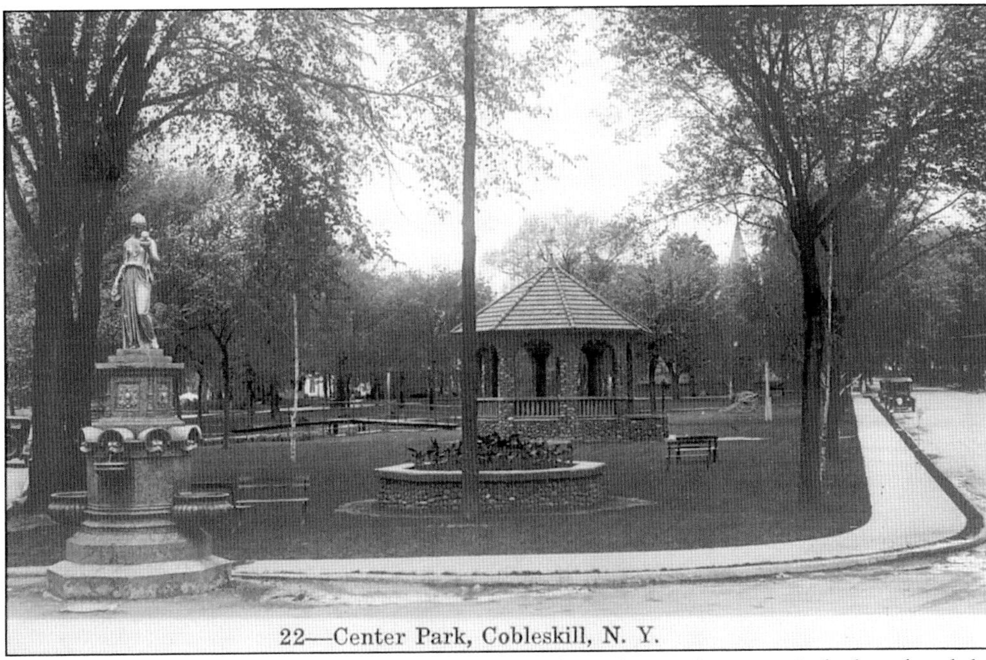

CENTER PARK. The view from the park has not changed much over the years. A clock replaced the statue of Minerva. Young and old enjoy Center Park throughout the year.

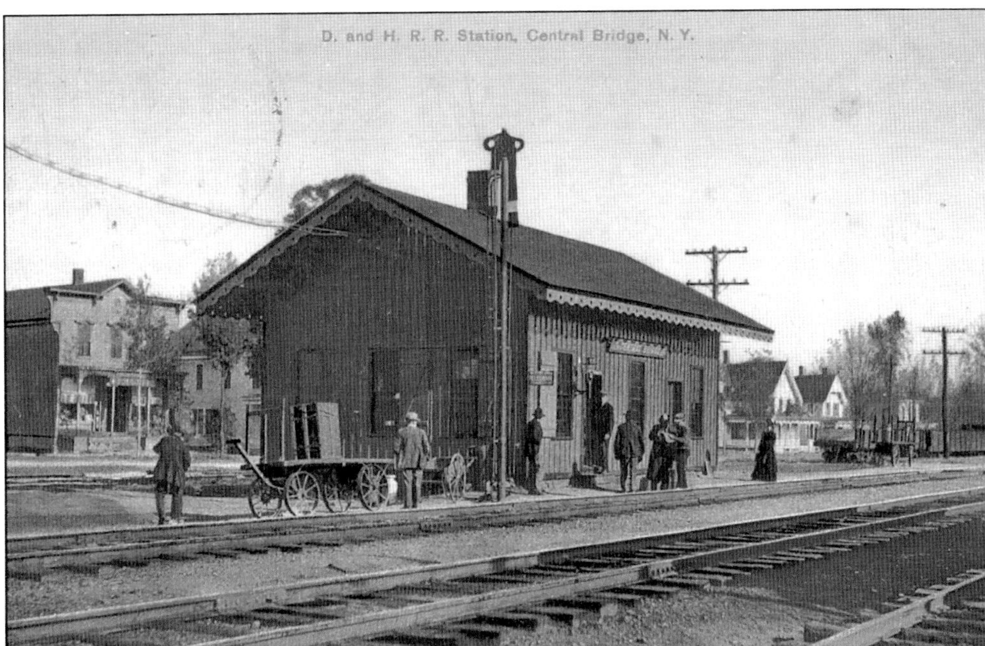

DELAWARE & HUDSON RAILROAD STATION. The Central Bridge Station was a beehive of activity in 1909. Note the fancy roof trim and vertical stick siding. The message on the card to Leah Wade from her brother states, "We started over toward Carlisle, got stuck fast in mud, had to come back toward Central Bridge take the train tonight." The train was very important to people in all the small communities along the Delaware & Hudson in the early 20th century.

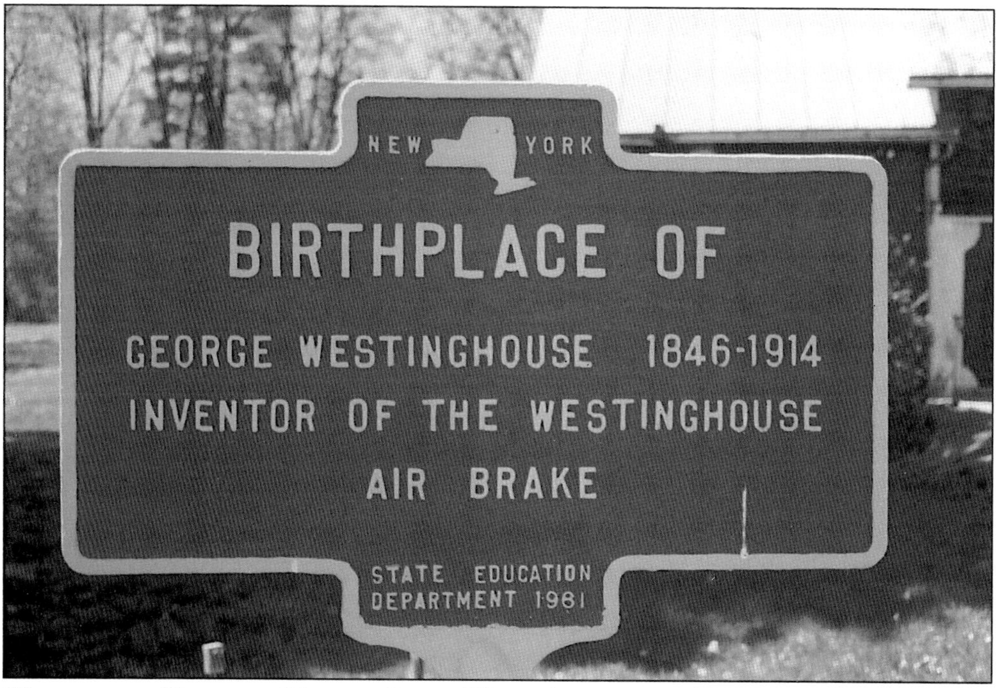

WESTINGHOUSE HISTORICAL MARKER. George Westinghouse Jr. was born on October 6, 1846, in Central Bridge. He became one of the greatest engineers, industrialists, and inventors of his day. He modernized the railroad with his air brakes. Included in his 360 patents was the invention of the reverse-action fail-safe system that remains standard today.

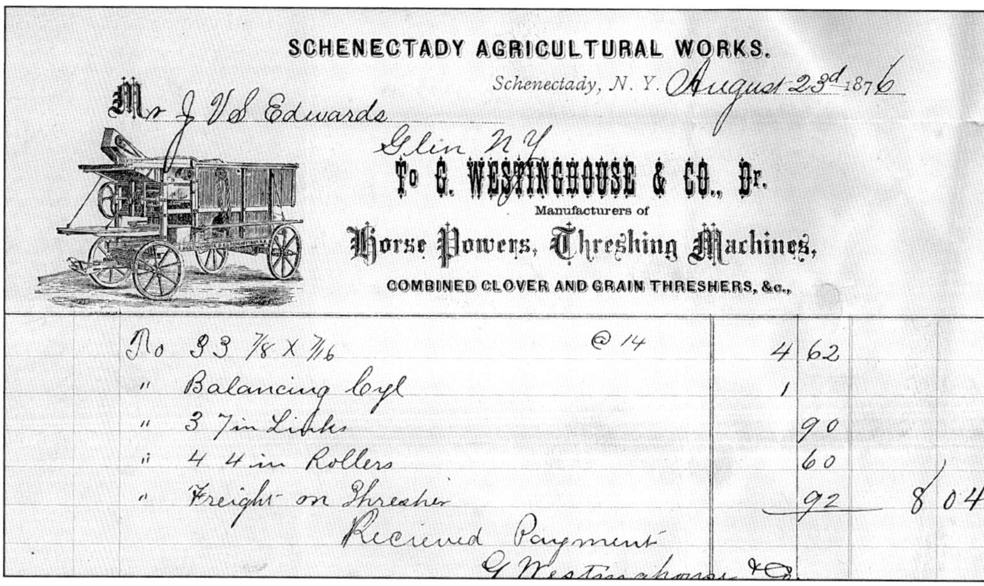
SCHENECTADY AGRICULTURAL WORKS.

Schenectady, N. Y. August 23d 1876

Mr J V S Edwards

Glin N Y

To G. WESTINGHOUSE & CO., Dr.

Manufacturers of

Horse Powers, Threshing Machines,

COMBINED CLOVER AND GRAIN THRESHERS, &c.,

No 33 7/8 X 7/16 @ 14	4	62	
" Balancing Cyl	1		
" 3 7in Links		90	
" 4 4 in Rollers		60	
" Freight on Thresher		92	8 04

Received Payment
G Westinghouse & Co

WESTINGHOUSE BILLHEAD. Westinghouse started a business in Schenectady. He is best remembered for his air brakes, horse-powered motors, and threshing machines. Many appliances still carry the Westinghouse name.

Two

RICHMONDVILLE

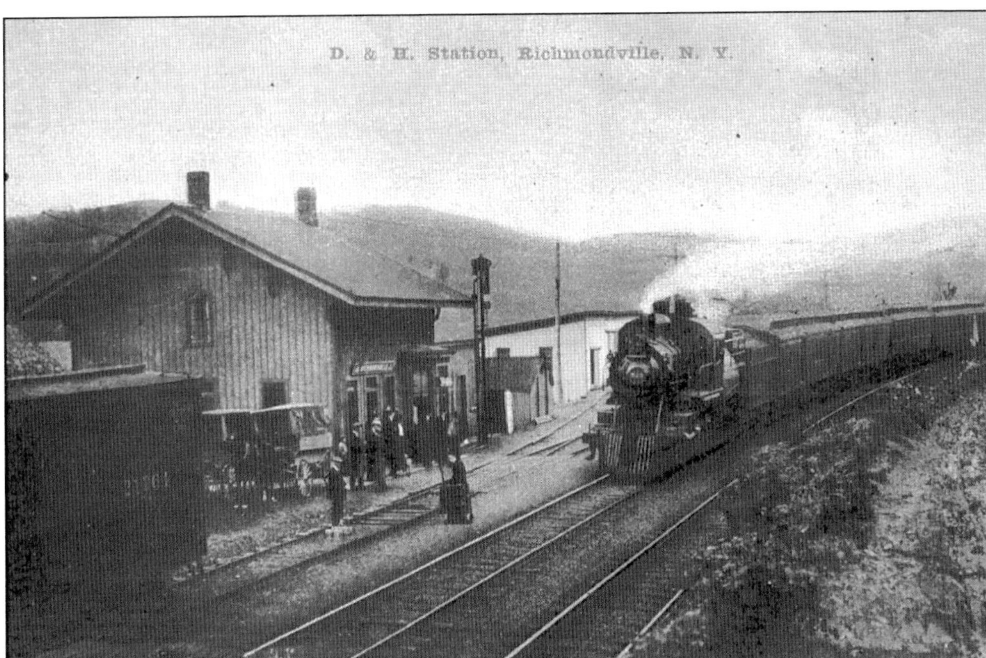

DELAWARE & HUDSON STATION, RICHMONDVILLE. In 1910, the Delaware & Hudson station was a popular place for travelers to meet. Drivers with their horse and wagons seem to be waiting for a passenger train to come steaming in from East Worcester way. The station was torn down several years ago.

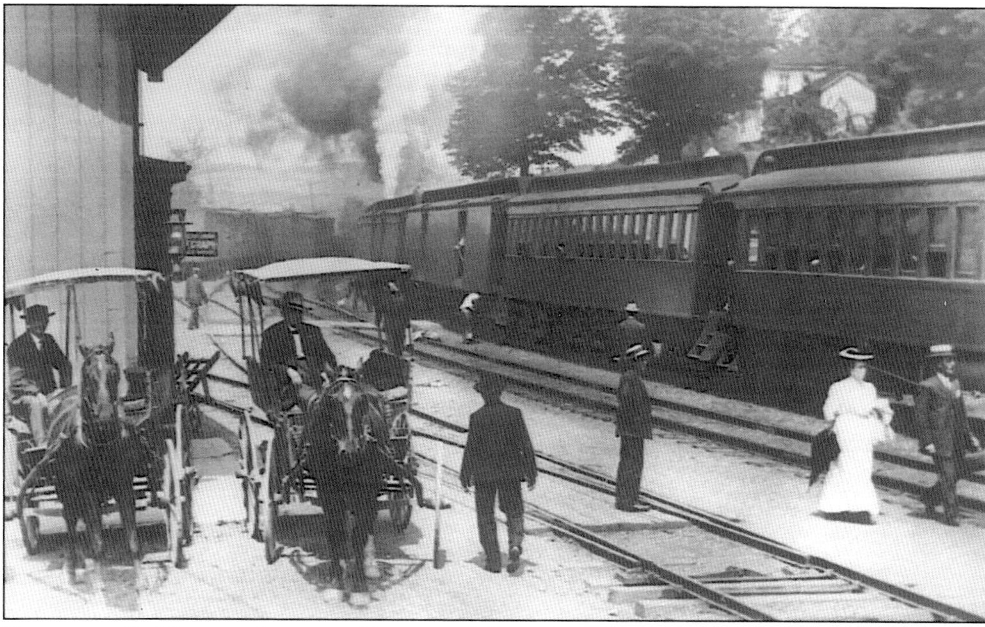

DELAWARE & HUDSON STATION. Henry and Etta Gott board the train for East Worcester after visiting in Richmondville. This 1907 photograph also shows rigs with drivers waiting for passengers disembarking in Richmondville.

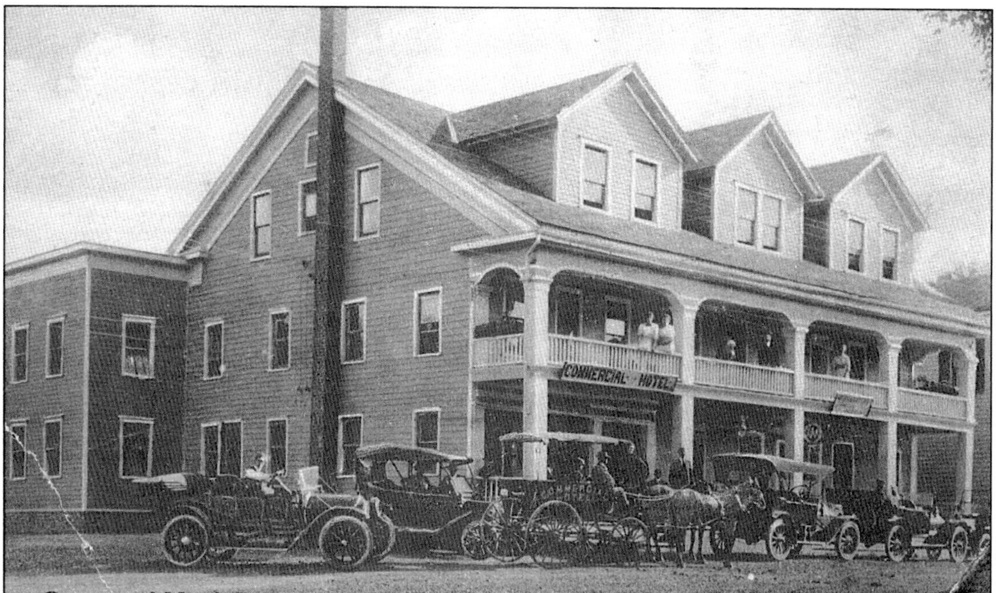

THE COMMERCIAL HOTEL. Folks out for a ride often stopped at the Commercial Hotel, one of the favorite spots for villagers in the early 1900s. Upon completion of the railroad, James Blodgett erected the Commercial Hotel near the station. It was known as Blodgett House and was convenient and comfortable for commercial travelers. Richmondville was a favorite summer resort because of the fertile, scenic valley that was known to be free from malaria. After a partial fire, the remains of the hotel were purchased by the village, torn down, and a new firehouse was built on the spot.

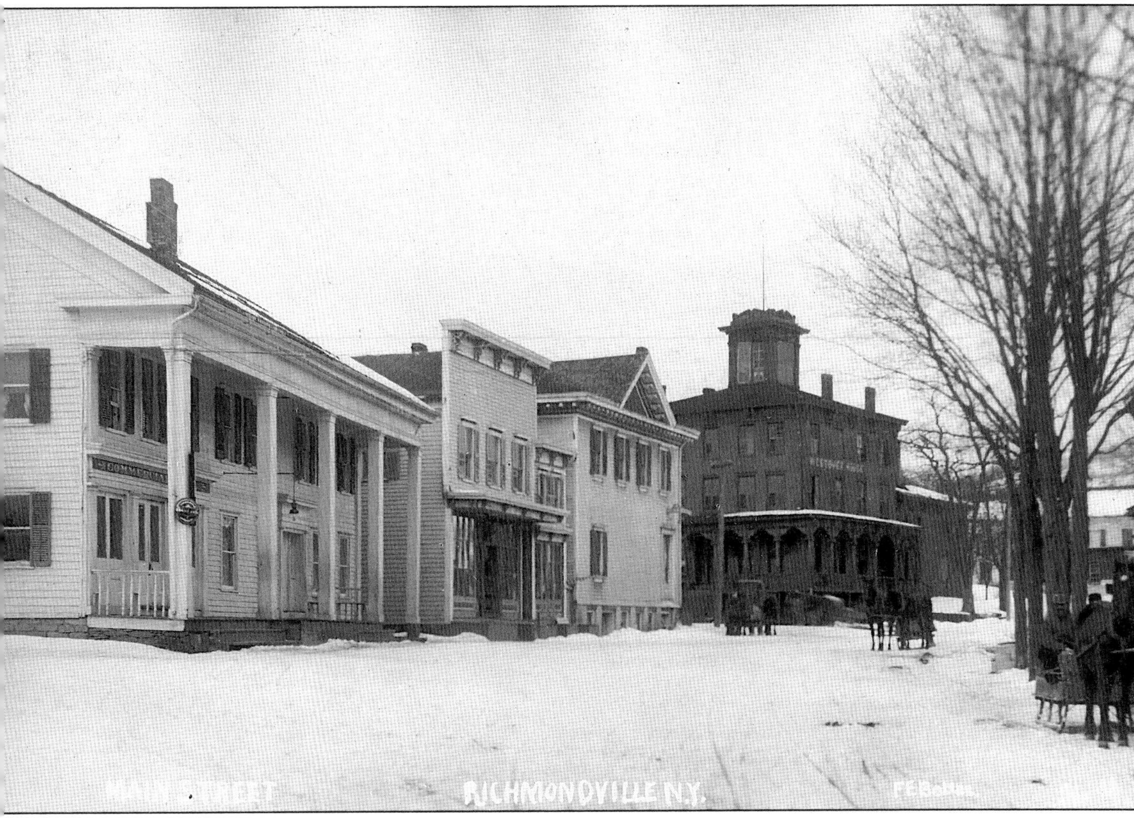

MAIN STREET. Sleigh bells ring on Richmondville's Main Street in the early 1900s. A trademark of an old-fashioned winter was riding in a horse-drawn sleigh. To take the chill off, thick robes and perhaps a warm soapstone or two at one's feet were the solution. The building with the cupola is no longer there; in its place is the post office. The hotel on the left is where the firehouse is now located. This is an F.E. Bolles postcard.

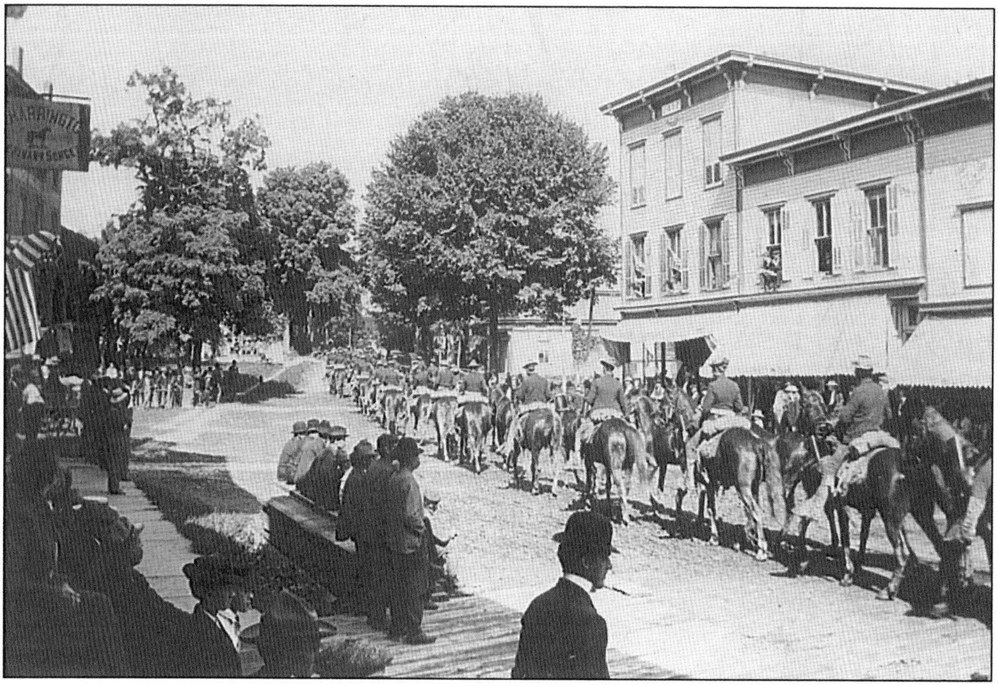

THE CAVALRY IN RICHMONDVILLE. Members of the U.S. Cavalry pass through Richmondville on August 28, 1904. The horses walk along the old plank road as a crowd gathers to watch.

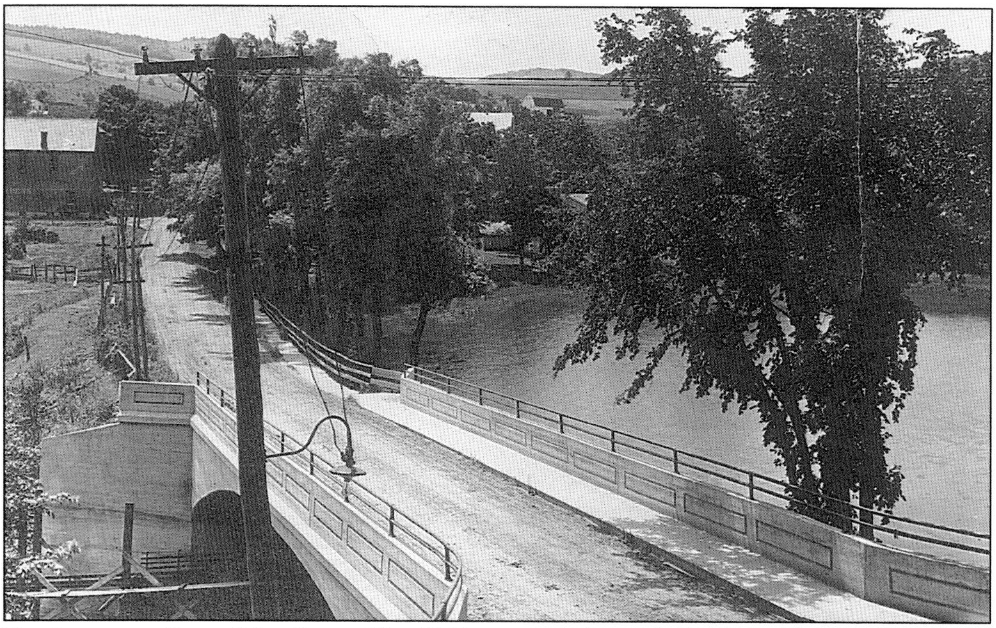

THE BRIDGE AT PAPER MILL POND. This 1911 postcard shows the bridge and the millpond site. Note the early streetlight on the left. Richmondville received electricity from East Worcester's Great Bear Light and Power Company at that time. The electricity was turned on one hour before sunset until 1:00 a.m. In the second decade of the 20th century, villagers felt fortunate to have electric lights for even a few hours a day. Soon, however, such hours would seem insufficient.

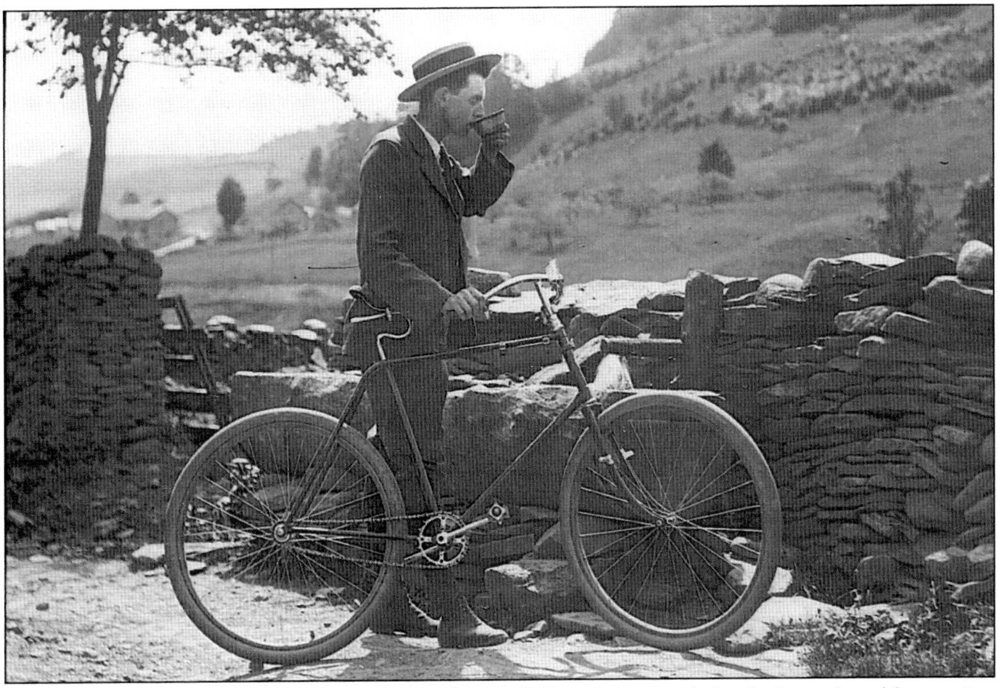

A BICYCLIST IN 1895. Everett Lawyer of Richmondville takes a cool drink from the old watering trough on Alvord Road in East Worcester. Lawyer does not seem to be worried about drinking water out of the rusty tin cup found at the site. Some travelers could be fussy and rinse out the cup first because of moustache hairs or tobacco-juice stains. Farmers providing water to passersby were often allowed a $5 deduction from their annual land tax.

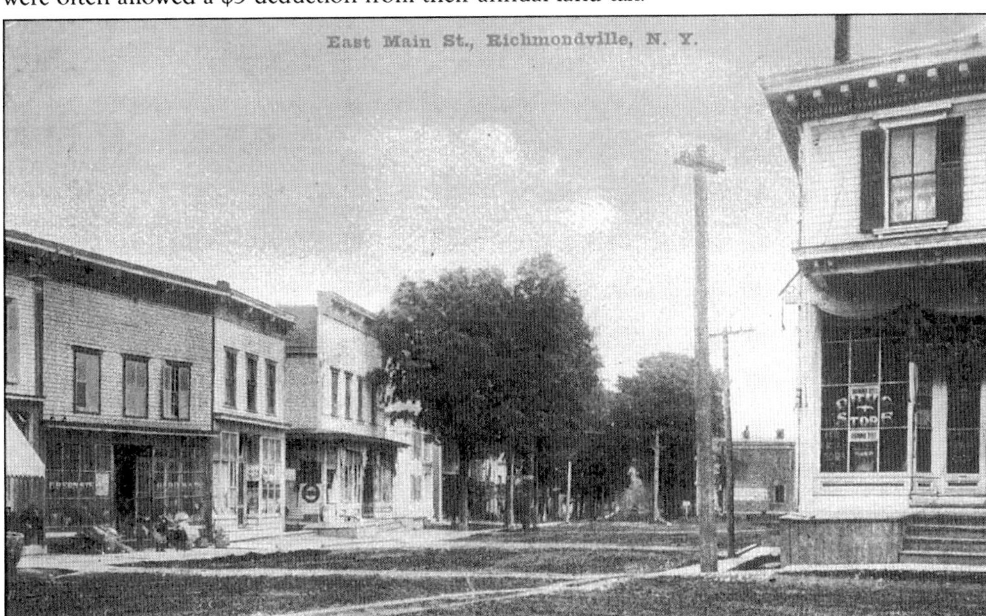

EAST MAIN STREET. It is 1910, the days of dirt roads, country stores, and hometown dedication. Many stores placed their wares outside in hopes of enticing customers. A man named Webb, the first mail carrier, brought newspapers on horseback from Cobleskill.

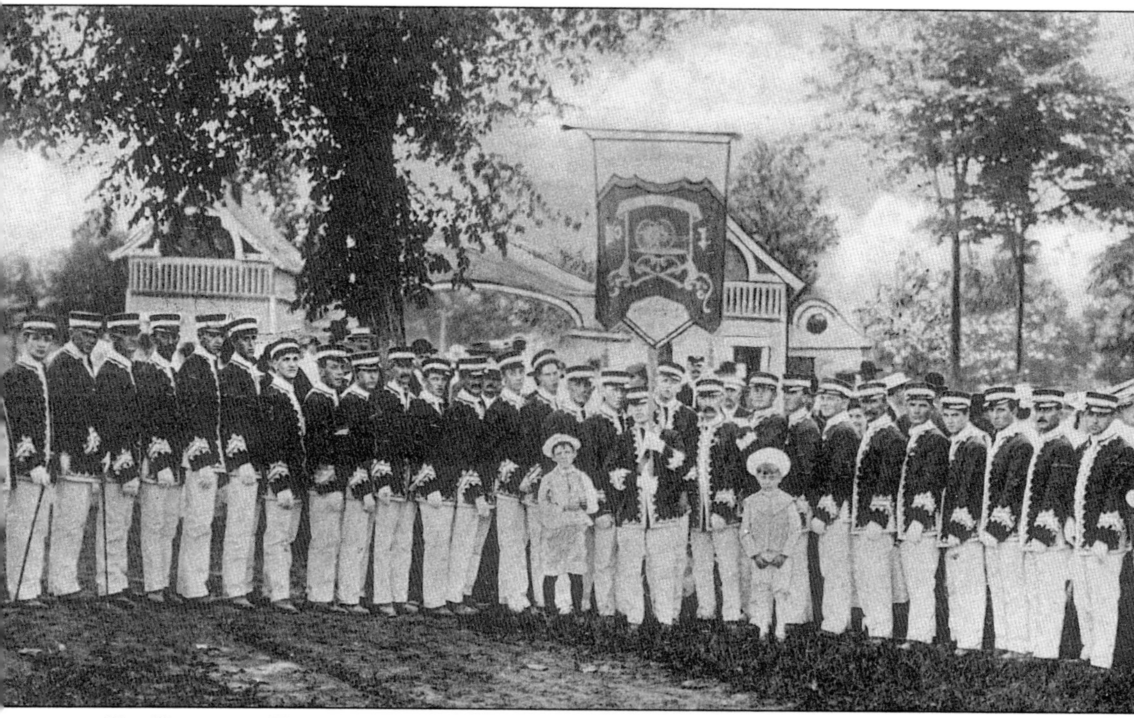

THE HARROWAY HOSE COMPANY. Members of the Harroway Hose Company of Richmondville line up in front of the entrance to the Cobleskill Fairgrounds to have their photograph taken *c.* 1909.

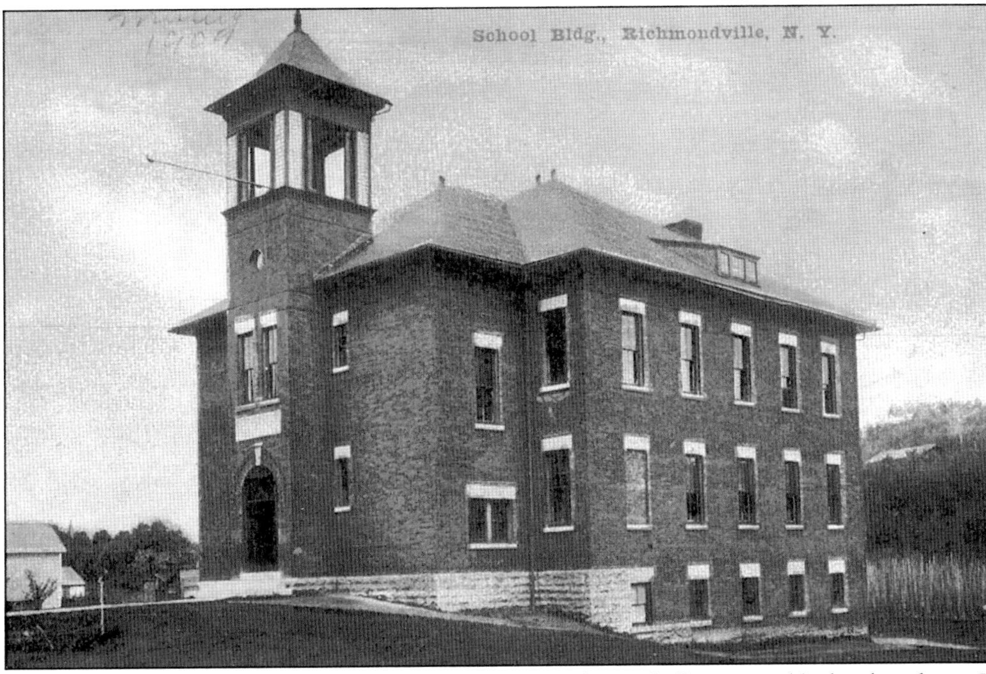

A SCHOOL BUILDING. In 1910, this school building in Richmondville was used by local students. It was later torn down, and a larger, light-colored brick school was built on the same site. Today the school is consolidated with Cobleskill.

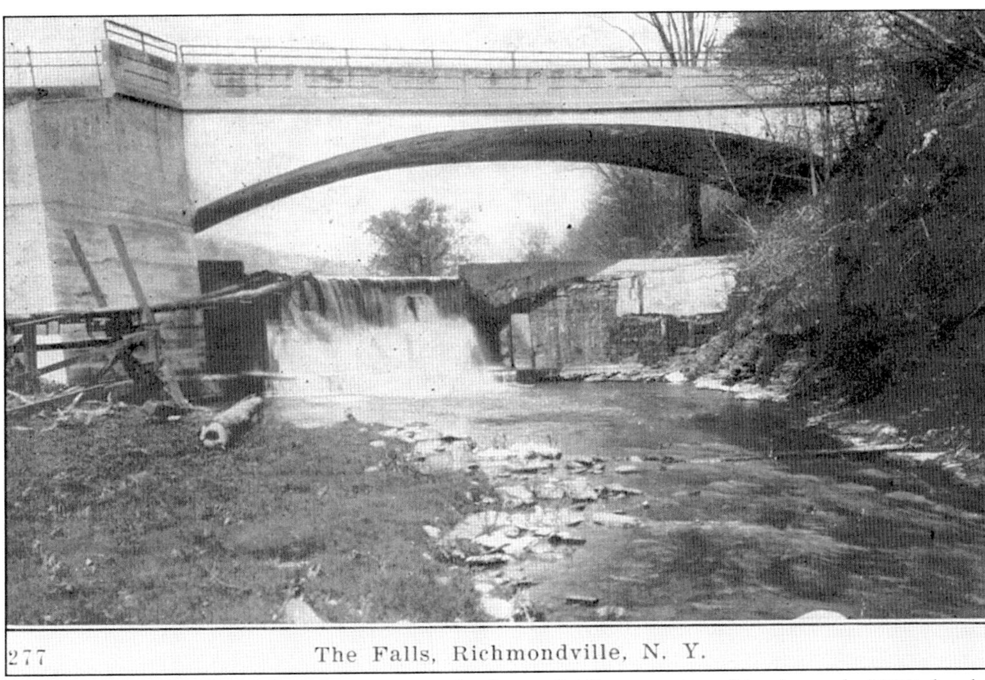

THE FALLS. This postcard depicting a scenic bridge and falls was printed in the early 1900s by the Greeting Card Manufacturing Company in Union Square, New York. The bridge and falls are still there but, after the construction of Interstate 88, cars can no longer drive over the span.

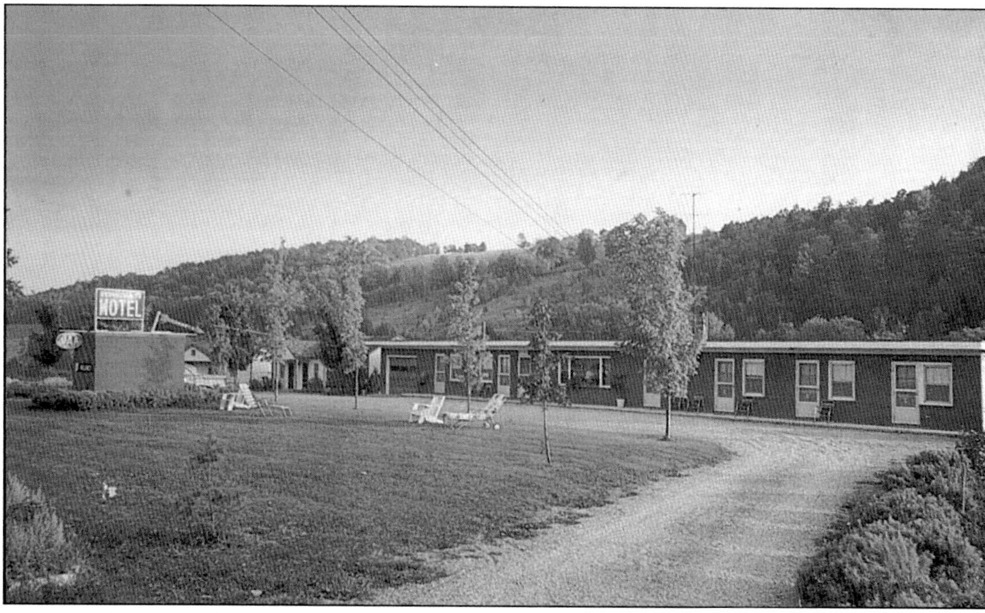

SCHULTE'S MOTEL. This motel, popular in the 1950s, advertised that it was only 12 miles from Howe Caverns and 7 miles from Cobleskill. The business, run by Gerhardt Schulte and his family, began with a restaurant and three double units. After the restaurant and family apartment upstairs burned, this motel was constructed in the 1950s. The business, sold in the mid-1980s, has been converted to apartments.

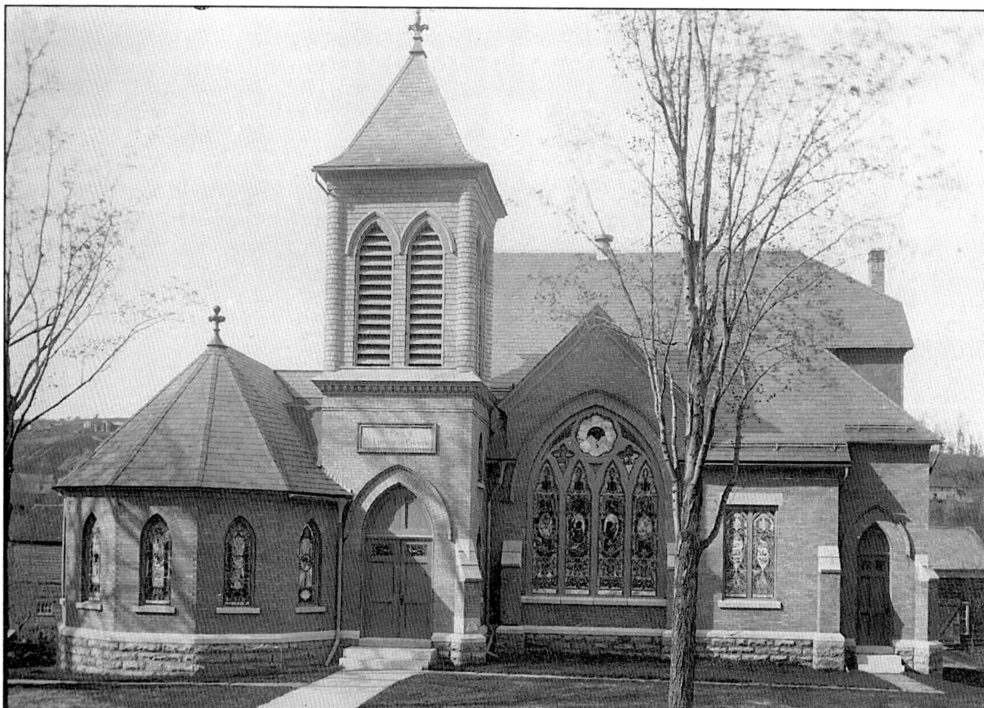

THE LUTHERAN CHURCH. This church is on Main Street near the traffic light. Its interior recently was renovated and its organ was rebuilt.

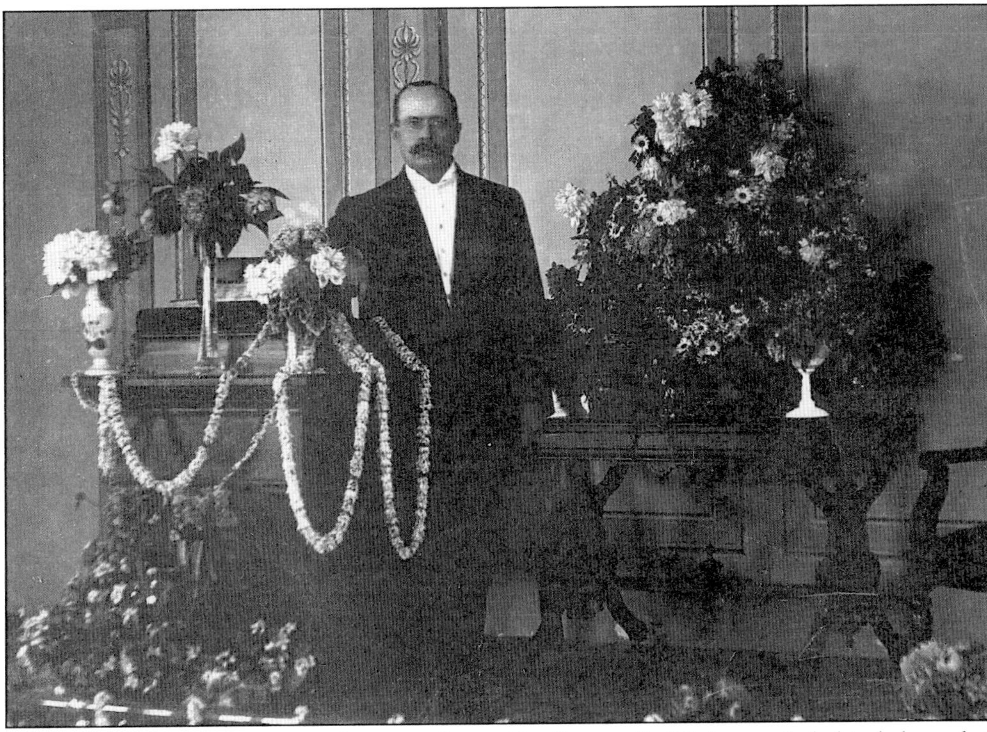

THE PASTOR OF THE LUTHERAN CHURCH. Pastor Dr. Eugene L. Wade stands behind the pulpit in the Richmondville Lutheran Church c. 1909. He also served as pastor of the Beard's Hollow Church, which is several miles away. Wade passed away in 1910.

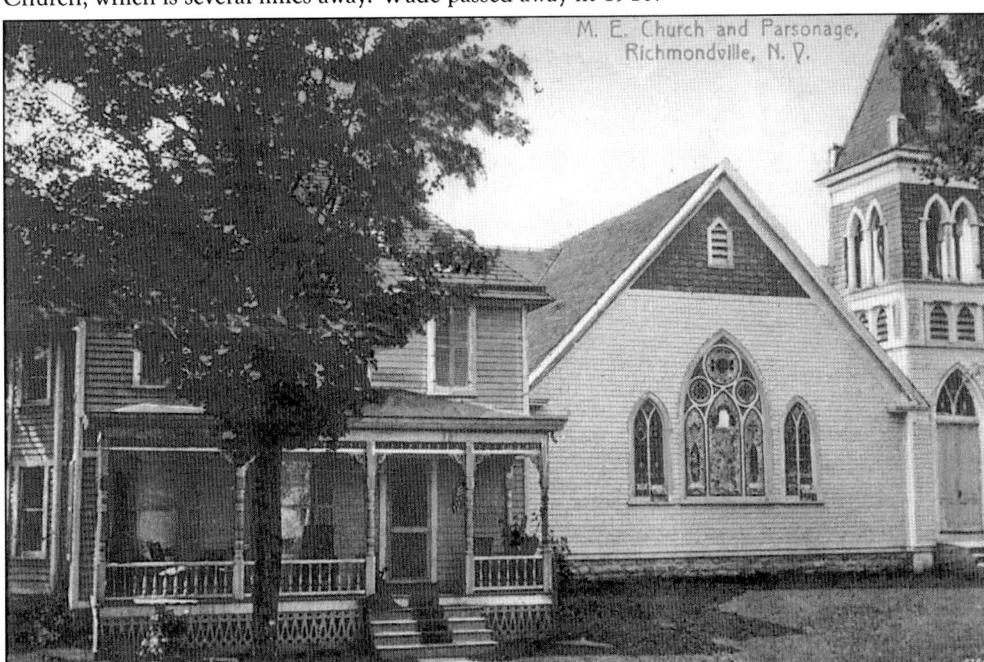

THE METHODIST EPISCOPAL CHURCH AND PARSONAGE. This postcard depicts the Methodist Episcopal church in 1909. Note the Victorian-style painting of the buildings.

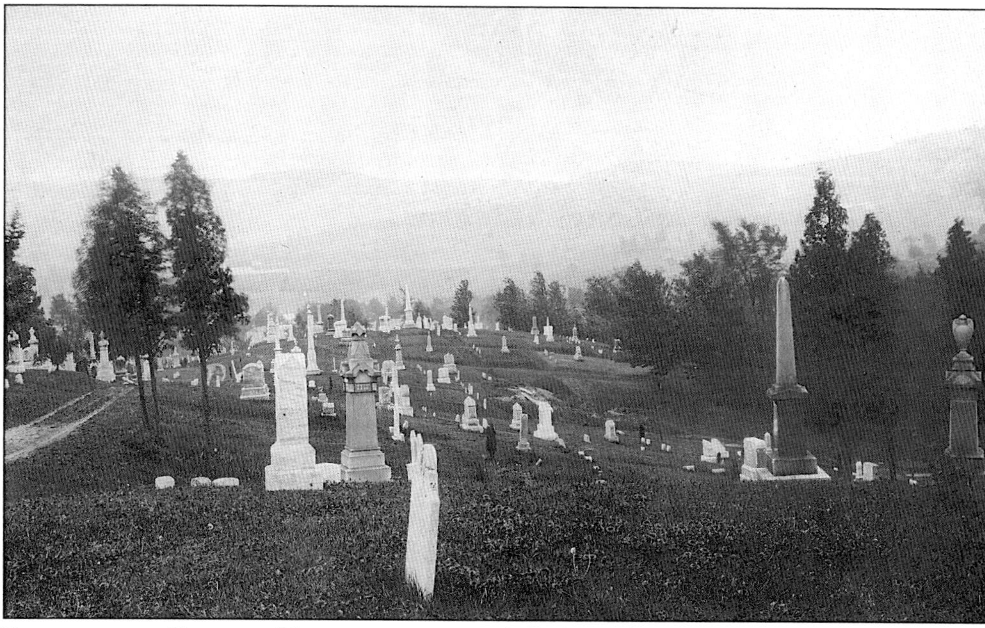

Richmondville Cemetery. This cemetery is on a hillside on the outskirts of Richmondville. This Dearstyne photograph postcard is from the early 1900s.

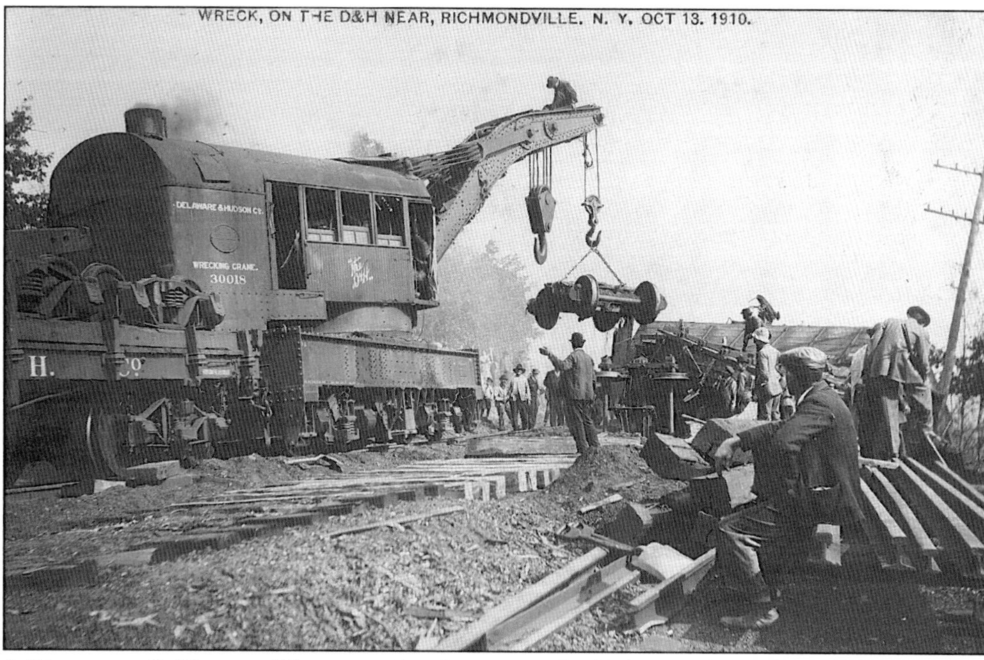

A Delaware & Hudson Wreck. A derailment on the Delaware & Hudson took place near Richmondville on October 13, 1910. A Delaware & Hudson crane was used to pick up the parts of the boxcars involved in the accident and place them back on the track. The man on the right sits on a load of new rails to be used to realign the track. H.B. Calkins of Hyndsville took this photograph.

Three

EAST WORCESTER

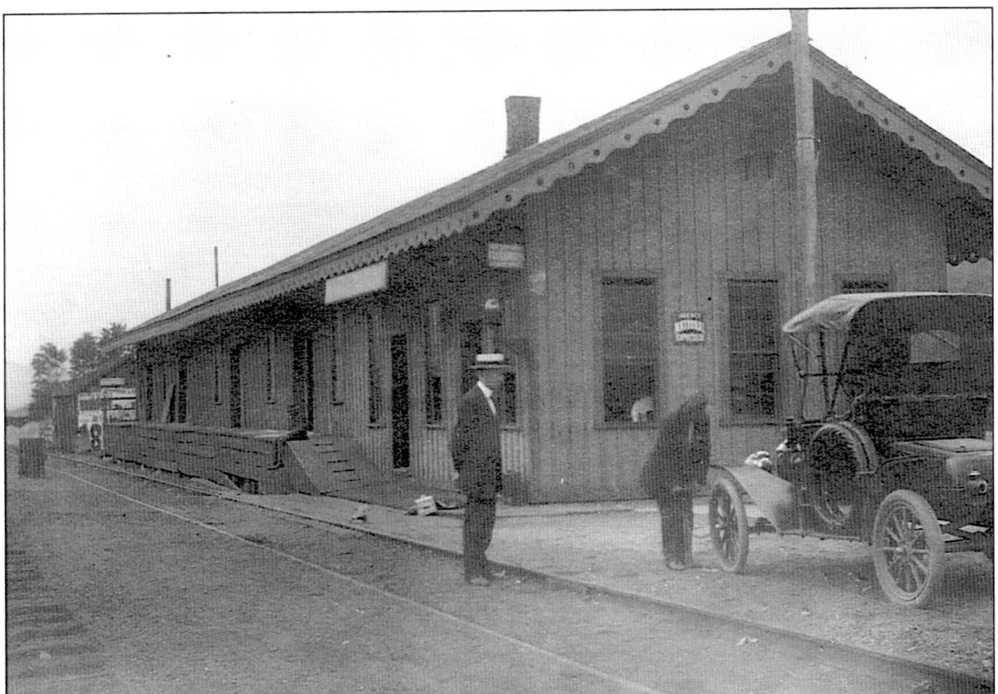

DELAWARE & HUDSON STATION. Like small stations along the Delaware & Hudson Railroad, this one was designed with fancy gingerbread-type scrollwork along the roof. Most of them were painted a dull, olive-drab color. The Albany & Susquehanna Railroad reached the East Worcester area on July 17, 1865. The Albany & Susquehanna, a forerunner of the Delaware & Hudson Canal Company, provided an immediate period of growth and prosperity for the area. Bluestone, which was an income producer from about six local quarries, was shipped by rail to the city for sidewalks.

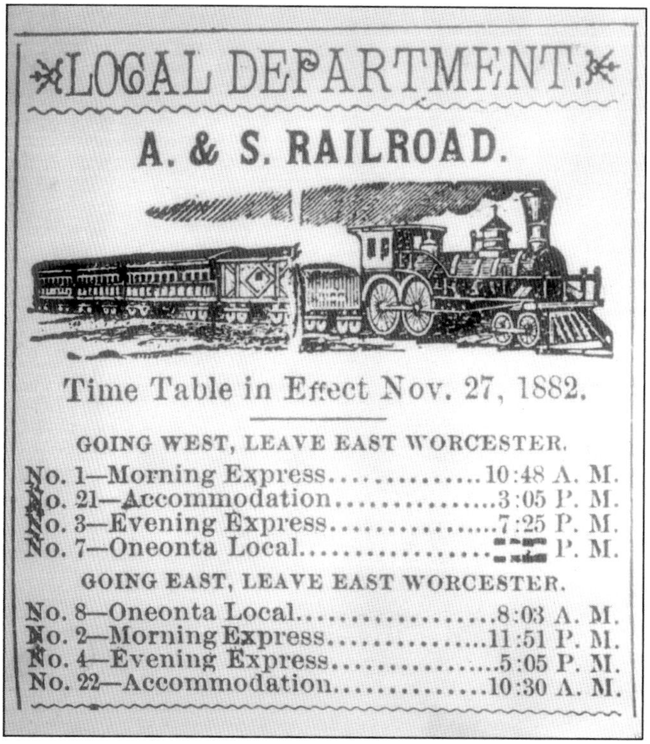

LOCAL DEPARTMENT.

A. & S. RAILROAD.

Time Table in Effect Nov. 27, 1882.

GOING WEST, LEAVE EAST WORCESTER.

No. 1—Morning Express..............10:48 A. M.
No. 21—Accommodation..............3:05 P. M.
No. 3—Evening Express...............7:25 P. M.
No. 7—Oneonta Local...............[illegible] P. M.

GOING EAST, LEAVE EAST WORCESTER.

No. 8—Oneonta Local..................8:03 A. M.
No. 2—Morning Express..............11:51 P. M.
No. 4—Evening Express...............5:05 P. M.
No. 22—Accommodation..............10:30 A. M.

The Albany & Susquehanna Railroad. This railroad timetable for the old Albany & Susquehanna dates to 1882, when many trains were arriving and departing.

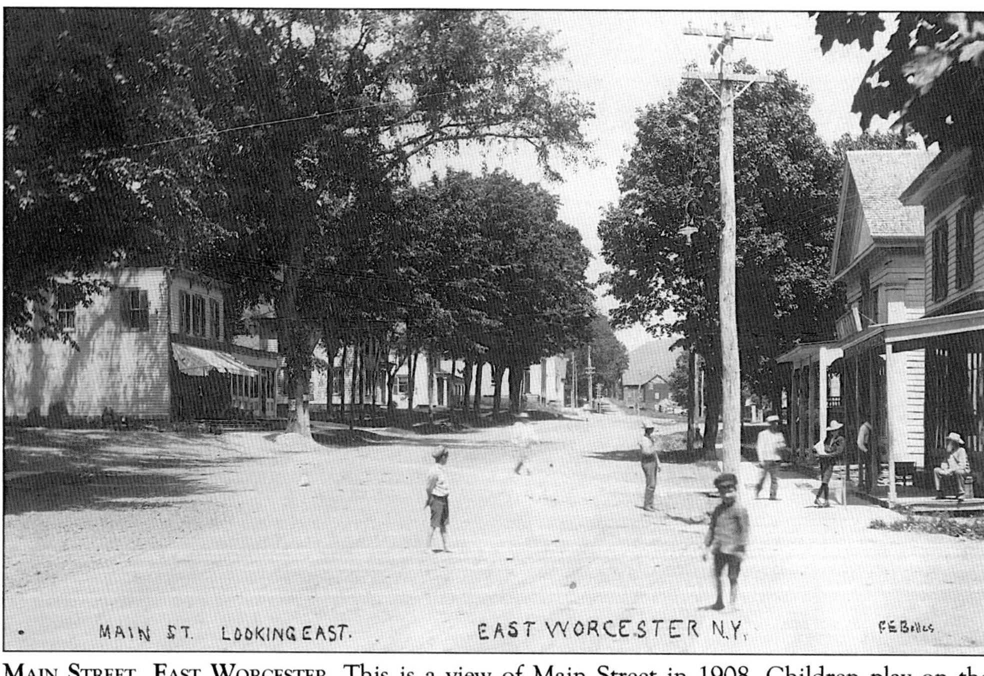

Main Street, East Worcester. This is a view of Main Street in 1908. Children play on the dirt roads with little danger of being run over. The card's message reads, in part, "Looking for a postcard from you telling us when to meet you at the station." In the foreground is a view of the early Great Bear street lamp, which was 25 candlepower (about 30 watts) and very dim by today's standards. The next street lamp to the east was a short block away.

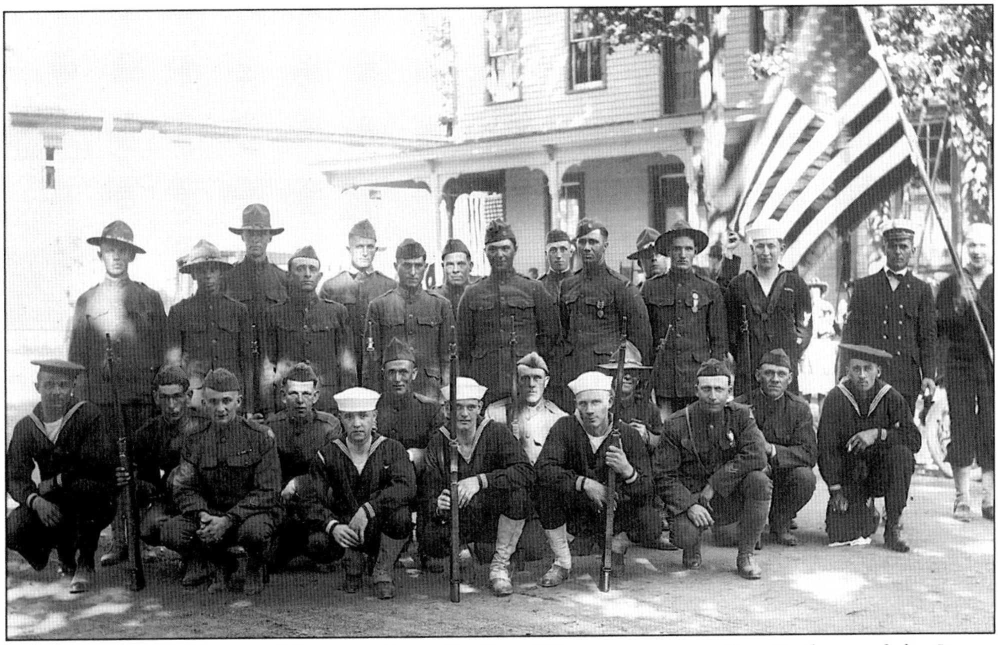

World War I Veterans. Veterans from the East Worcester area gather in front of the James Dante residence on Main Street during a Memorial Day exercise in 1920. Cpl. William H. Anthony is in the front row to the far right.

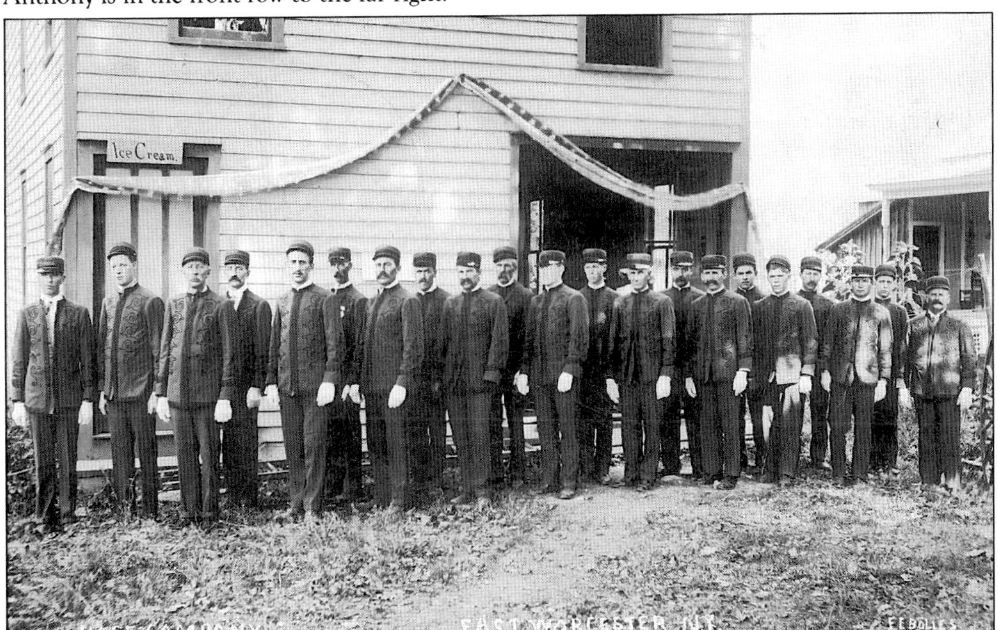

The East Worcester Hose Company. The hose company was organized in 1898. It was said that the men made an impressive appearance at parades with their new uniforms and strict training. The first firehouse was located at 7 Maple Street and contained a hose cart and one pumper. This photograph of the 21 firefighters in line was taken c. 1900. In 1956, a brick building was constructed on Main Street for the men and their equipment. This postcard is one of many taken by photographer F.E. Bolles.

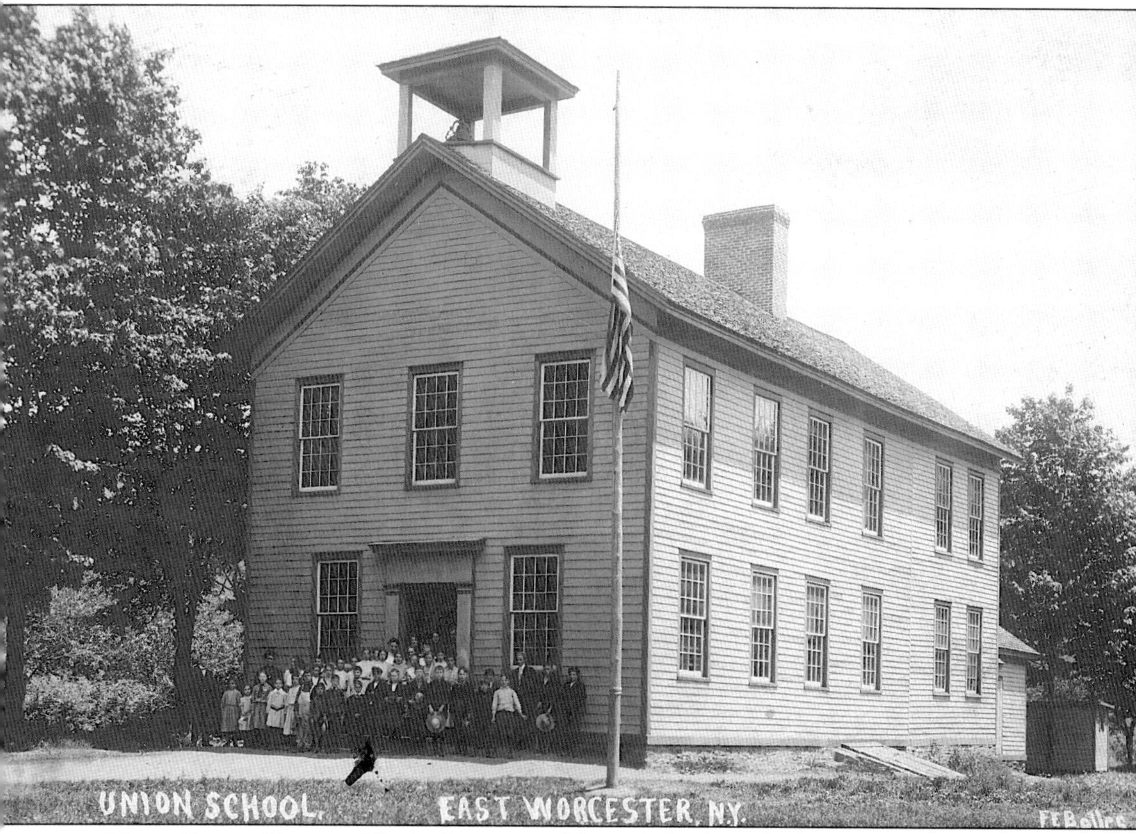

UNION SCHOOL DISTRICT NO. 3. A two-story Union School was built in East Worcester c. 1867. Principal Andrew S. Draper of Westford became the first commissioner of education in New York State. The wooden structure consisted mainly of two rooms, with the lower grades occupying the ground floor. An outhouse and shed were located in the back. In 1870, there were two teachers and 99 pupils. The building was remodeled in 1900, with the addition of a laboratory and cloakroom upstairs and two rooms with cloakroom downstairs. A brick building replaced the school in 1915, and the old wooden one was moved to the center of East Worcester, where it housed the post office. This building was later replaced by a new post office and firehouse. This photograph postcard is from the camera of F.E. Bolles.

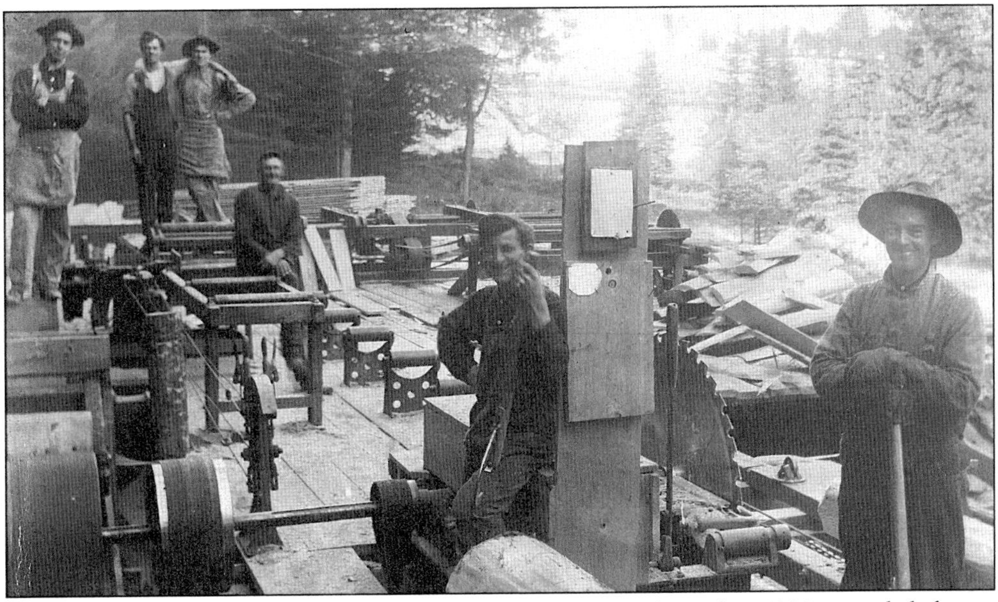

THE GREAT BEAR LIGHT AND POWER COMPANY. This company, formed in 1908, provided electric lights to East Worcester, Schenevus, and Richmondville. William F. Shup Inc., the major stockholder, operated a hydro-steam system that could function by water pressure acting on a steam engine. Harry Shafer, owner-operator of the Worcester Electric Company, objected to Great Bear placing electric lines along Worcester streets to Schenevus. The matter was settled by the Public Service Commission, which ruled in favor of the East Worcester system.

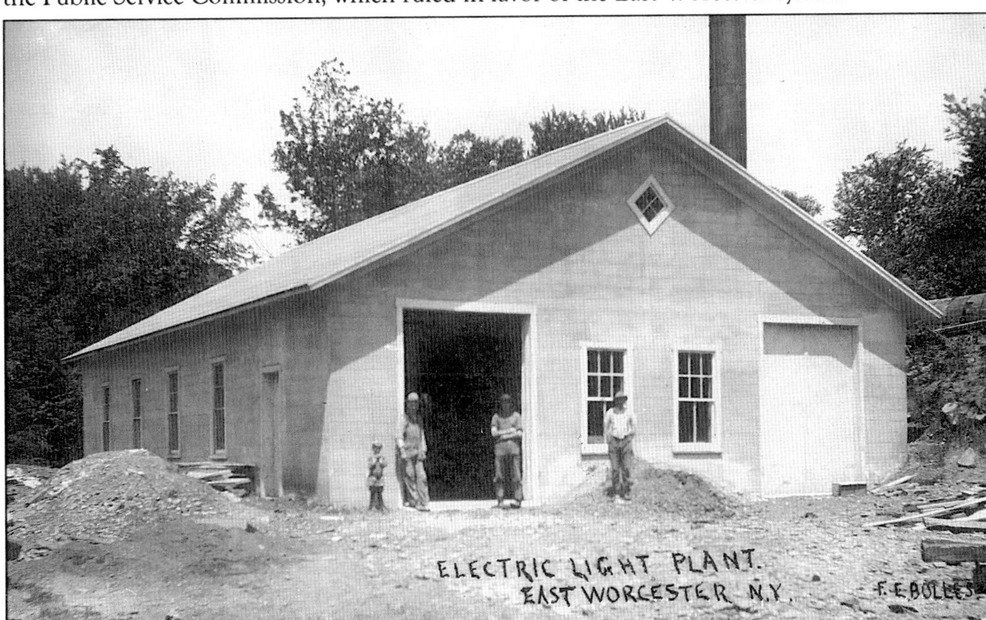

THE POWERHOUSE UNDER CONSTRUCTION. This postcard shows the partly completed Great Bear powerhouse. The smokestack has been erected, but the guy wires are not yet in place. It also appears that transmission lines have not been strung. In addition, the coal annex and steam exhaust vents have not been built. The plant seems to be vacant, and the machinery has not arrived. This is a photograph by F.E. Bolles.

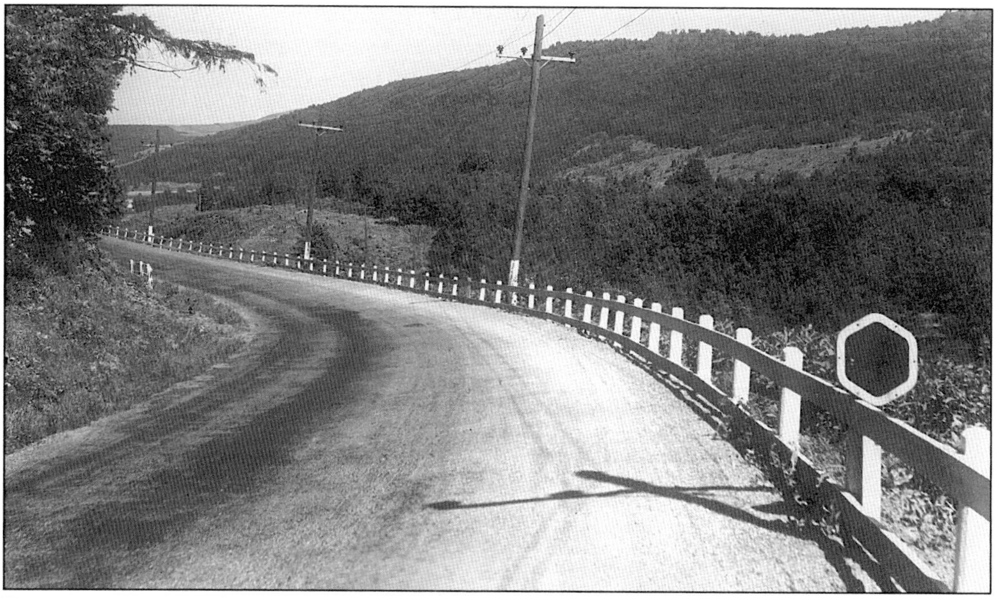

TRANSMISSION LINE. The Great Bear transmission line to Schenevus followed Route 7, also known as the Old Schohanna Trail. The size of the insulators suggests that this was a 110- or 120-volt line. It is thought that the three wires shown provided two circuits, one wire serving in common. One circuit supplied the homes in Schenevus, and the other (controlled independently by the light company in East Worcester) supplied power to the street lamps.

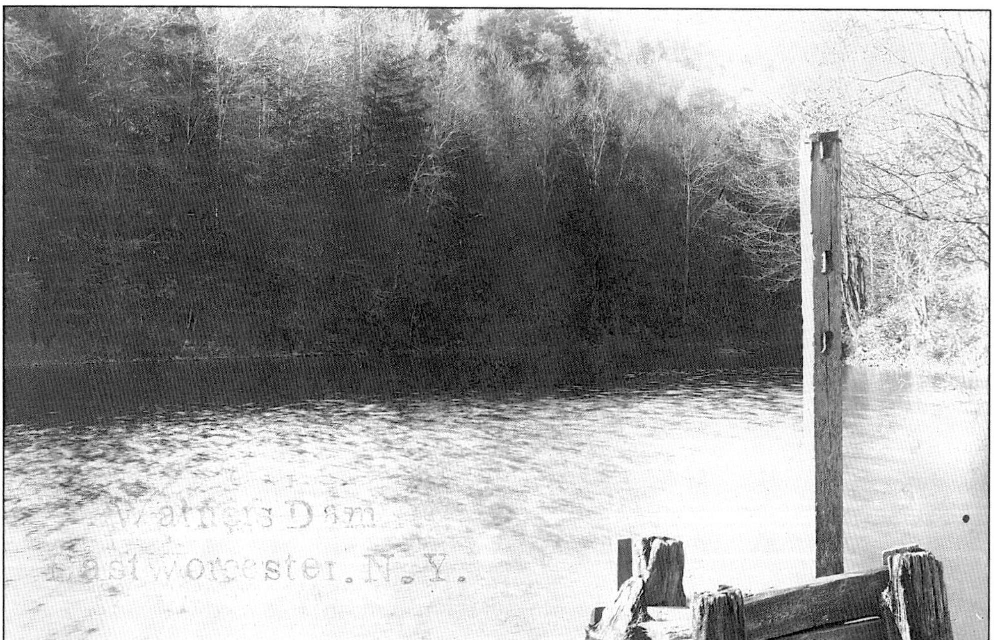

WARNERS DAM. This is the head gate for the Warner Brothers Mill Pond in 1908. Mill water entered the tubelike penstock through this head gate, which could be opened or closed by using a lever—the long pole shown in the foreground. The dam was dismantled when the Great Bear Light and Power Company took over.

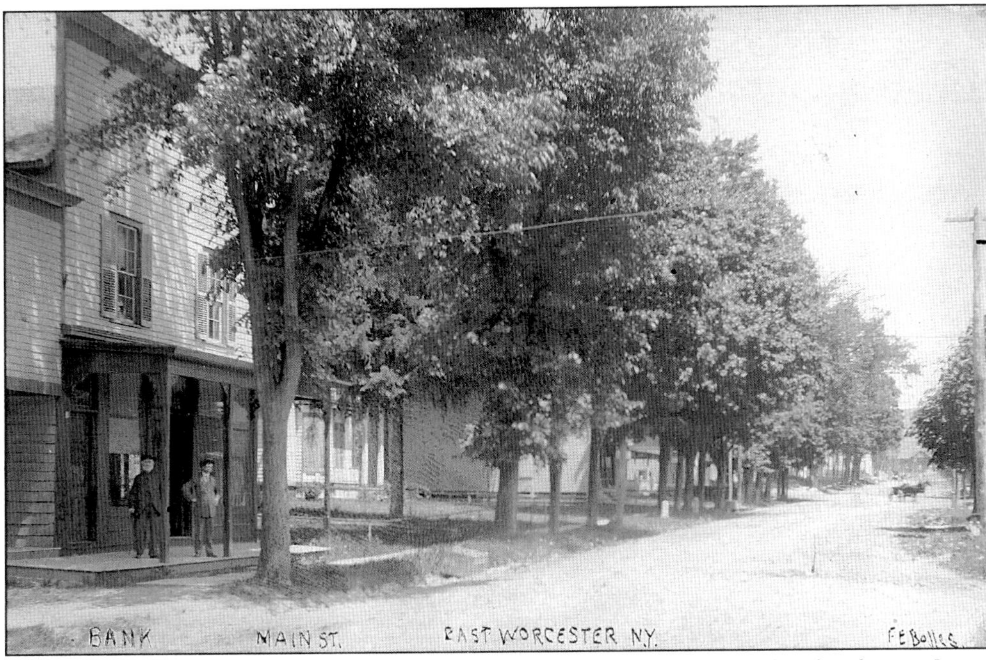

THE EAST WORCESTER NATIONAL BANK. The bank was located on the north side of Main Street, east of Oak Creek, in a building purchased by William E. Dante. He opened the bank in 1908 with a capital of $25,000. On December 5, 1916, the bank was forced into liquidation. This photograph was taken c. 1908.

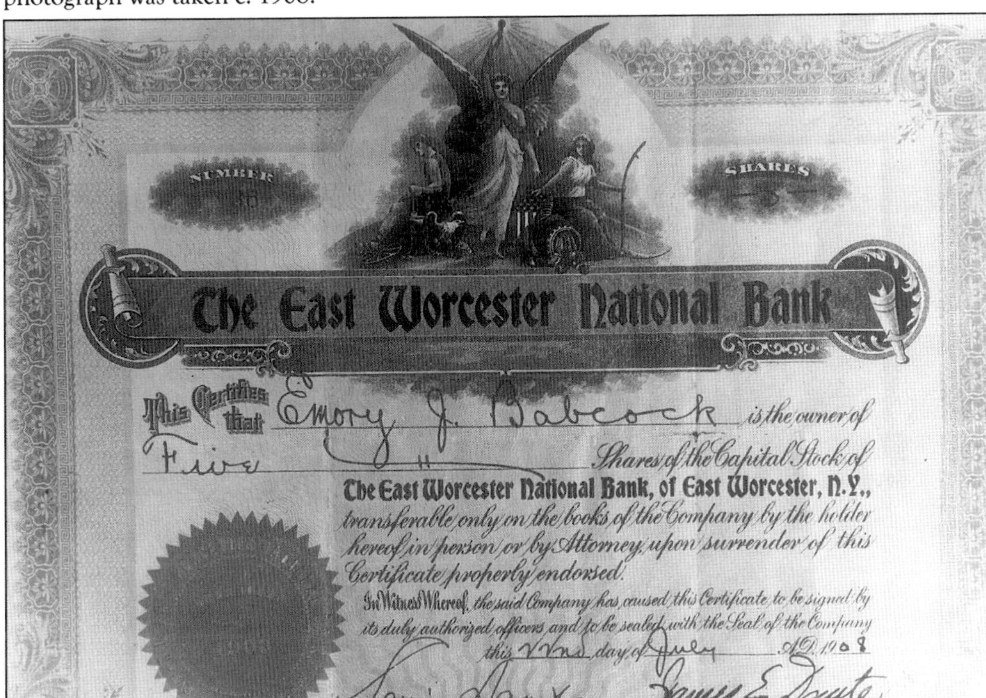

STOCK CERTIFICATE. This is a copy of the stock certificate from the East Worcester Bank, which was forced into liquidation on December 5, 1916.

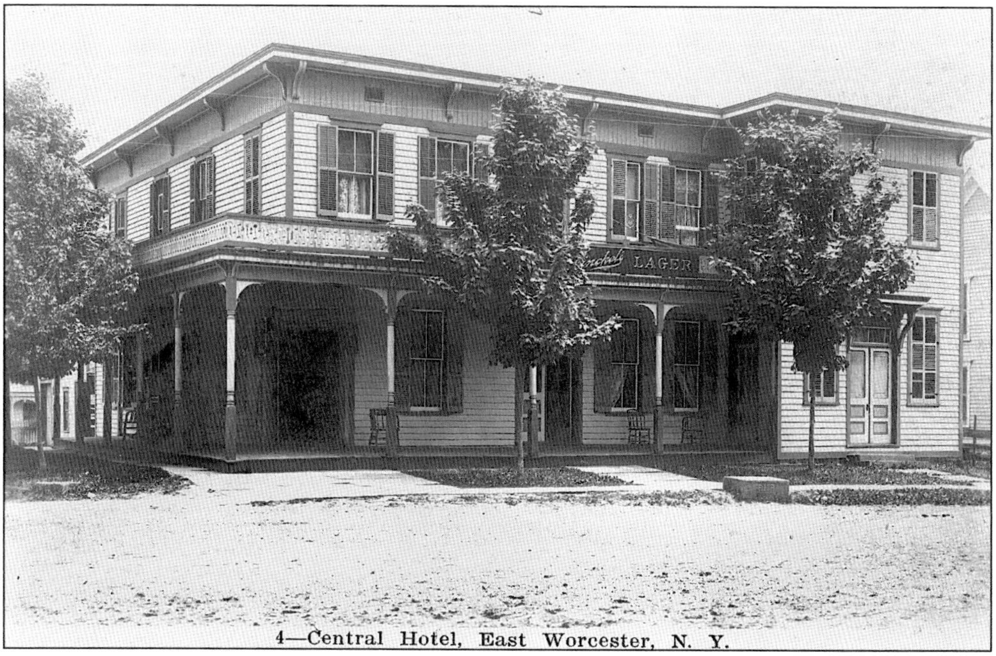

THE CENTRAL HOTEL. This 1907 photograph shows the Central Hotel, adorned with a Lager sign. The building, located on Main Street, served as a hotel and restaurant over the years. It is now a private residence.

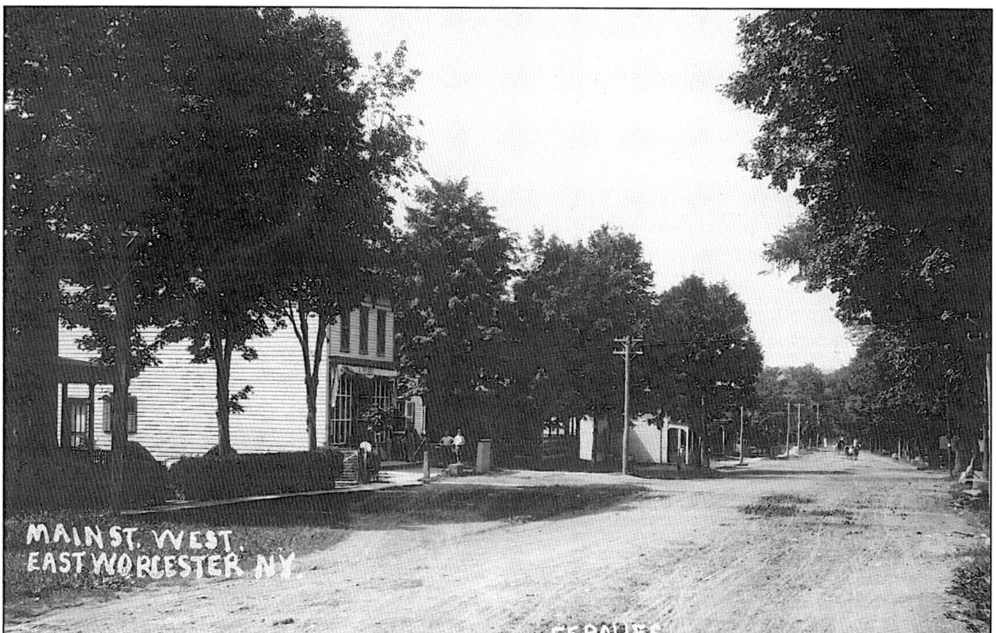

WEST MAIN STREET. This view of west Main Street shows a dirt road, horse and wagons coming into view, and young maple trees. The postcard is by F.E. Bolles.

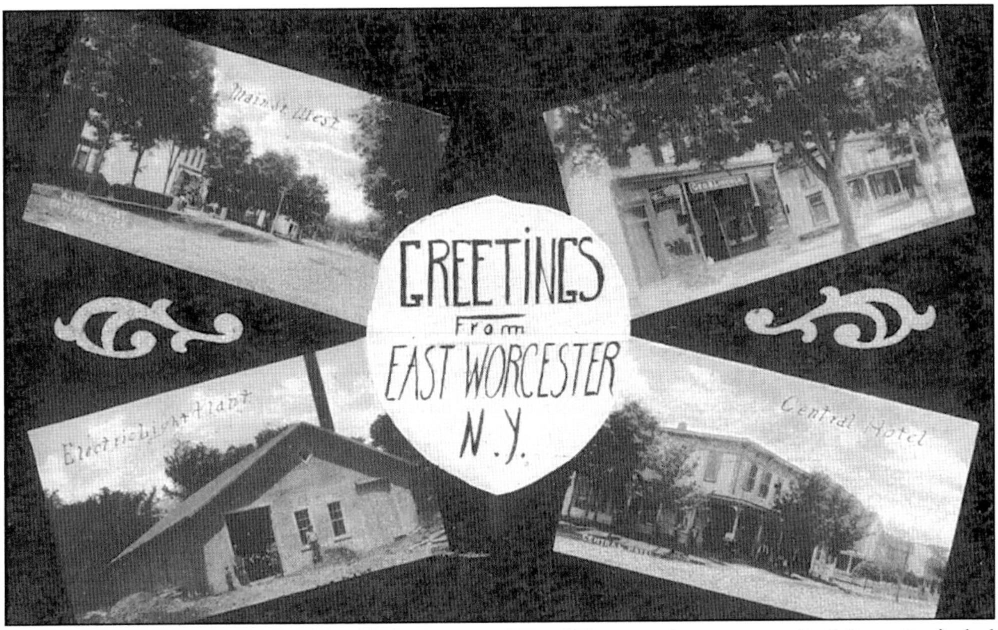

GREETINGS. This 1910 postcard highlights some of East Worcester's important buildings. Included on Main Street are the George B. Lincoln Store, Great Bear Electric Plant, and the Central Hotel.

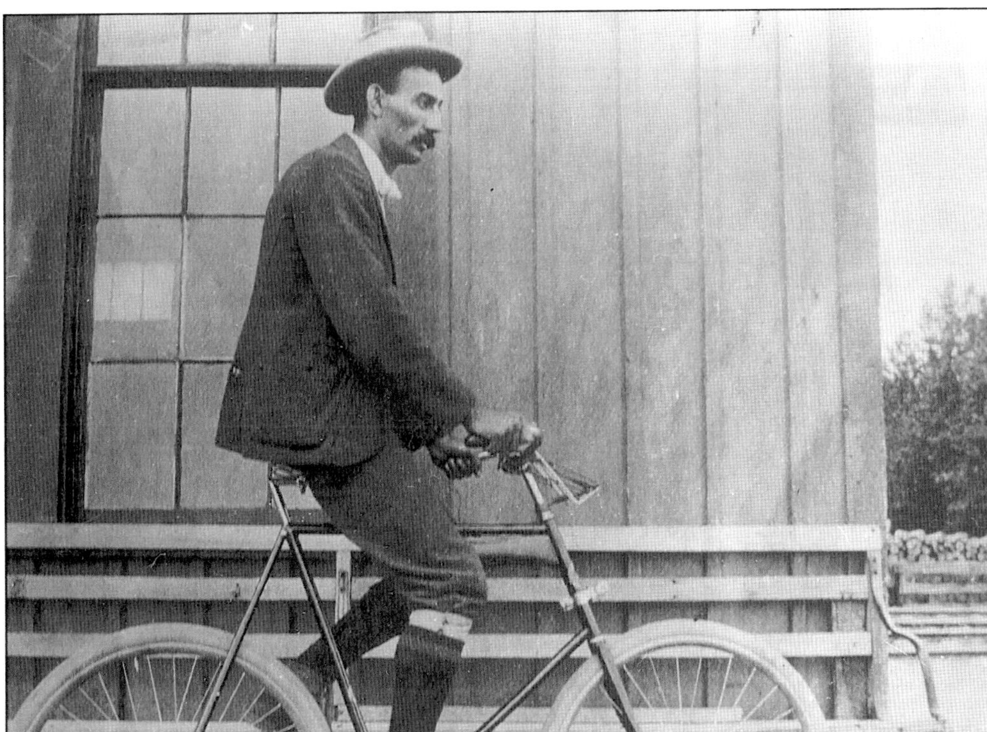

A CHAINLESS BICYCLE. In this 1890s postcard, L. Reightmeyer gets ready to pedal off on his bicycle. He is wearing the appropriate biking attire of the day—bicycle pants, stockings with garters, and high shoes.

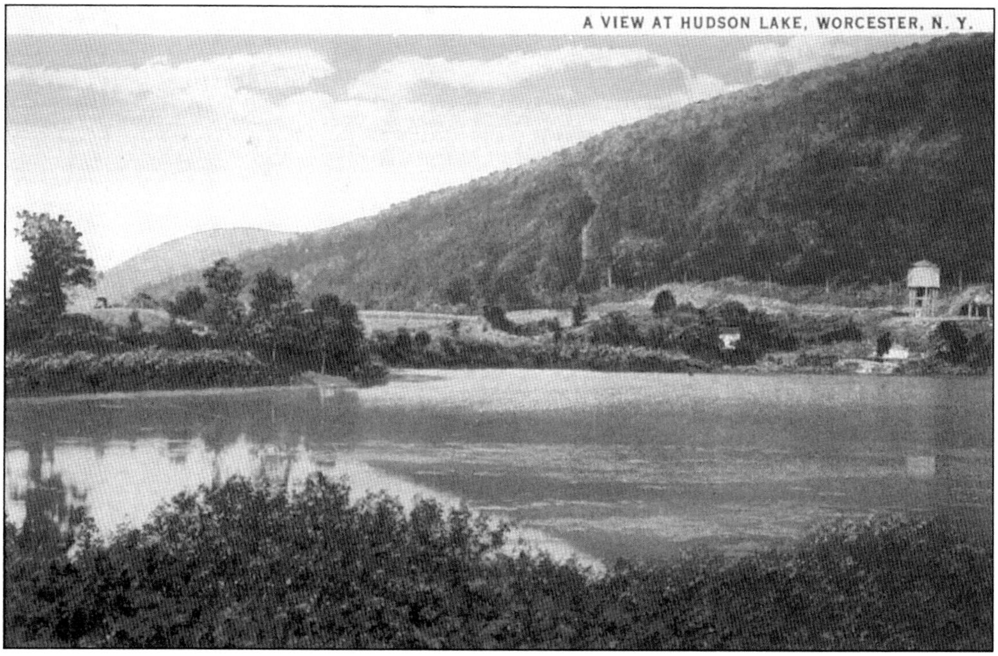

HUDSON LAKE. This is a view of Hudson Lake, located between East Worcester and Worcester. The Delaware & Hudson water tank on the upper railroad track was removed many years ago. John A. Hudson and his wife, Freelove, settled in the area c. 1808 on a 200-acre tract of land known as Hudson Farm. It is thought that John may have been a descendant of the English explorer Henry Hudson, for whom the Hudson River was named.

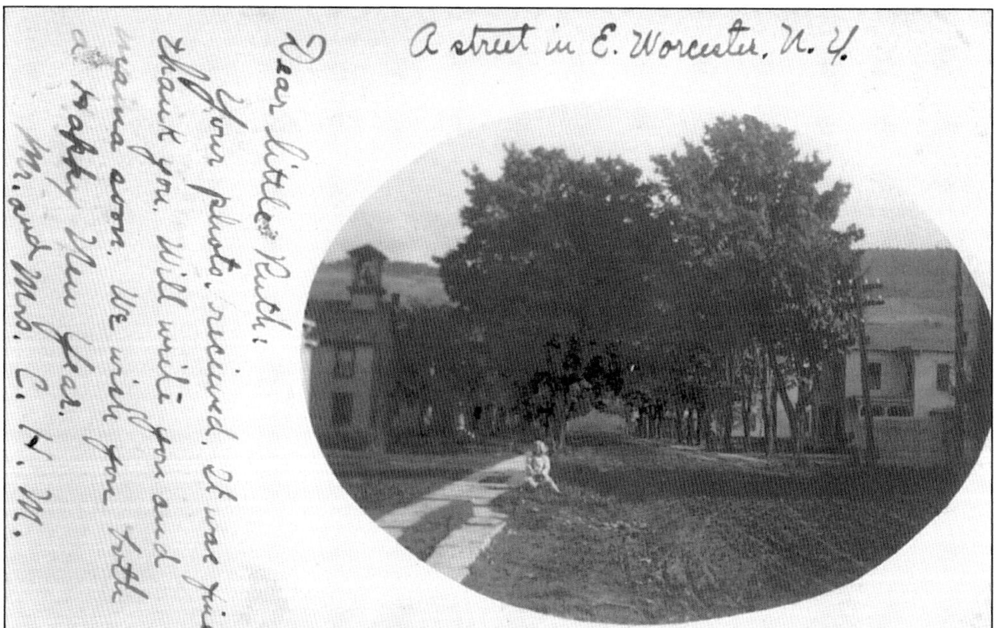

SIDE STREET. A little girl sits by the side of the road in this 1906 postcard. The Union School District No. 3 building is on the left. Maple trees line Depot Street, which leads to the station.

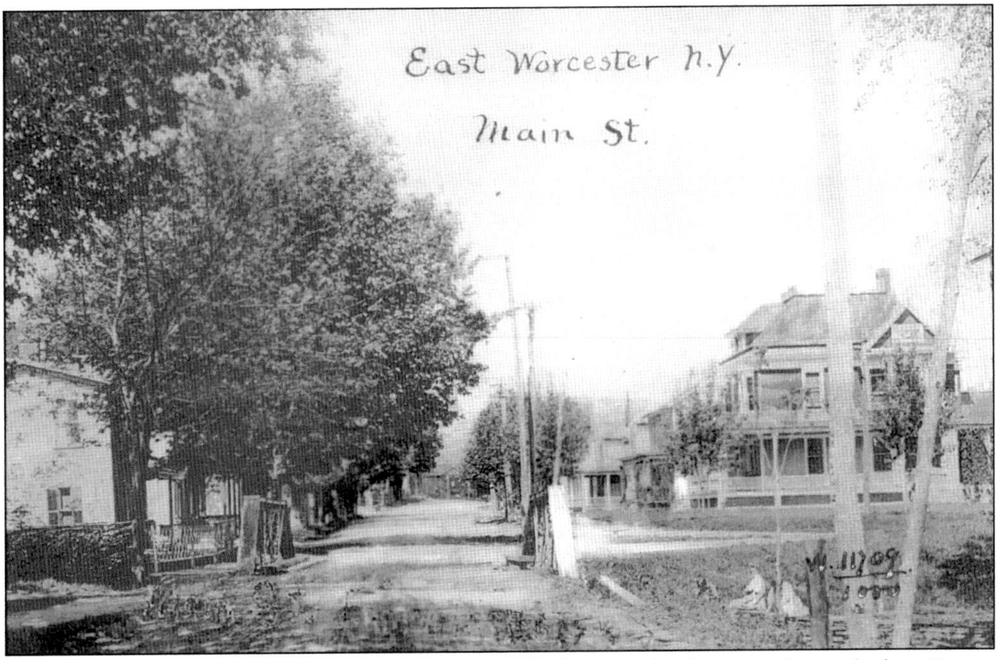

MAIN STREET. EAST WORCESTER'S MAIN Street once had an iron bridge over the creek along Route 7. Note that the road still was dirt and unpaved in early 1900.

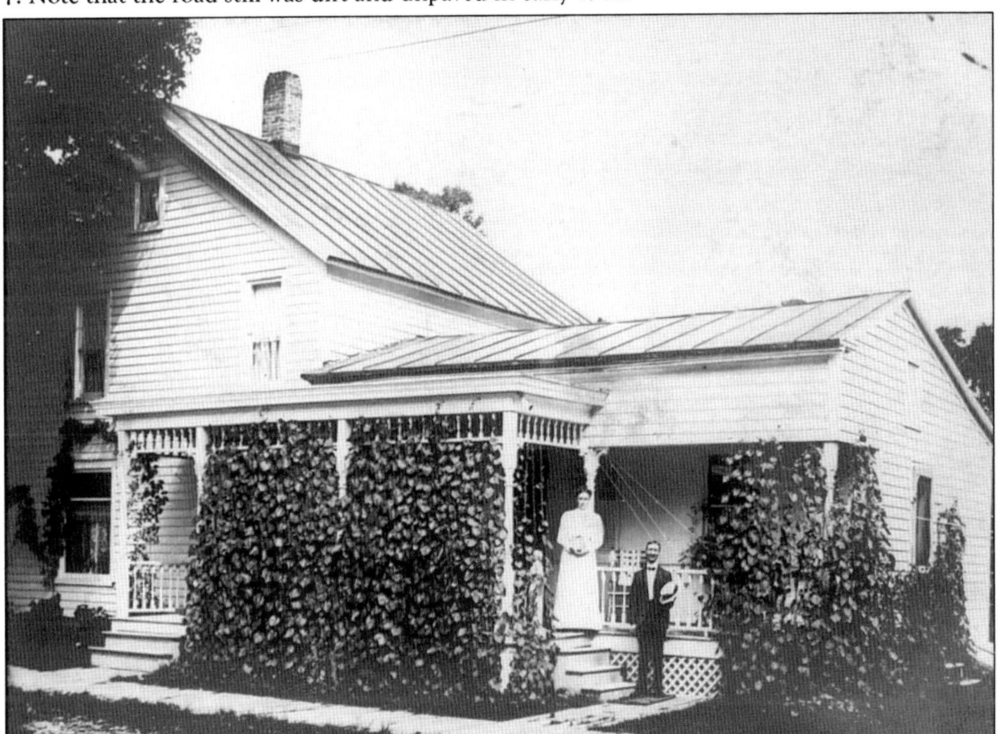

A LOCAL HOME. The reverse side of this 1908 card says it is from the Strobeck farm and Uncle Albie and Aunt Maude. The old-fashioned vine climbing up portions of the porch could be Dutchman's-pipe.

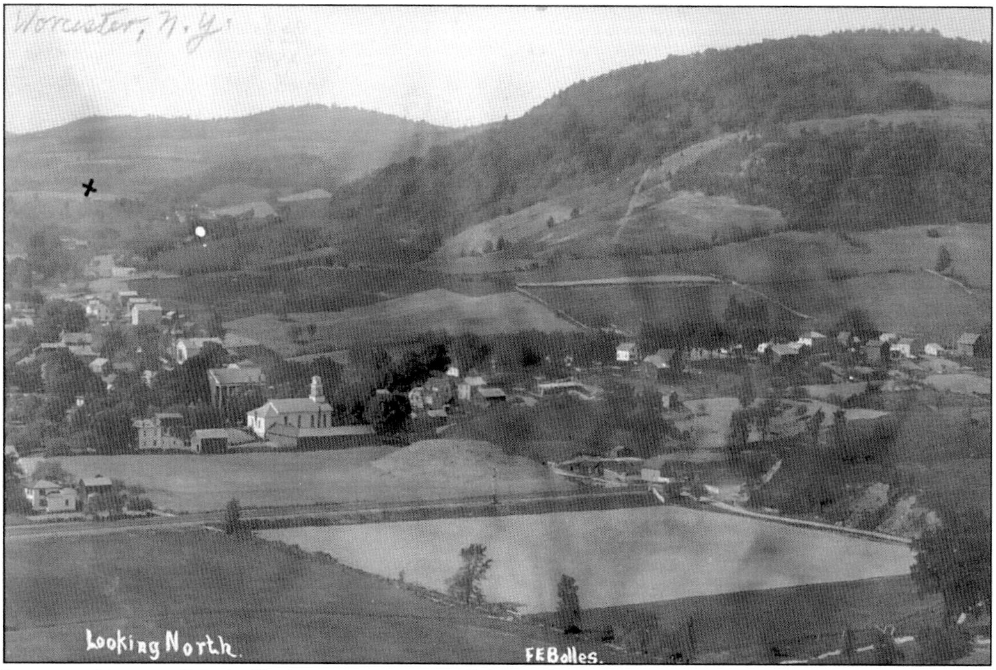

Looking North. F.E. Bolles's camera captured this village panorama from East Worcester's South Hill. The railroad tracks and the Methodist church are easily identified.

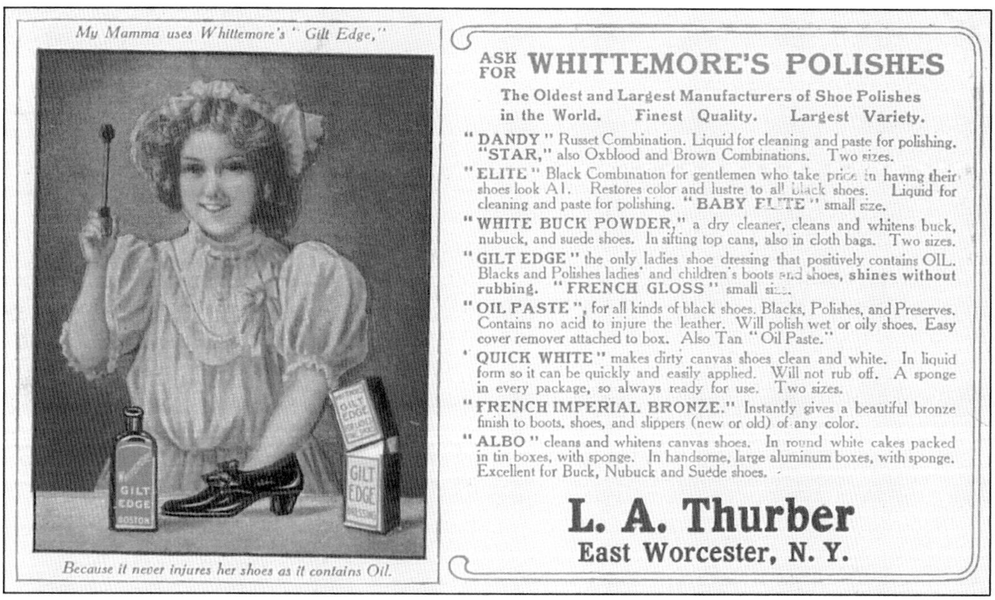

An Advertising Blotter. L.A. Thurber's East Worcester Country Store handed out blotters advertising "Gilt Edge" shoe polishes. East Worcester residents patronized Thurber's store in the early 1900s.

Four

WORCESTER

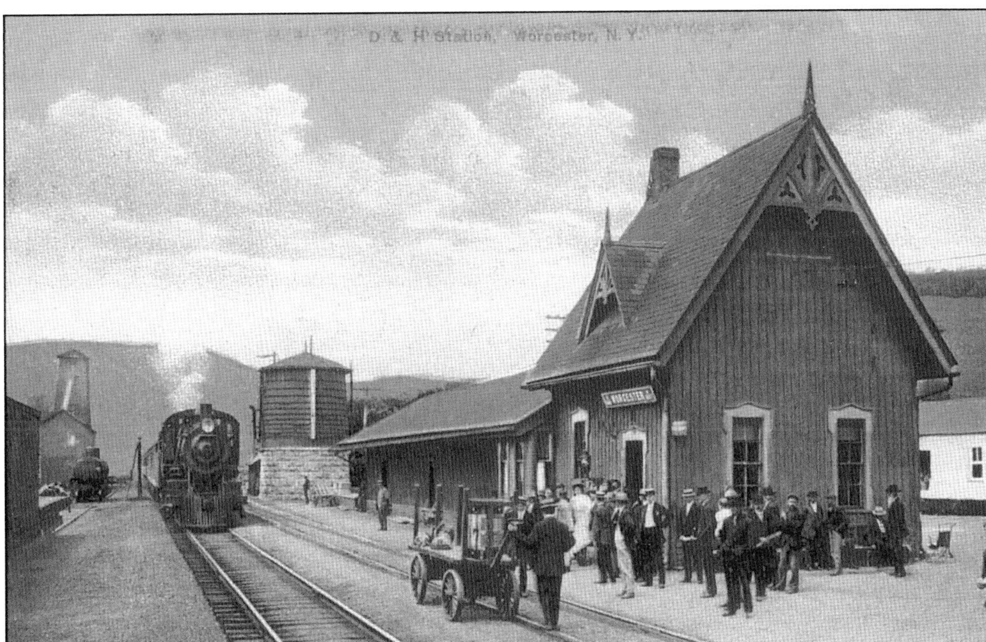

DELAWARE & HUDSON STATION. The first Albany & Susquehanna train from Albany reached Worcester on July 17, 1865, amid much excitement. The site was determined after a struggle between businessmen who all wanted it at a different location. Directors of the Albany & Susquehanna–John Cook and Aborn Bigelow–won out with their decision to place it in the general area of South Hill Road and South Church Street. Worcester got a significant boost with the arrival of four and five passenger trains a day.

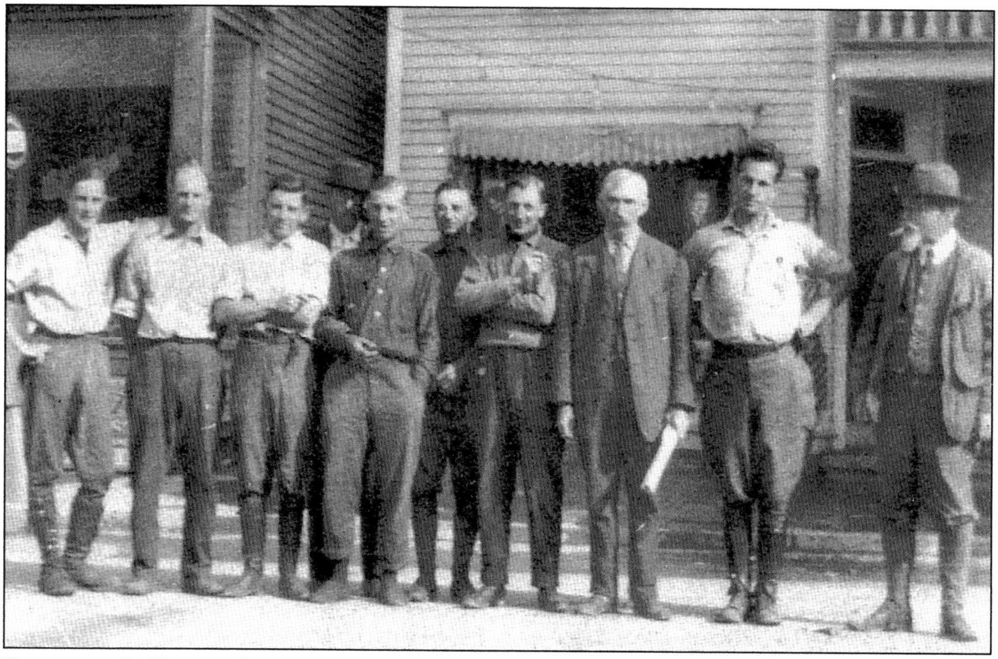

DELAWARE & HUDSON SURVEYORS. Surveyors and other Delaware & Hudson employees line up for a photograph in front of the Central Hotel (now the Worcester White House Inn). This 1913 photograph shows the inn's quarters, which were occupied by a barbershop that was operated by Raymond Potter.

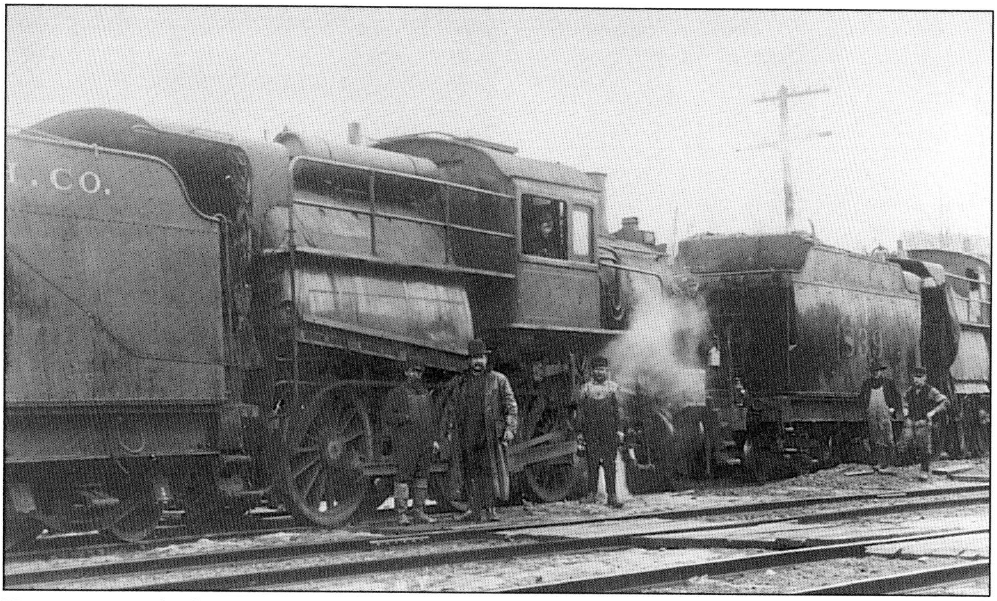

THE PUSHER. The heavy freight trains of the 1890s required a "pusher" to boost them up over the gap from Worcester to Richmondville. At one time, the grades were as steep as 1.31 percent but were later reduced to a maximum of .8 percent. Near the engine is brakeman-switchman Will Rector, who lost his hand in an accident and wore a hook. Hand-coupling of railroad cars caused many injuries in the early days. The engine and the men were stationed in Worcester. The other workers are unidentified.

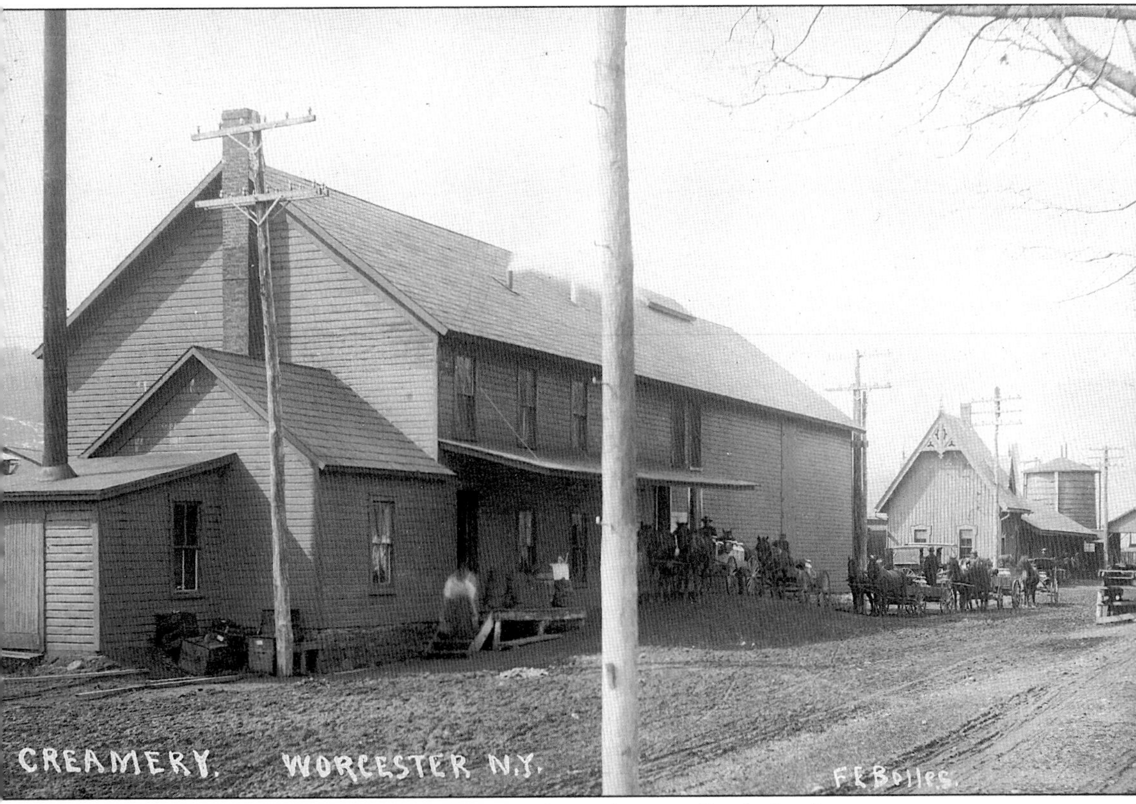

CREAMERY. In 1907, the creamery on Depot Street became Borden's. An ice-storage area was located at the west end of the building. Farmers increased the size of their dairies and brought in milk, which was processed and shipped daily to New York City on the milk train. A huge vat was used in the manufacture of pot cheese. At one time, 600 pounds of butter and the same amount of pot cheese were shipped to New York City on a regular basis. The Grange League Federation purchased the building and used it for its feed business. Once used for storage, the structure is now vacant.

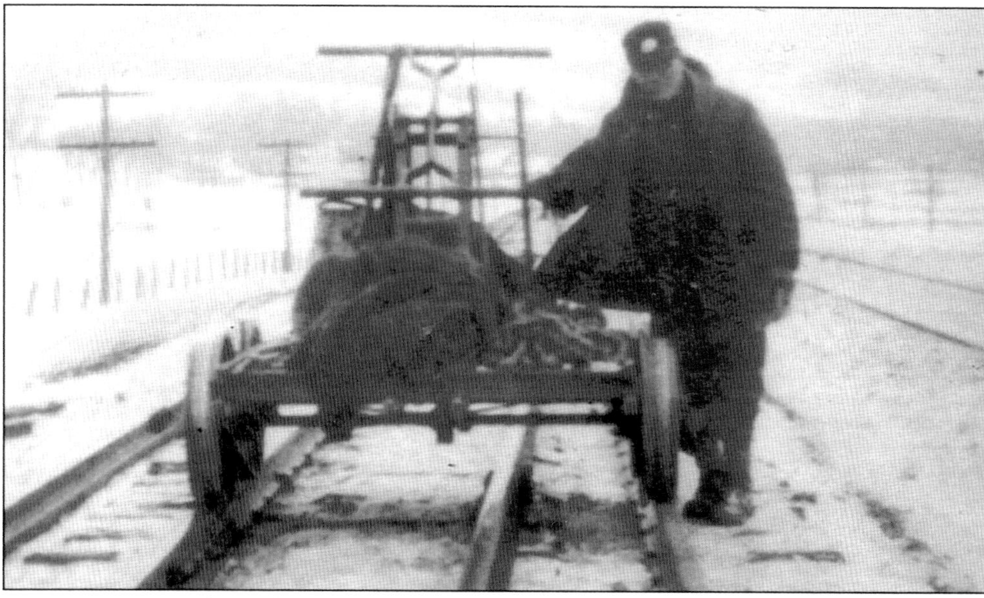

THE HANDCAR. In the early days of railroading, the lowly handcar was an important piece of equipment. Trackmen used their little handcars to cover their section of track to scout for a broken rail. The men pumped the bar of the handcar up and down to make it run. Harry Miller, whose father, uncle, and grandfather were all Delaware & Hudson trackmen, is pictured here. Their history goes back to the Albany & Susquehanna.

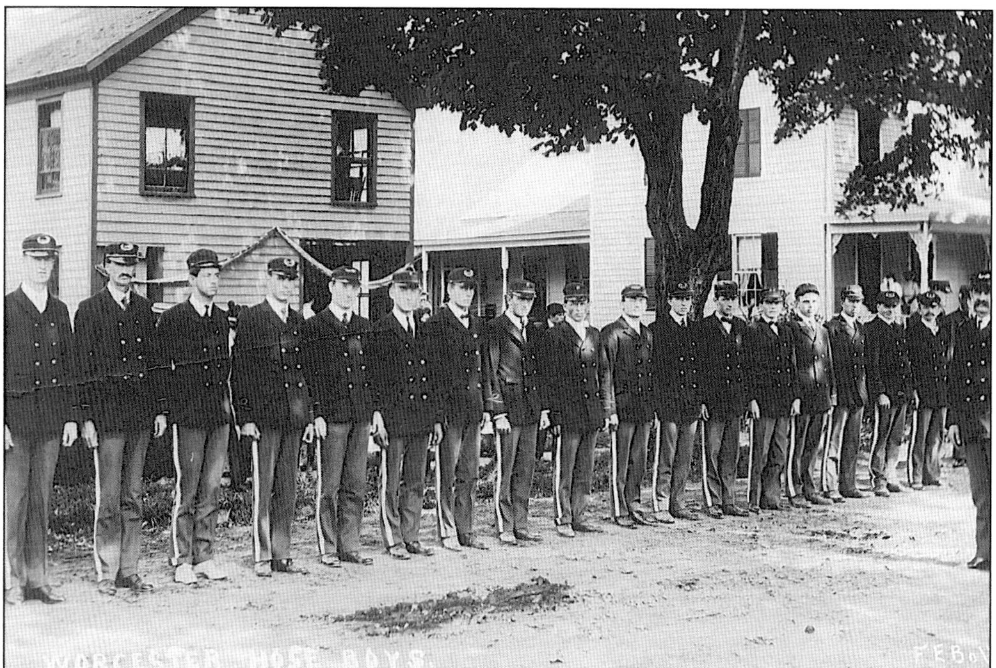

WORCESTER HOSE BOYS. The Wilder Hose Company was organized in October 1887. The new village water system was turned on in November. Members of the new hose company, accompanied by the band, marched victorious through the streets of Worcester, turning on the hydrants as they went. In this postcard, the men pose in their new uniforms before a parade.

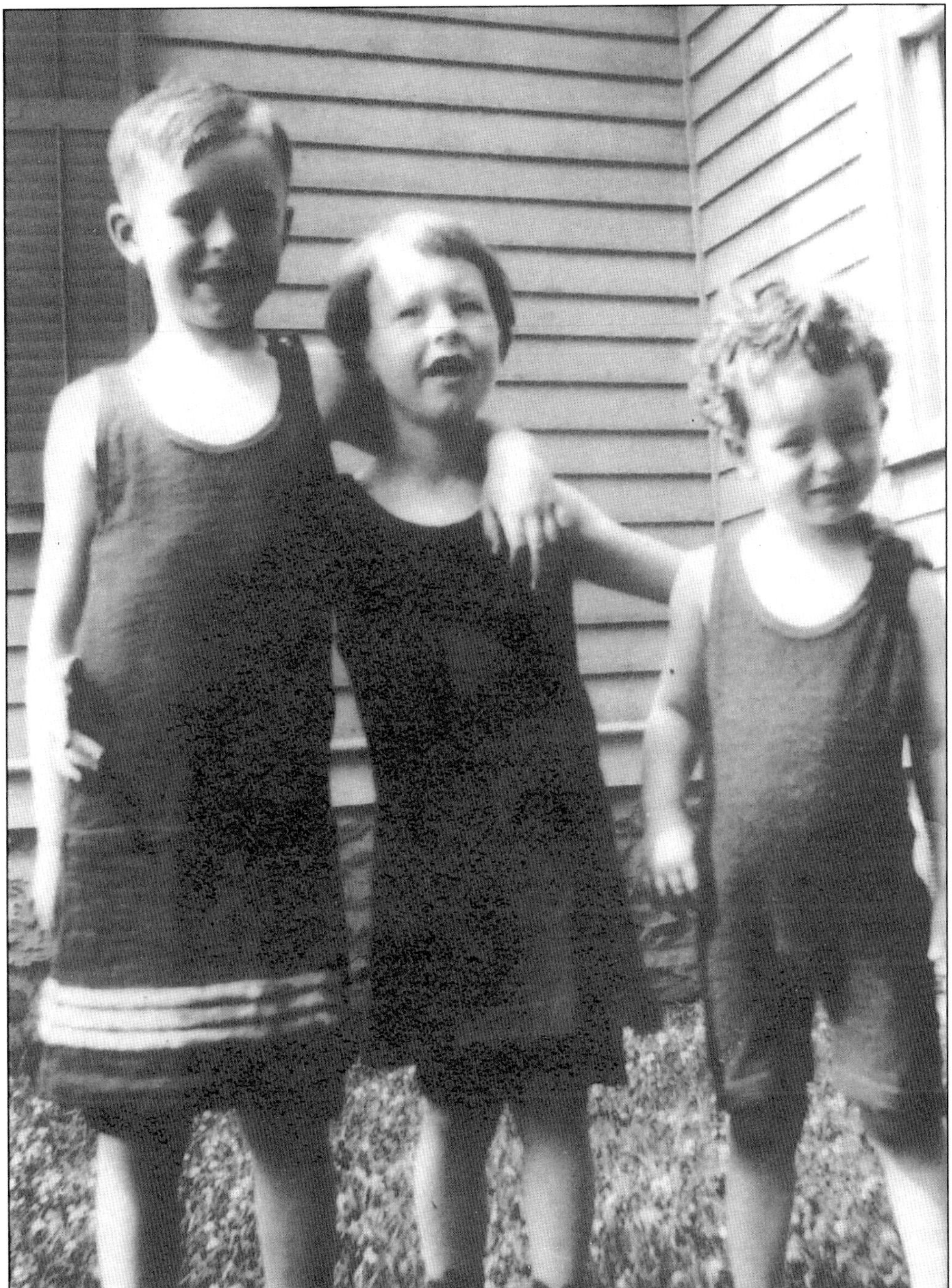

BATHING BEAUTIES. Willard, Milton, and George Wright grew up during the Great Depression. Willard (left), the oldest, got the new jackets, which were large so he could grow into them. The clothes were then handed down to the other two. Sunday dinners were usually chicken, but sometimes their father would buy a quarter of beef from a farmer. As a teenager, Willard often pulled mustard for a local farmer for 15¢ an hour. He also got 50¢ a week for driving farmer Cummings's cows from the pasture to the barn.

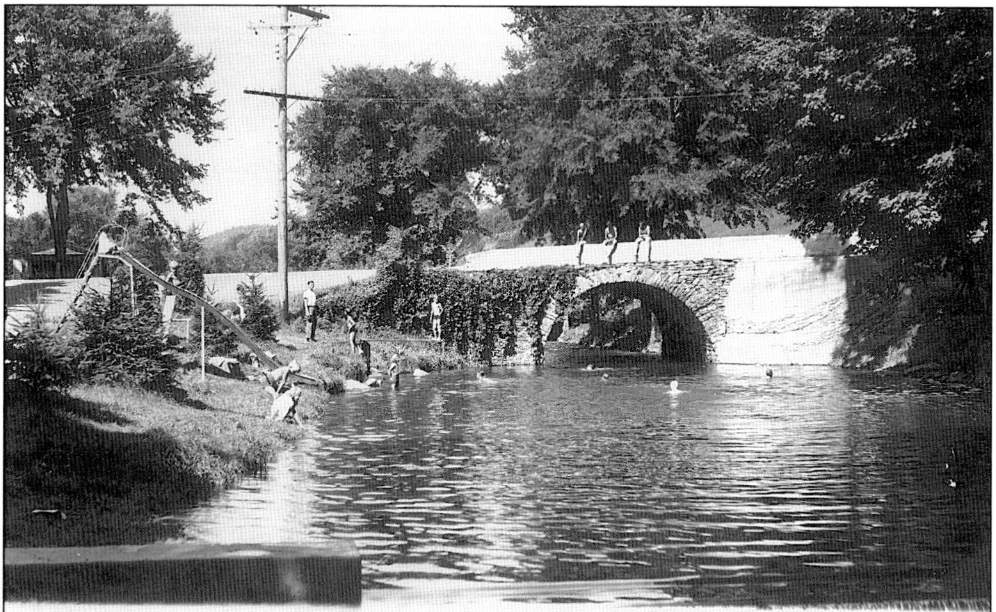

26—Swimming Pool, Worcester, N. Y.

SWIMMING POOL. Local children and adults used the swimming pool near the old stone arch bridge over Decatur Creek during the 1930s. A group of people raised enough money to build a cement dam and two bathhouses. The dam caused the creek to back up, forming a deep pool for swimming. Often, those daring enough would dive off the bridge.

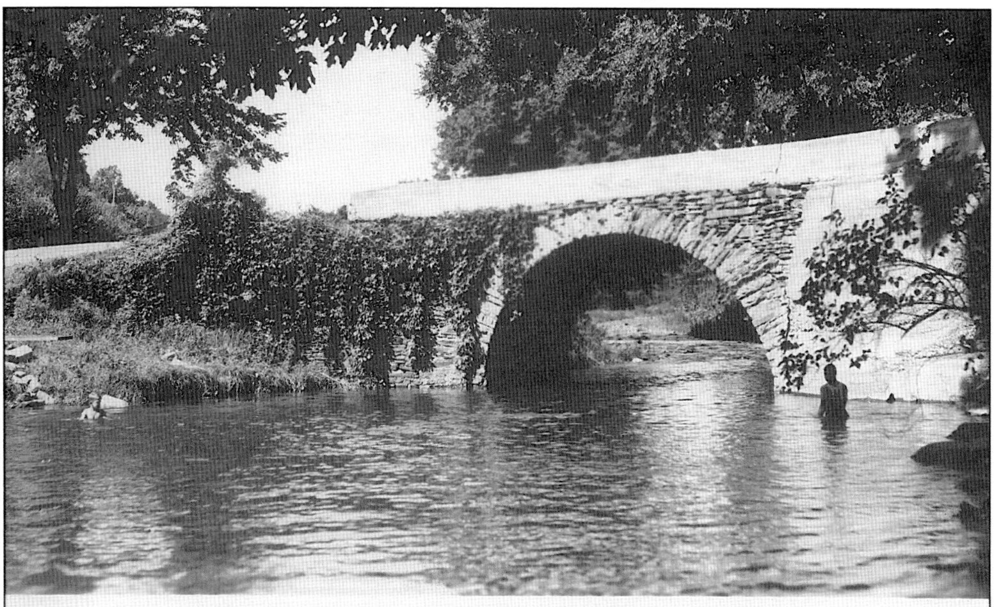

3—Arch Bridge, Worcester, N. Y.

THE STONE ARCH BRIDGE. This beautiful stone arch bridge at the end of Decatur Street was lost in a flood on September 21, 1938. Before the disaster, young and old enjoyed swimming in a portion of the creek beneath the bridge. The town's damages from the flood amounted to $100,000. The bridge was built in 1884 from local fieldstone. There is a painting of the bridge on one of the drop curtains in the Wieting Theatre.

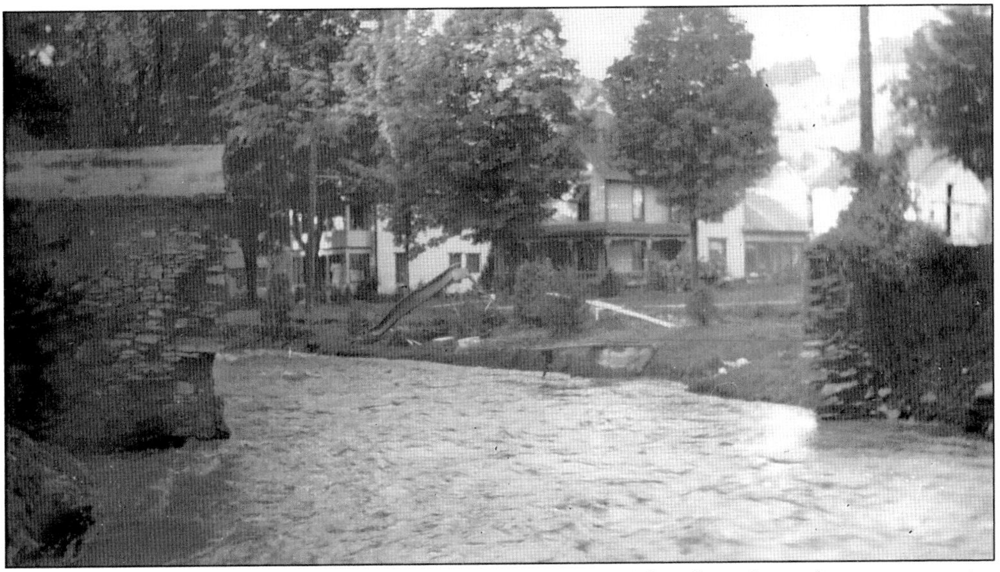

The Great Flood. Disaster struck on September 21, 1938. After three days of continuous rain, Decatur Creek sent roaring floodwaters through the area, causing extensive damage. This bridge on Water Street was swept away, roads washed out, homes wrecked, and meadows ruined when deposits of stone and gravel changed the course of the creek bed. Nine bridges in town were destroyed during the flood.

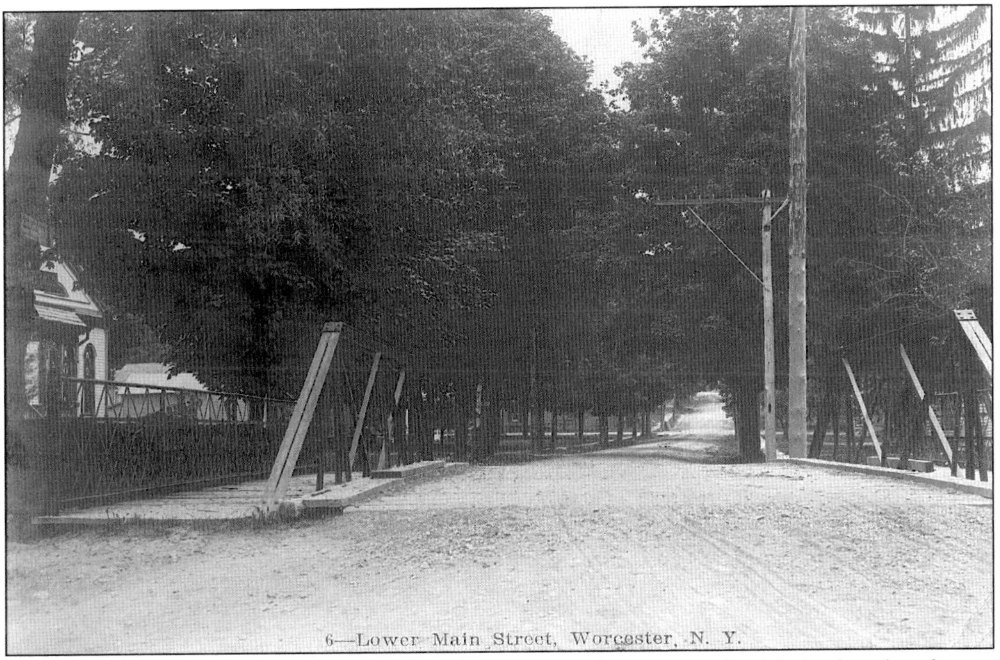

The Bridge on Main Street. The iron bridge on Main Street, near the Methodist church, was also taken out during the flood. Residents were without water for about a week after the water main beneath the bridge was destroyed. A cement bridge was built over Route 7 in addition to an above-ground water main.

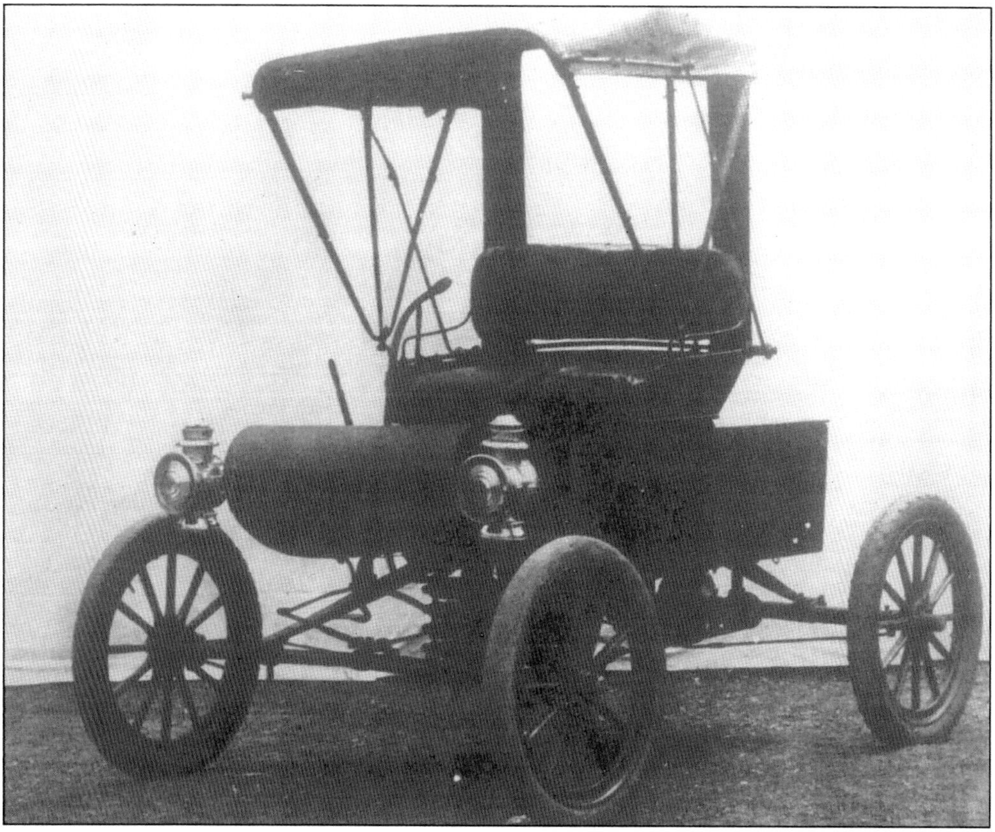

THE FIRST CAR IN TOWN. This 1902 Oldsmobile Runabout, the first car in town, cost $625 and was owned by Louis W. Bellinger, Worcester's first automobile dealer. He built a garage and service station at 30 Main Street and installed the town's first curb gas pump.

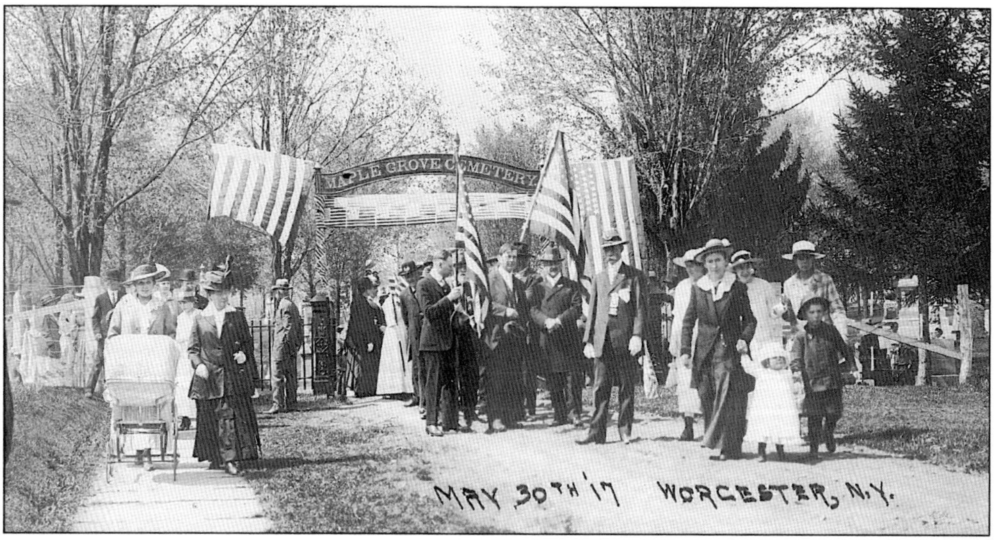

MEMORIAL DAY 1917. People leave Maple Grove Cemetery following the service at the Soldier's Monument. Seth Flint is the tall, slender man with the mustache. Flint, a Civil War bugler, wears his Grand Army of the Republic ribbons.

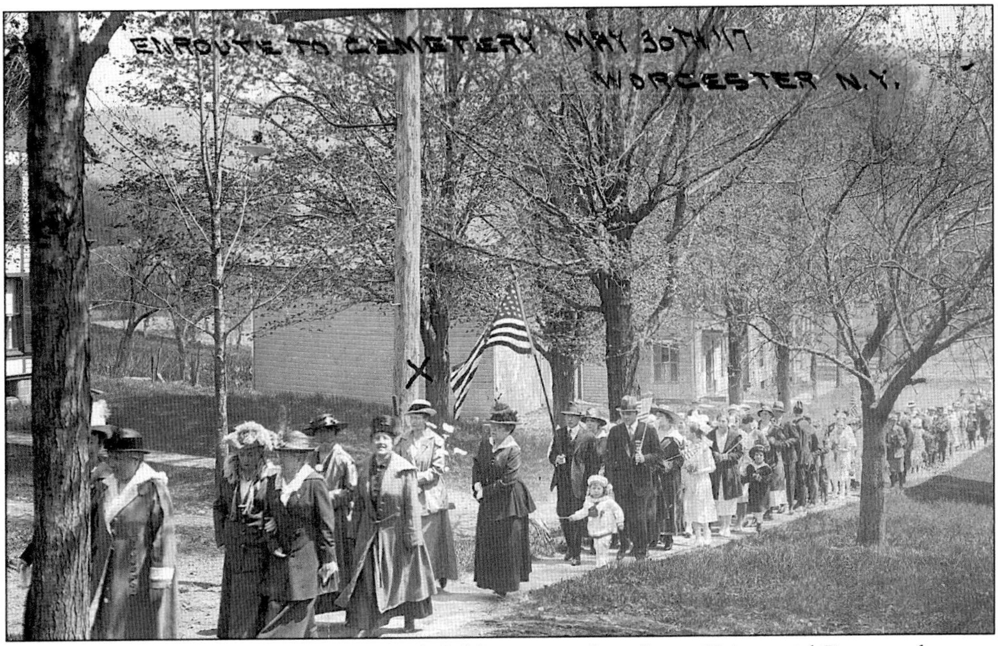

MEMORIAL DAY 1917. Women, men, and children join a long line of Memorial Day marchers up the sidewalk bordering Cook Street to Maple Grove Cemetery. This postcard provides a good example of clothing styles of the day. Women wore hats with plumes, long dresses, and gloves. The men wore hats and suits, and children had sailor suits, tams, and big bows.

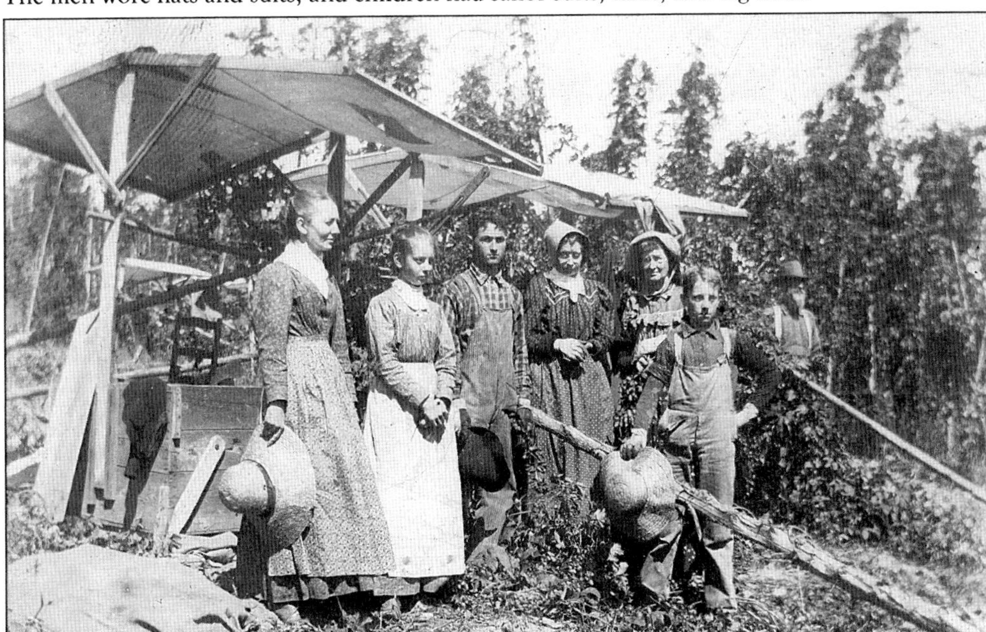

HOP PICKERS. This 1900 photograph shows hop pickers at Howard W. Flint's farm on Decatur Road. Sometimes the heat was overwhelming. One day, a Mrs. Key died while picking in the field. Pickers wore wide-brimmed hats and baggy clothes with long sleeves to protect against scratchy, prickly hop vines. Gloves also were worn as well as long stockings and a scarf around the neck so insects could not gain entry.

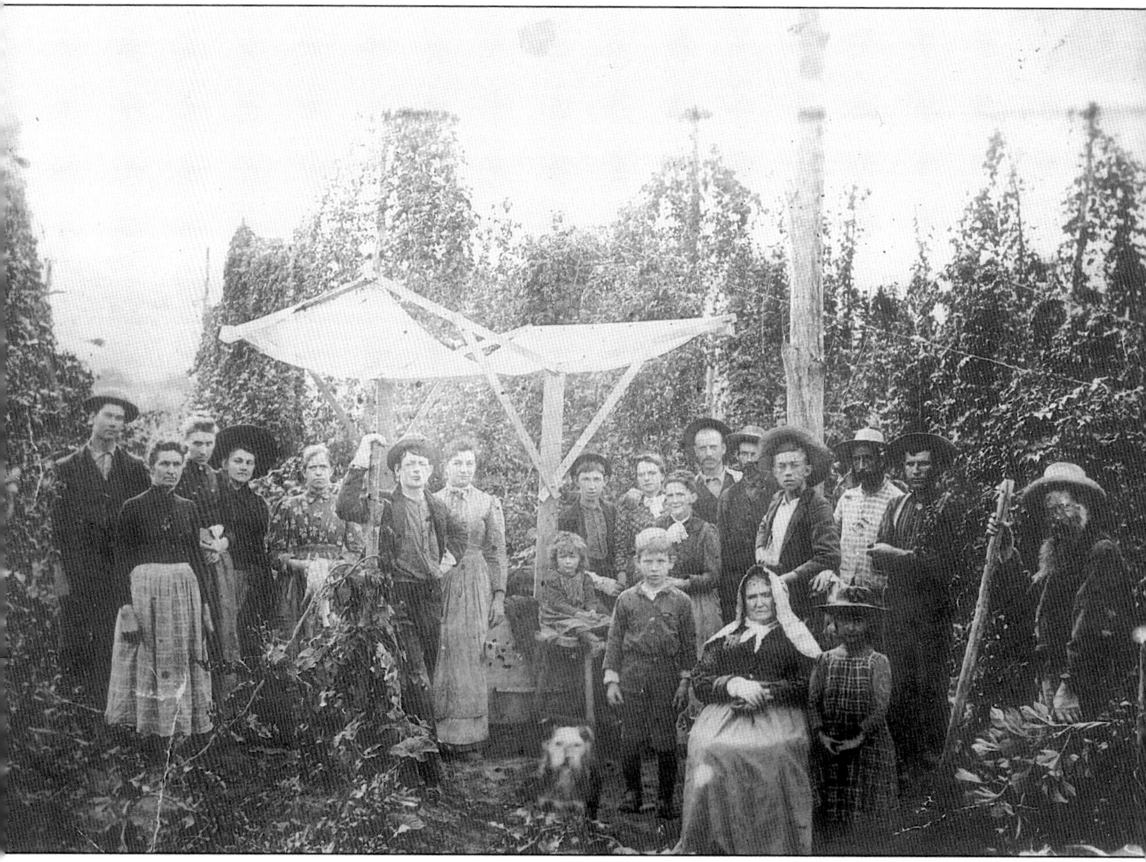

Hop Pickers. This is another view of hop pickers in a field near Worcester. Men, women, and children all help with the picking chores. A picker finding a vine shaped into a circle, called a "kissing loop," could kiss anyone he or she wanted. Sometimes the kiss recipient had to be chased around the yard before a kiss could be obtained. The hop yard was known as a place of talking, gossiping, singing, joking, flirting, and making up poems. Hop picking was described as hot, sweaty, scratchy, and buggy work.

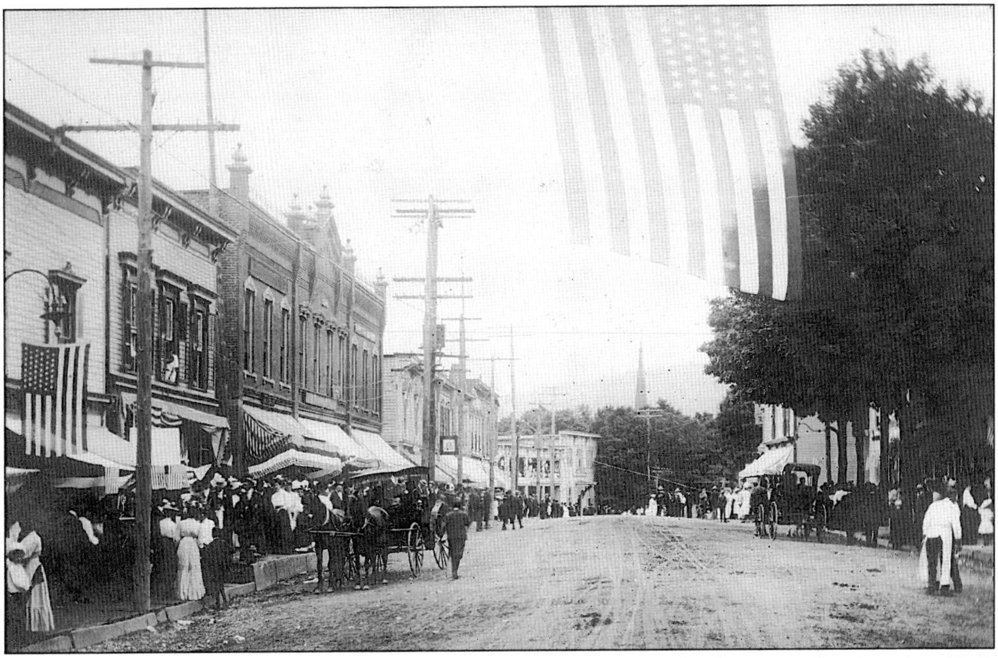

The Fourth of July 1908. Spectators came to town by the hundreds to see the Fourth of July parade. Fireworks could be sold legally in the 1920s and 1930s. Both Earl F. Johnson's variety store and Pete Natale's store sold firecrackers, Roman candles, skyrockets, and sparklers. Children could buy a pack of 50 firecrackers for 25¢. The packs had a main fuse that was designed to discharge the firecrackers one at a time within a few seconds.

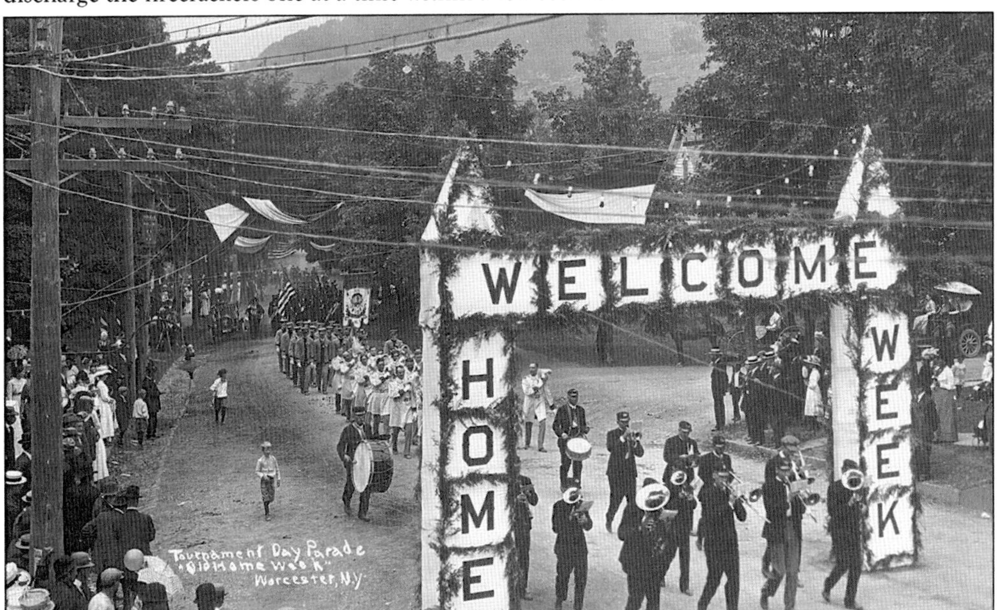

Old Home Week. The Tournament Day Parade was part of Old Home Week, July 31 to August 4, 1911. Crowds came out to enjoy the giant parade, which was a highlight of the five-day celebration.

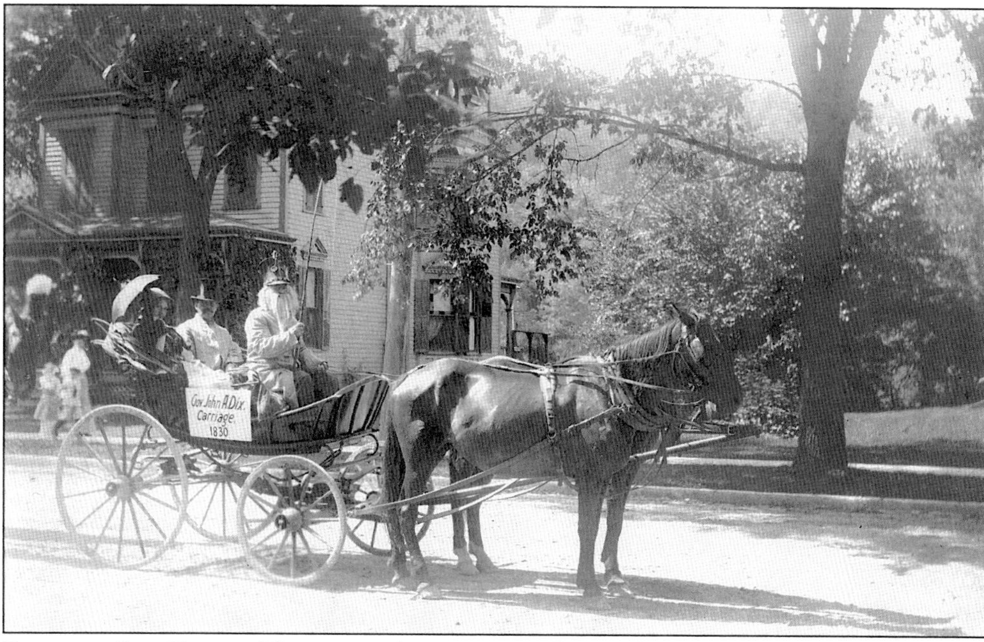

FOURTH OF JULY PARADE. The sign on the wagon says, "General John A. Dix Carriage 1830." The horse-and-wagon float may be celebrating a 100th anniversary.

WERE I to choose, dear Berta, a husband for you,
I'd seek a man, brave, tender, devoted and true.
'T would not be 'mid proud fashion's bold pomp and vain blare,
Nor yet 'mid wealth's gay, showy enticements and glare;
Nay, nay, I would not seek for position nor pride
Nor wealth nor power nor title for you as a bride.
For what are all these for a soul to live on?
A flame—nay, flash—nay, twinkle—and then they are gone.
What are all these and travel and palace and dome
Beside the sweet, calm joy of a dear little home?
Nay, not a Croesus, nobleman, nor other than
An earnest, honest, loving yes, God-fearing—man,
To bring you peace, contentment and happiness, too,
I'd seek if I were choosing a husband for you.

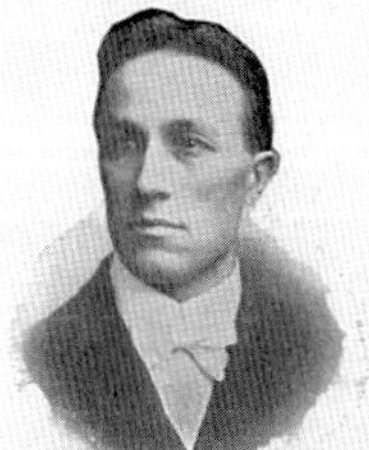

Carl C. Countryman

CARL C. COUNTRYMAN. Little is known about Carl C. Countryman, who lived in the area during the 1950s. He ran for president of the United States but never made the news enough for people to learn about him.

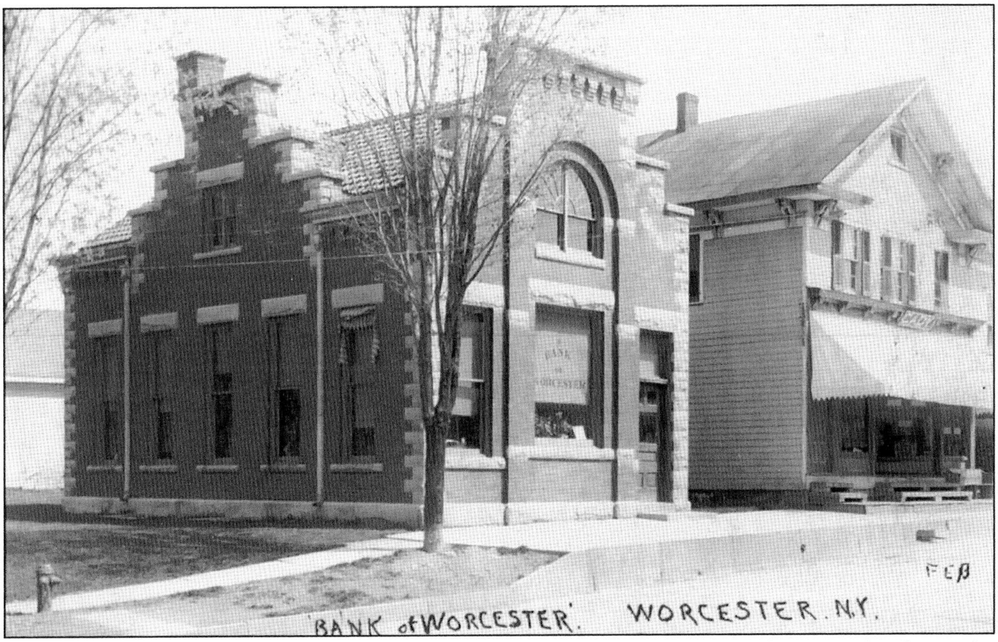

Bank of Worcester. The bank secured the right from the town to build a new bank on the site of the graves of the ancestors of Pres. James A. Garfield. The matter was settled after a bitter clash between the citizens of the town and bank officials. While excavating, many bones were discovered as well as rotten pieces of wood. Three generations of Garfields lived in town. Before his assassination, Garfield wrote a letter expressing his hope to be able to visit Worcester.

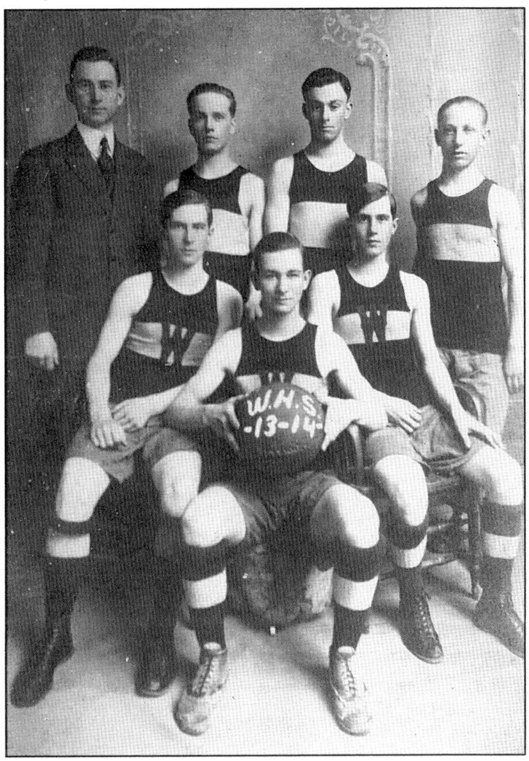

Worcester High School. Pictured are six members of the 1913–1914 Worcester High School basketball team. From left to right are the following: (front row) Fred Moak, unidentified, and Frank Moak; (back row) unidentified, unidentified, Van Wright, and Melvin Simmons.

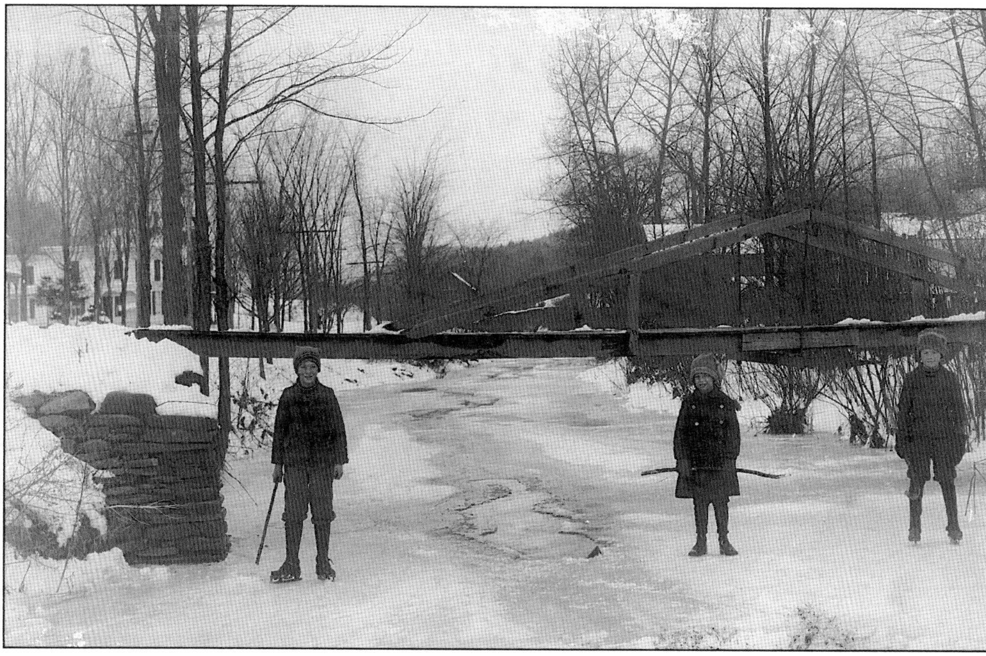

SKATING ON DECATUR CREEK. These children enjoy skating on Decatur Creek on a winter day in 1908. The old wooden footbridge is in the background. From left to right are Howard Galer, unidentified, and Van Wright.

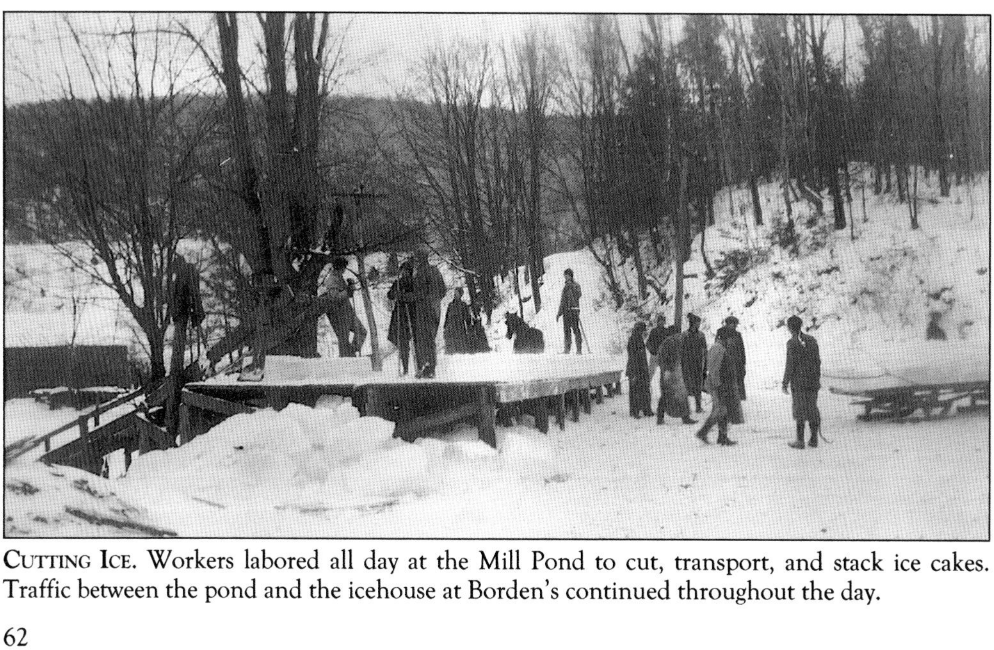

CUTTING ICE. Workers labored all day at the Mill Pond to cut, transport, and stack ice cakes. Traffic between the pond and the icehouse at Borden's continued throughout the day.

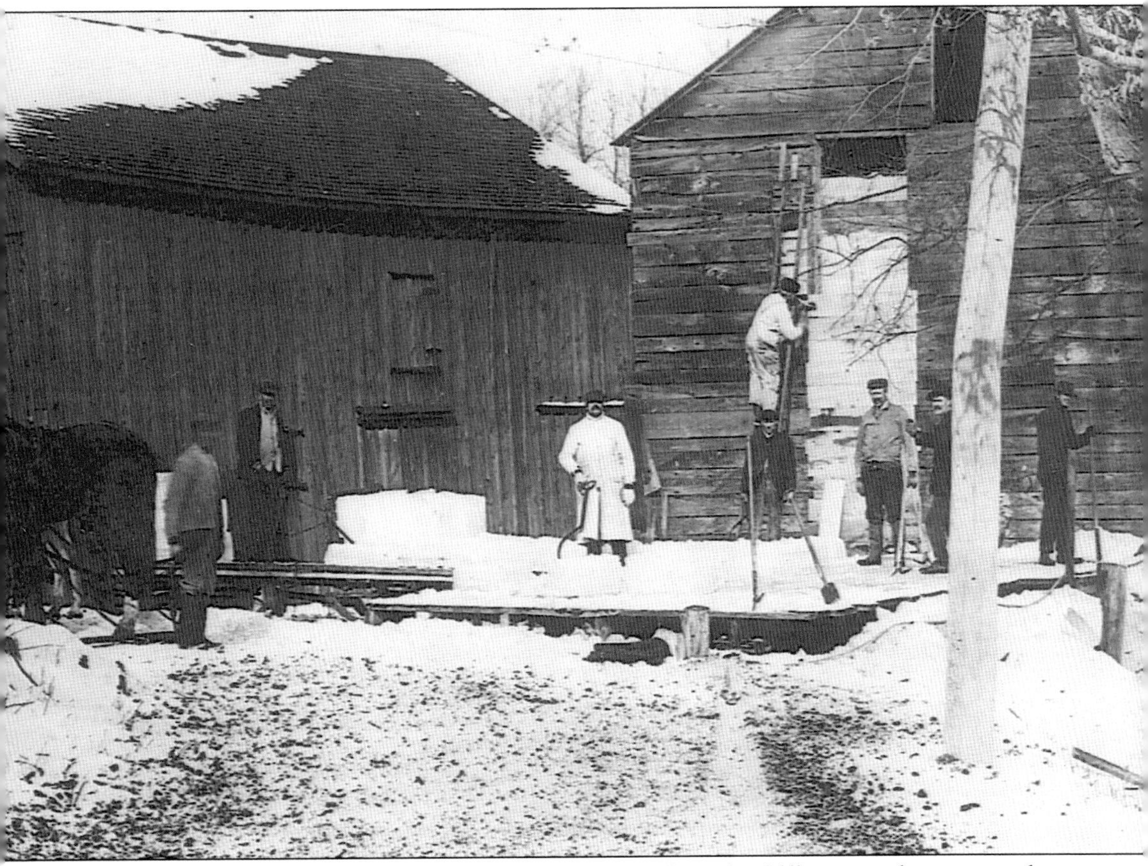

Ice Harvest. Borden's Creamery, on Depot Street, began the task of filling its icehouse once the Mill Pond reached a thickness of one foot. A crew on the ice cut and floated the ice cakes to a loading dock. The cakes were then transported by horse and sleigh to the creamery, where they were stacked in sawdust to keep them during the summer months. Once Borden's had its limit of ice, the icehouse at the Mill Pond was filled. Harry Shafer delivered the ice in the hamlet during the summers in the 1930s before most homeowners had refrigerators.

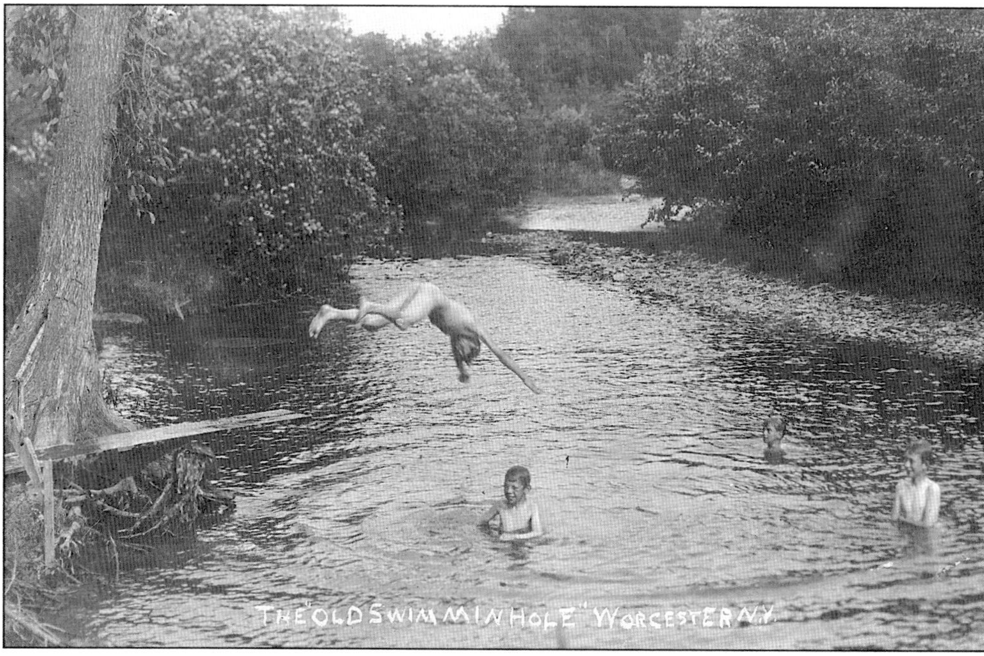

THE OLD SWIMMING HOLE. In the early days of the 20th century, the old swimming hole was near the Mill Pond in the stream that flows into Schenevus Creek. In this view, local boys in their birthday suits jump from a homemade diving board and enjoy the cool water on a hot summer day.

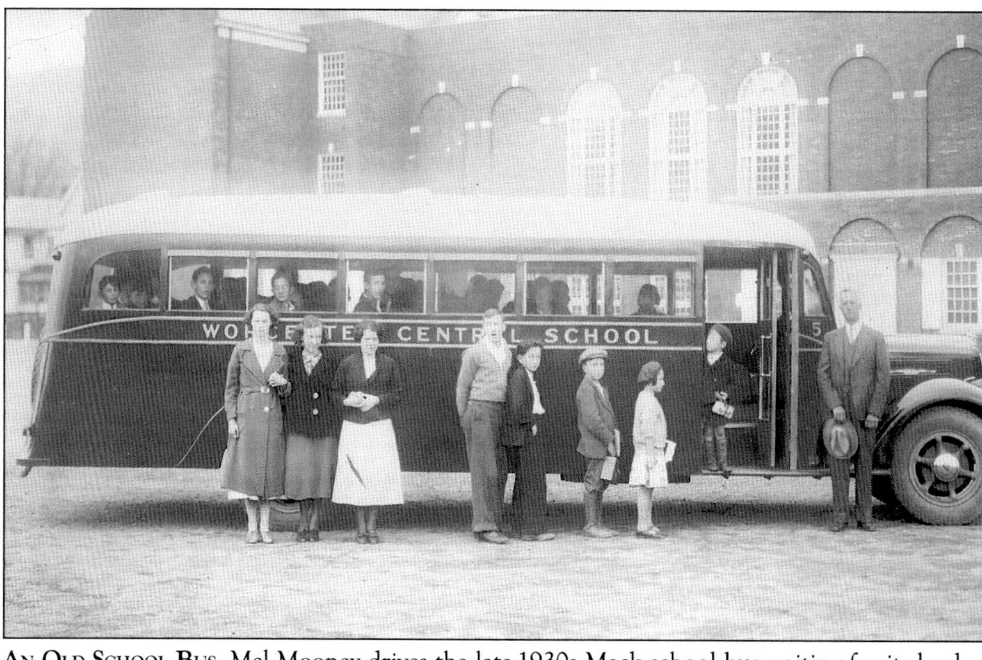

AN OLD SCHOOL BUS. Mel Mooney drives the late-1930s Mack school bus waiting for its load of children before taking off on the afternoon run. Worcester Central School's buses at that time were dark green, before state law mandated the yellow school bus. Margaret and Ellen Mooney are on the left.

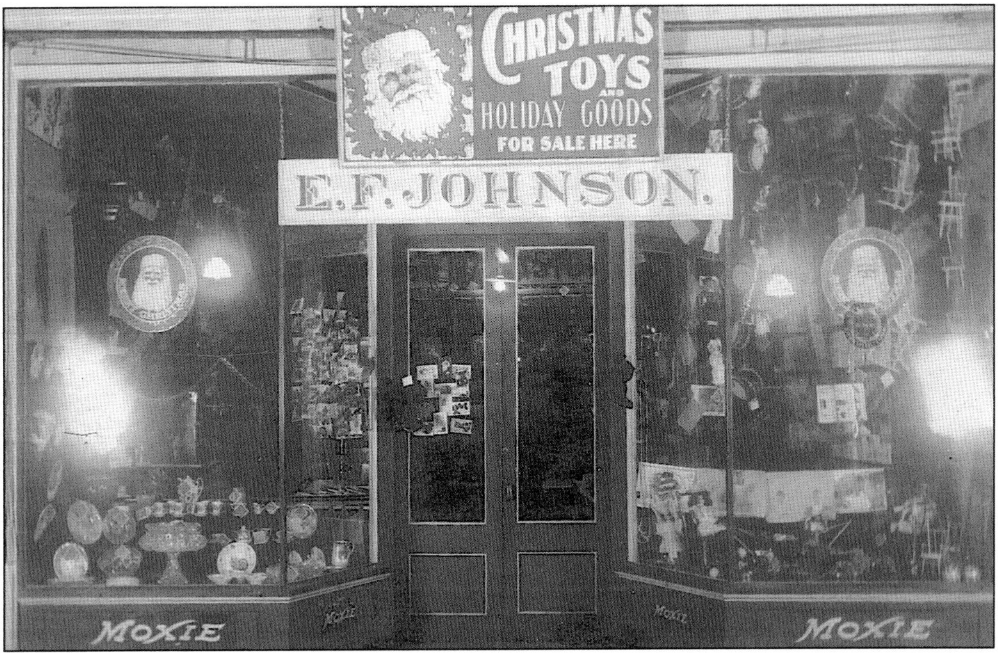

E.F. Johnson's Variety Store. This festive Christmas display fills the window of Earl F. Johnson's variety store *c.* 1912. His business survived two world wars and saw many political and economic changes. His store was sold to Carl Brownell in 1945, and the building was destroyed by fire on May 3, 1994.

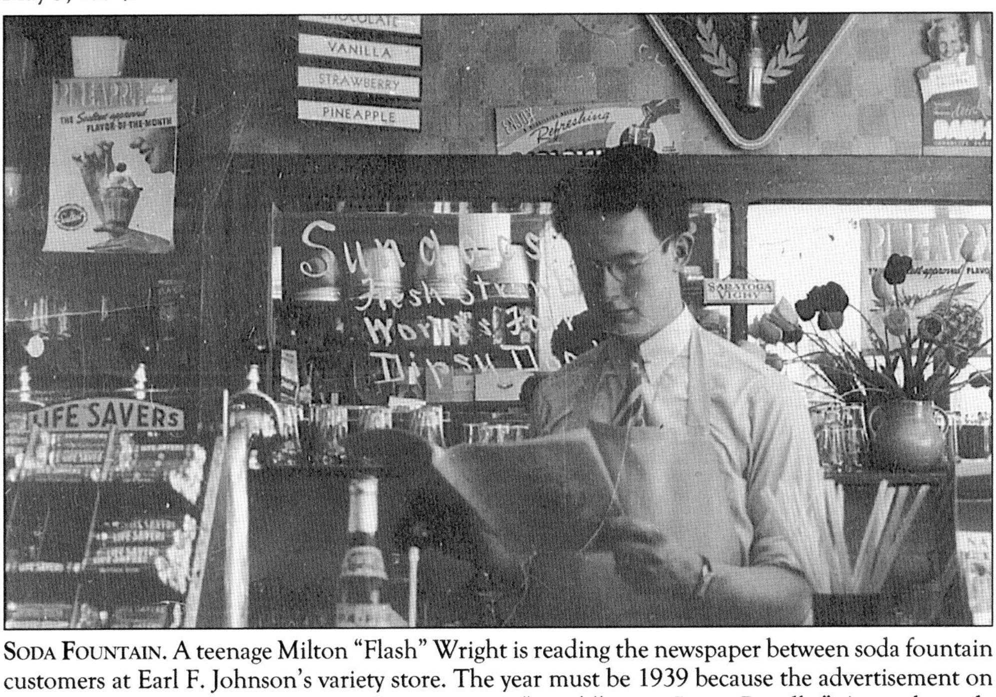

Soda Fountain. A teenage Milton "Flash" Wright is reading the newspaper between soda fountain customers at Earl F. Johnson's variety store. The year must be 1939 because the advertisement on the mirror behind the fountain suggests trying a "World's Fair Dipsy Doodle." As in the soda fountain era, Johnson's facility included a long marble counter with stools where customers could sit down and enjoy a sundae or soda.

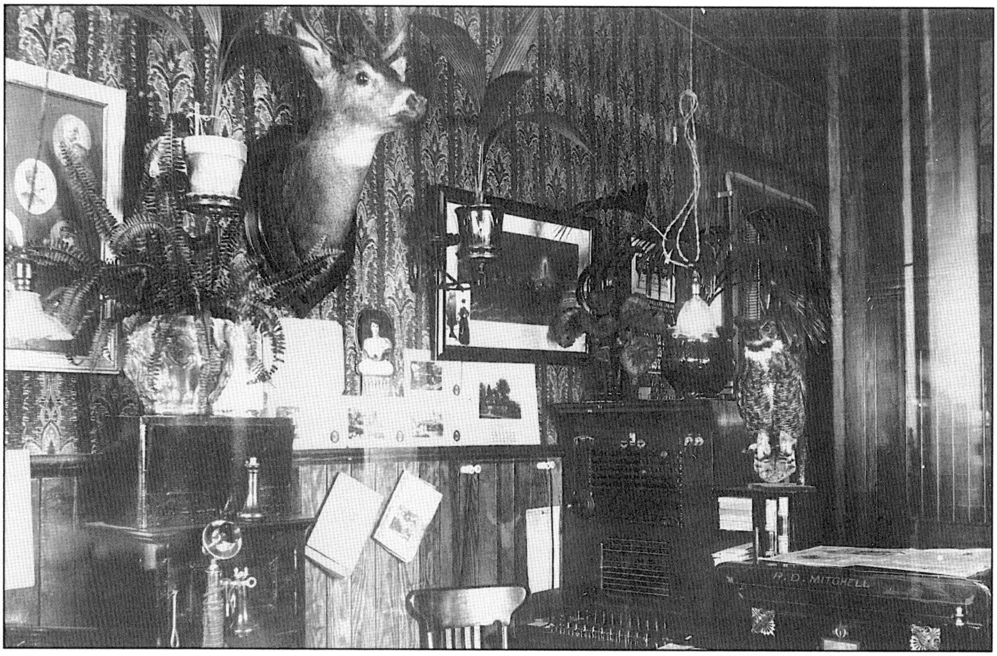

The Central Telephone Office. This is an F.E. Bolles postcard of the Central Telephone Office in Worcester. In 1905, the company was incorporated by a group of local people with headquarters and switchboard located in the Central Hotel. A mounted deer head and plants complement the office, which has a candlestick-style telephone.

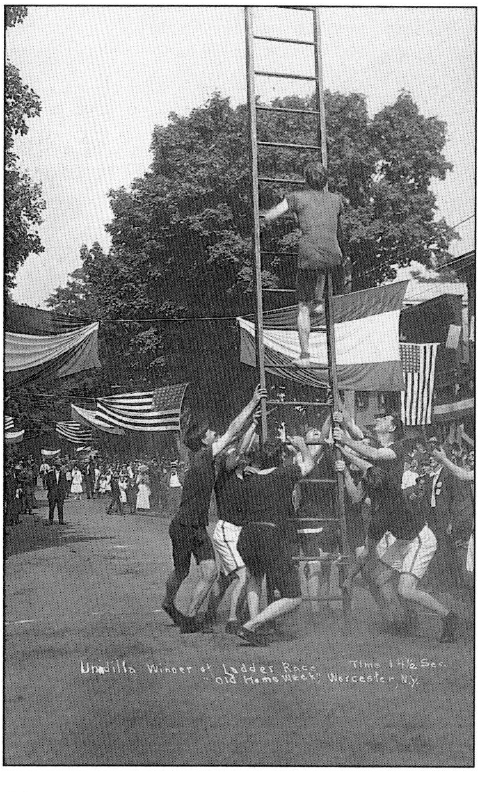

Old Home Week. Firematics was an event during the 1910 Old Home Week. These races are between the local department and Unadilla firefighters. Unadilla won this ladder race in 14.5 seconds.

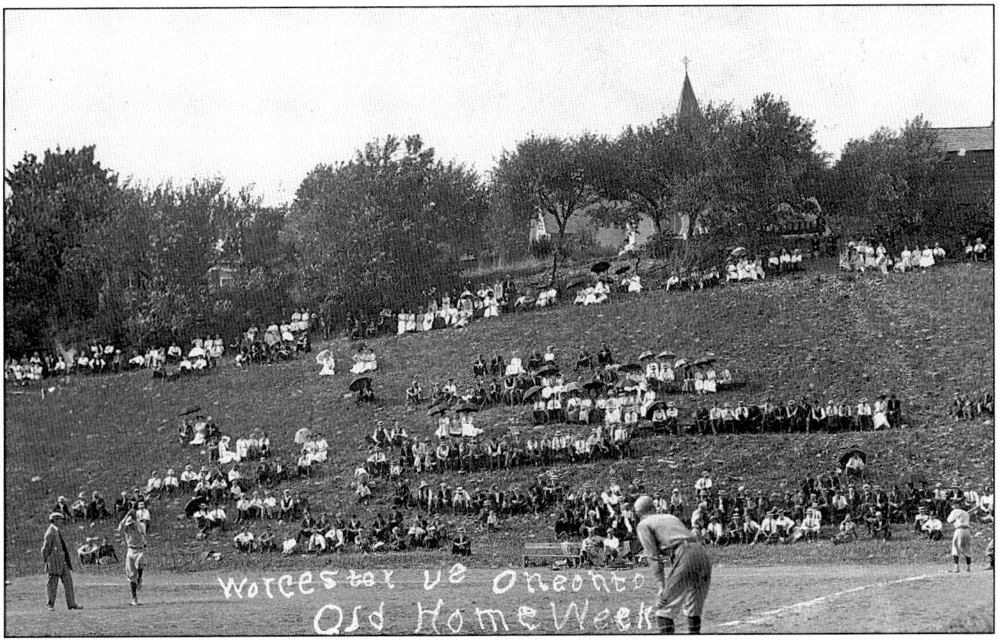

A Baseball Game. Spectators line the hill by the playing field to watch a game between Oneonta and Worcester during Old Home Week. The area is now part of the Worcester Park. In the background, the steeple of the First Presbyterian church is visible.

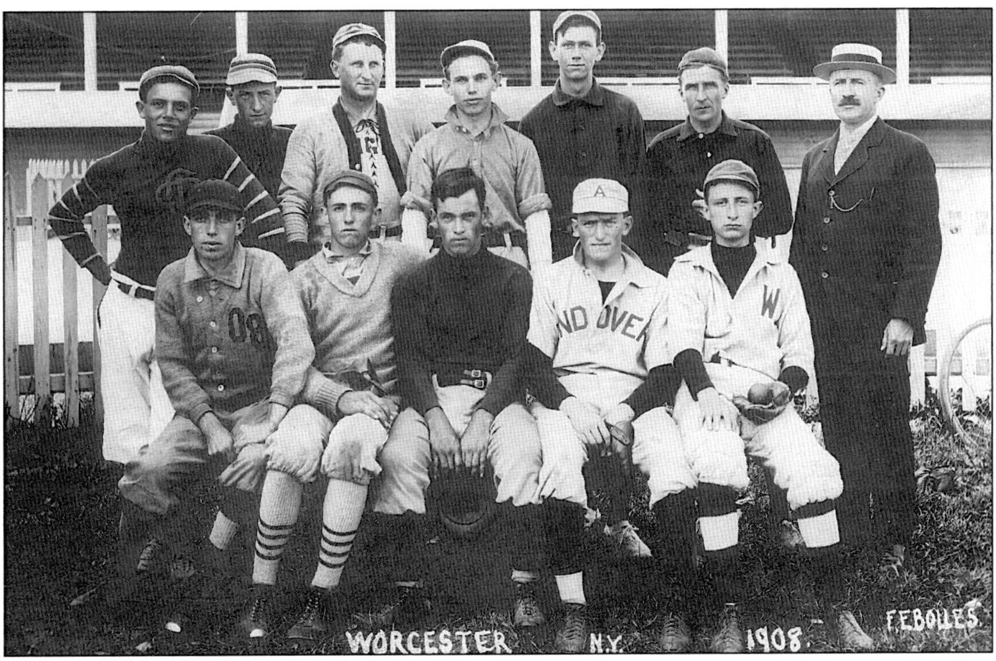

A Baseball Team. This is an F.E. Bolles postcard of baseball team members in Worcester in 1908. From left to right are the following: (front row) Van Wiem, John Sterricker, Willard Wright, Orrin Pierce, and Carl Gillette; (back row) Roy Goodell, Fred Pierce, ? Flint, Harry Simmons, Carroll Lehman, Norman Martin, and Prof. Menzo Burlingame.

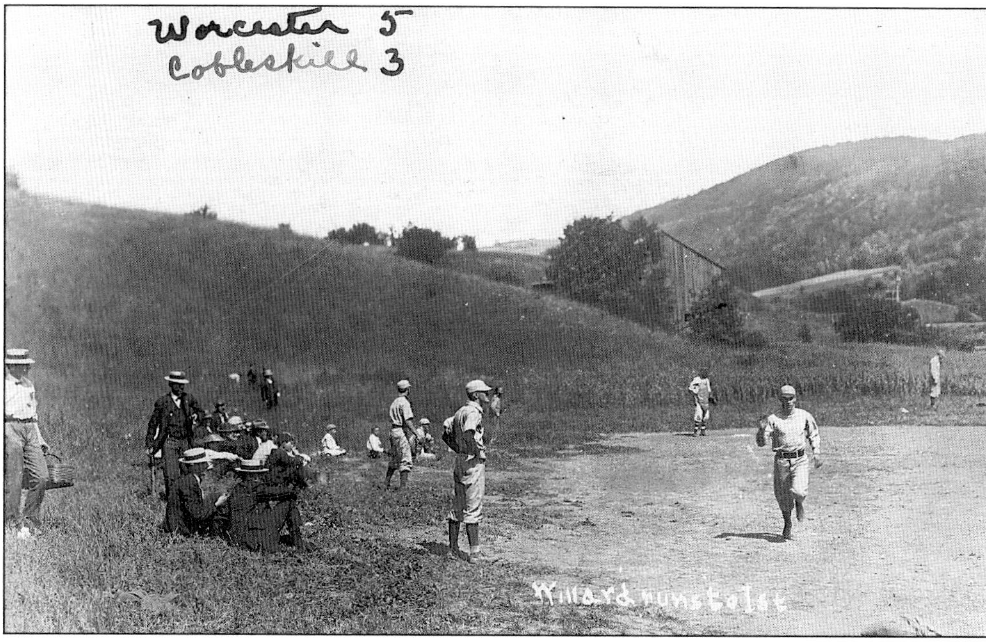

A BASEBALL GAME. This baseball game played by the town team resulted in a final score of Worcester 5, Cobleskill 3. The games were played on the field behind the stores in the town's business district. Willard Wright, who later played professional baseball, runs to first base. Wright briefly played for the Brooklyn Tip/Tops in the Federal League in 1915.

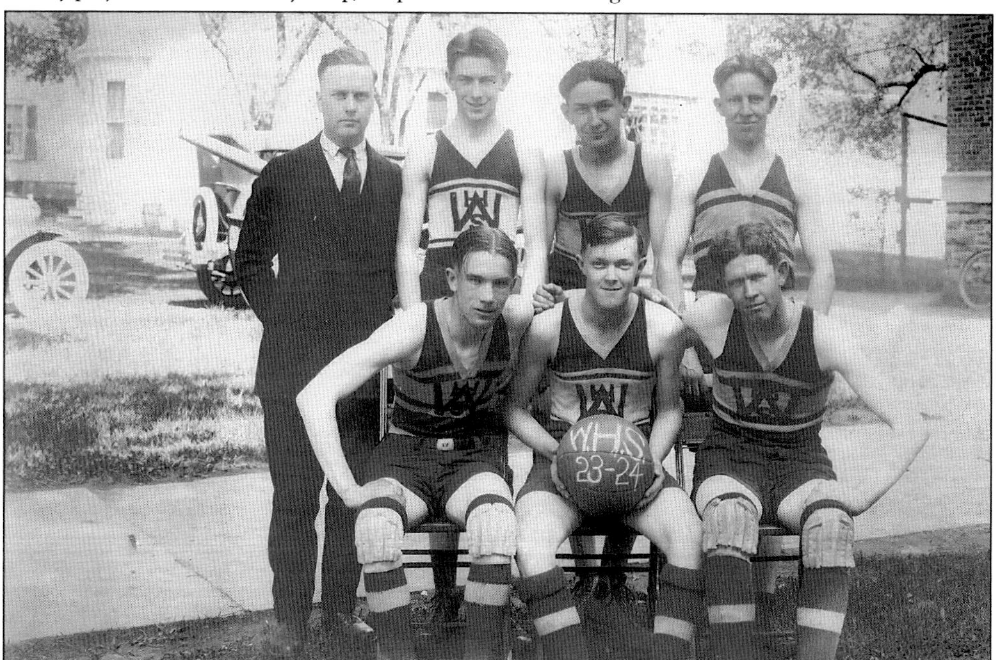

A BASKETBALL TEAM. The Worcester Central School boys' basketball team in 1923–1924 included these players. From left to right are the following: (front row) Bill Whitcomb, Willard Chase, and Melvin N. Ferguson; (back row) coach John Wilcox, Leonard Whitcomb, George Lesh, and Clement Moore.

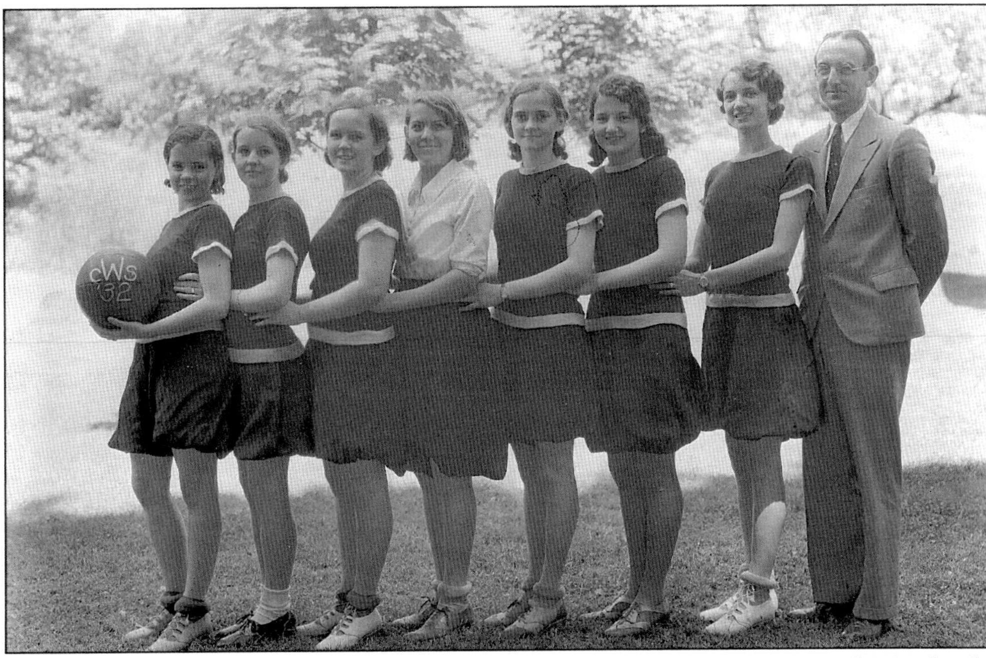

A Girls' Basketball Team. Pictured are members of the 1932 Worcester Central School girls' basketball team. From left to right are Leah Wade, Theresa Graham, Elizabeth Kelso (Caiazza), Helen Osier, Emma Bingham, Mary Burlingame (Konstanty), Ivah Sommerville (Reploeg), and Prof. Arthur B. Doig.

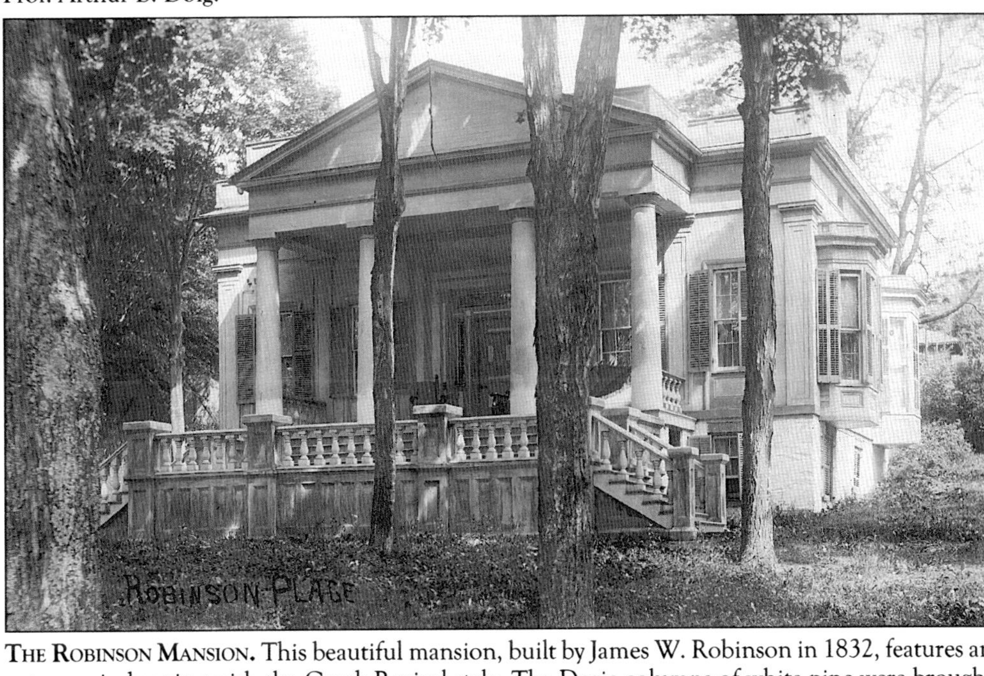

The Robinson Mansion. This beautiful mansion, built by James W. Robinson in 1832, features an entrance in keeping with the Greek Revival style. The Doric columns of white pine were brought from Albany by an oxen team. The Robinson family came from Omagh, Tyrone County, Ireland, in 1804. James W. Robinson's grandmother Jane Barber was the daughter of Jane Hamilton, a sister of Alexander Hamilton.

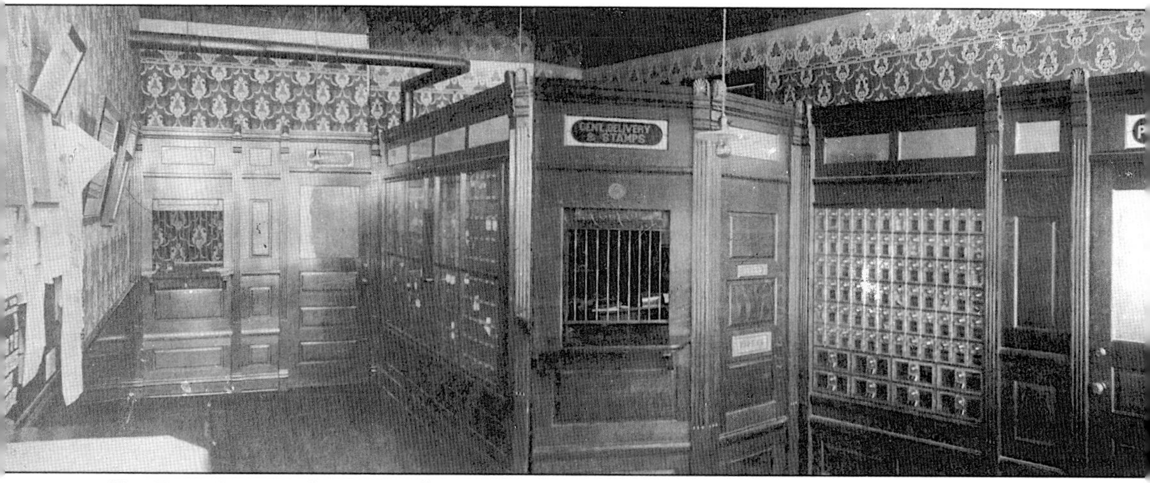

THE POST OFFICE. This F.E. Bolles postcard shows the interior of the post office, which was in the brick building at 74 Main Street. The new equipment arrived and was placed in position. The case was finished in golden oak and there were 280 call boxes and 80 keyless lock boxes and drawers. The bottoms were made of wire to avoid dust accumulation. The up-to-date post office has a fireproof vault formerly used by the bank. The postmaster informed the *Worcester Times* that the entire cost came out of his pocket.

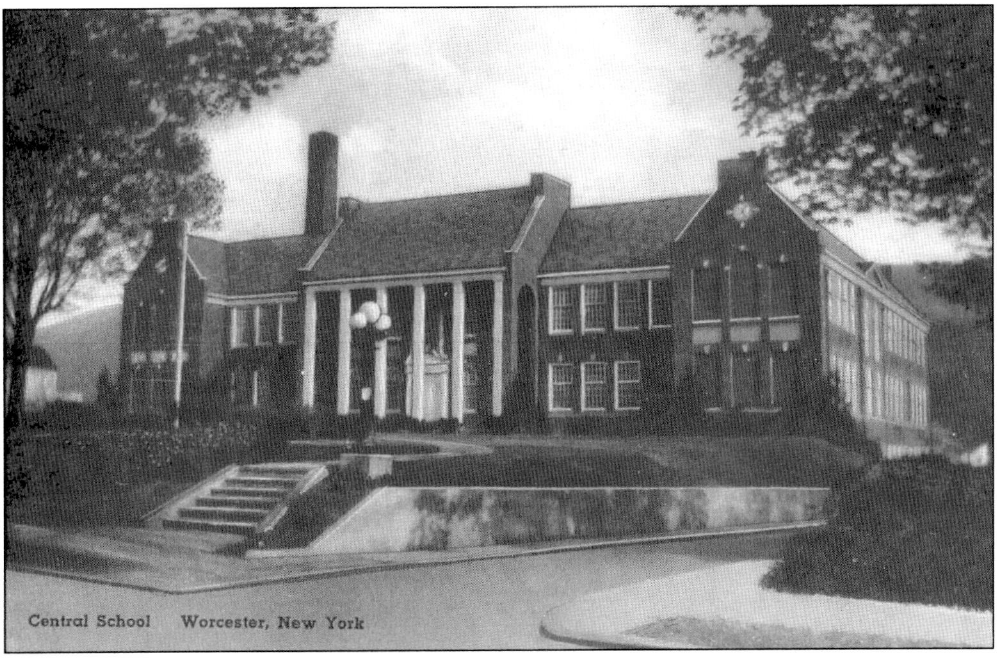

WORCESTER CENTRAL SCHOOL. This view of the school at 182 Main Street, which was built in 1932, shows the Harry Bigelow Jr. memorial globe electric lights along the sidewalk steps. Grace and Harry Bigelow lived across the street from the school. Bigelow, a promising young lawyer, was killed in an automobile accident.

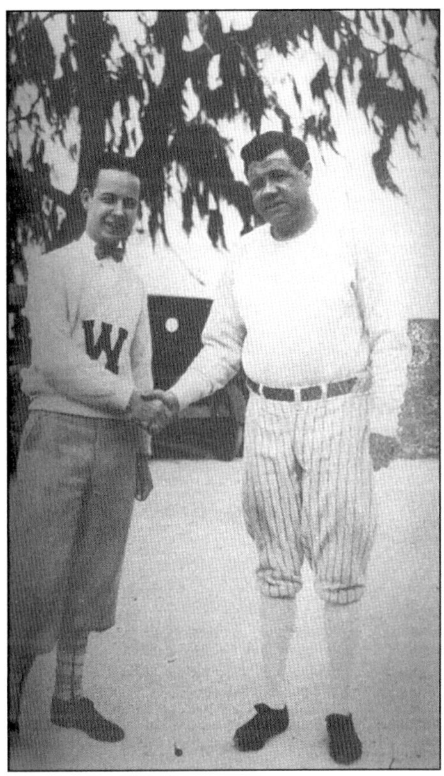

A WORCESTER BOY MEETS BABE RUTH. Harry Bigelow Jr. was lucky enough to meet Babe Ruth after one of the New York Yankees games. Bigelow was killed in an automobile accident in the Cooperstown Junction area when he was in his thirties. Bigelow's great-grandfather Cyrus Bigelow was one of the early settlers of the Tusculum area of the town.

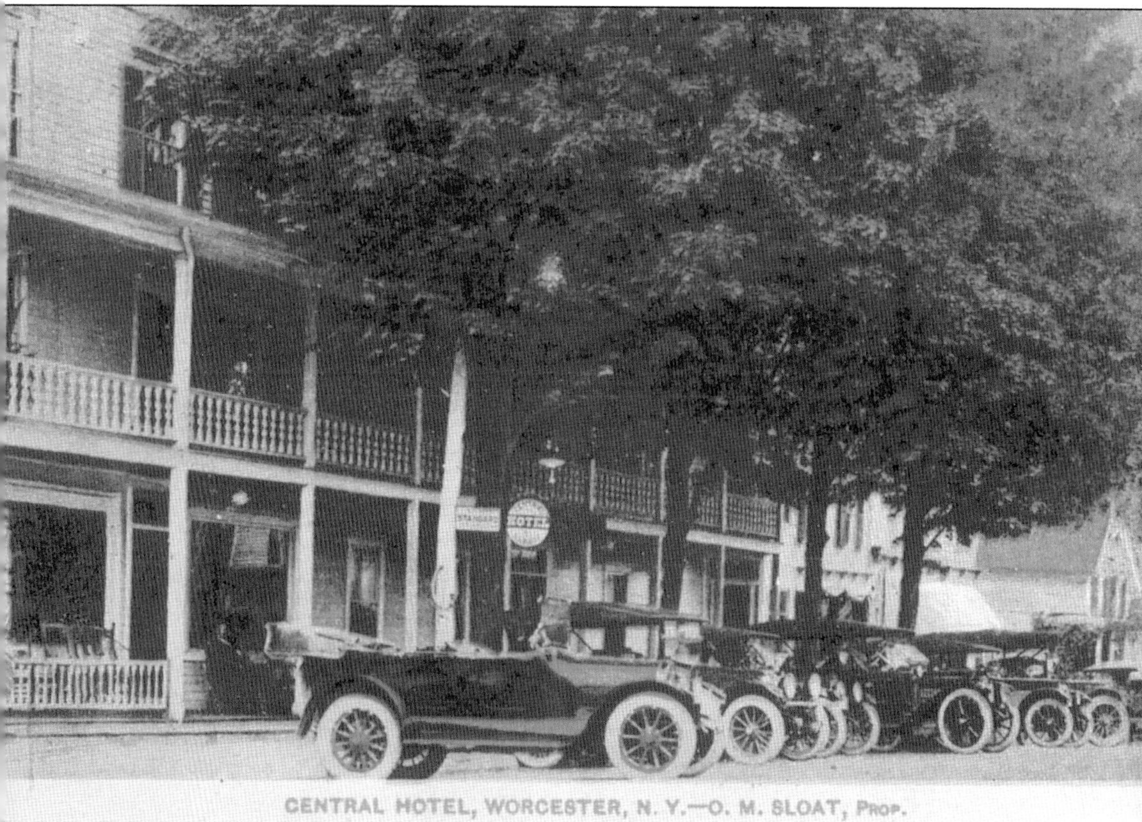

The Central Hotel. Omar M. Sloat was proprietor of the Main Street Central Hotel, which he purchased from Squire Shafer in 1905 for $13,000. Sloat added a street-floor suite, which was the living quarters of Hellen Wieting for many years. She donated the Wieting Theatre to the town in 1909. The hotel played host to many motorists out for a jaunt. The message on the back of this card refers to a motor trip from May 29 to June 2, 1918, from Owego to Troy, New York. "May 29 – Unadilla House, Unadilla and supper at Ninevah church porch. May 30 – lunch just beyond Oneonta. Fresh tar and a "blow-out." May 31 – drive to Watervliet, Cohoes and Albany. June 1 – Homeward bound via Schenectady, Altamont, Cobleskill and Oneonta. 8 p.m. tire off at Cobleskill for puncture. 9 p.m., bound for Worcester and arrival at 10 p.m. June 2 – at 10:30 a.m. left for Binghamton. 12 to 4 p.m. carburetor fixed at Oneonta. Dinner at Oneonta Hotel."

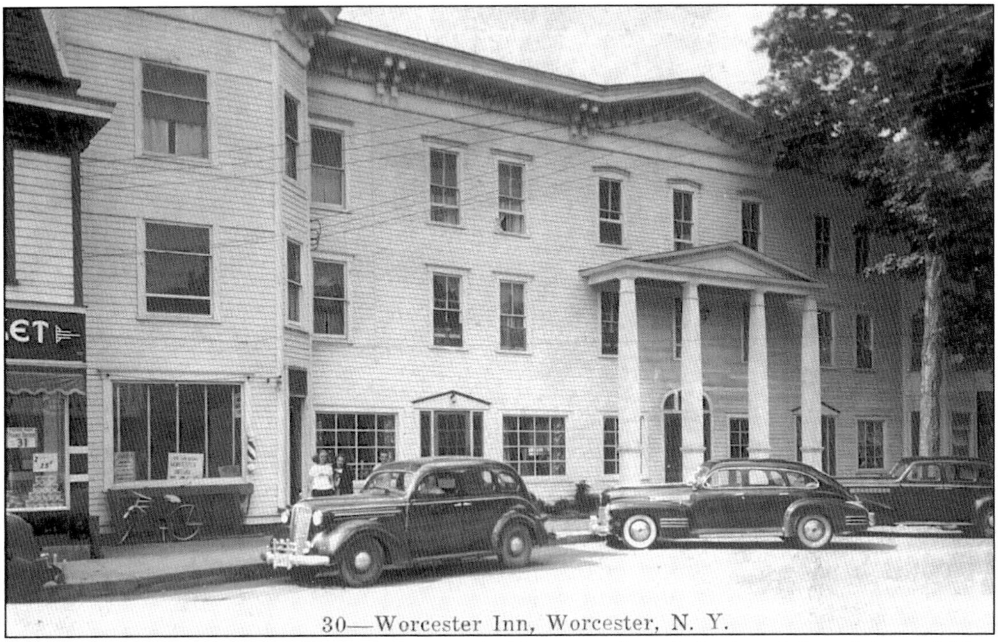

THE WORCESTER INN. Nine years after Peter A. Farro purchased the hotel from Mr. and Mrs. Harrison Crippen in 1938, he did extensive remodeling. Farro, who now called the business the Worcester Inn, removed the double front porches and completely remodeled the main floor. The dining room was enlarged and a coffee shop added. Later, he added a modern bowling alley, which has since been removed.

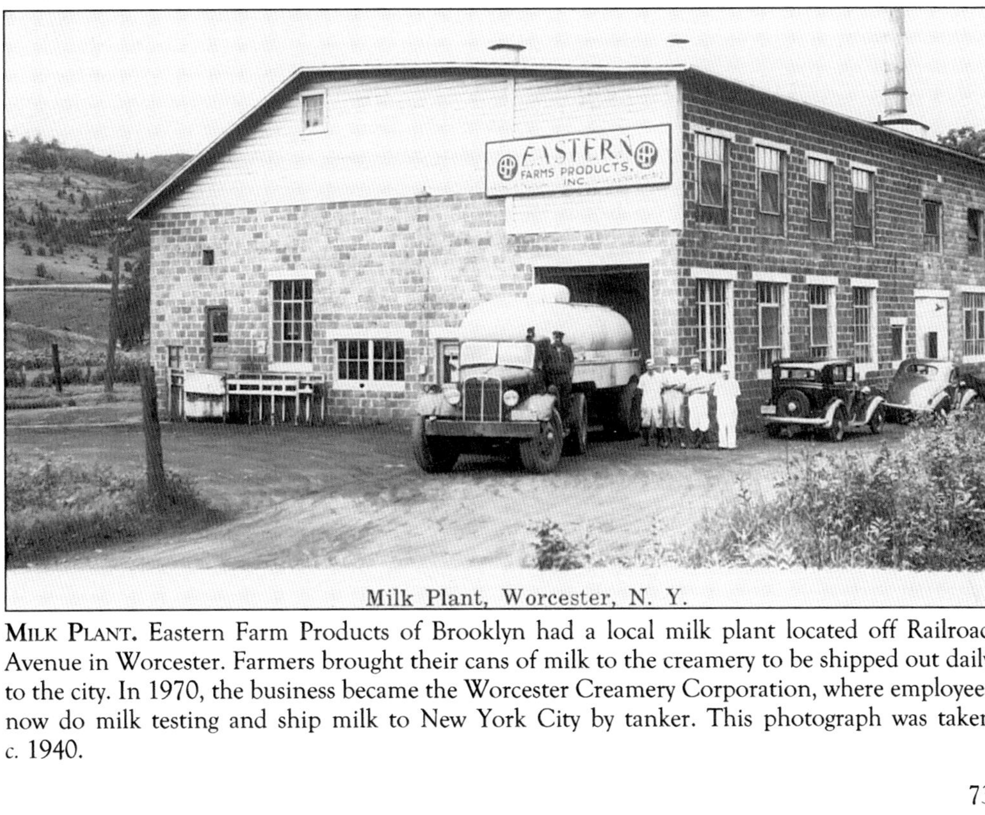

MILK PLANT. Eastern Farm Products of Brooklyn had a local milk plant located off Railroad Avenue in Worcester. Farmers brought their cans of milk to the creamery to be shipped out daily to the city. In 1970, the business became the Worcester Creamery Corporation, where employees now do milk testing and ship milk to New York City by tanker. This photograph was taken c. 1940.

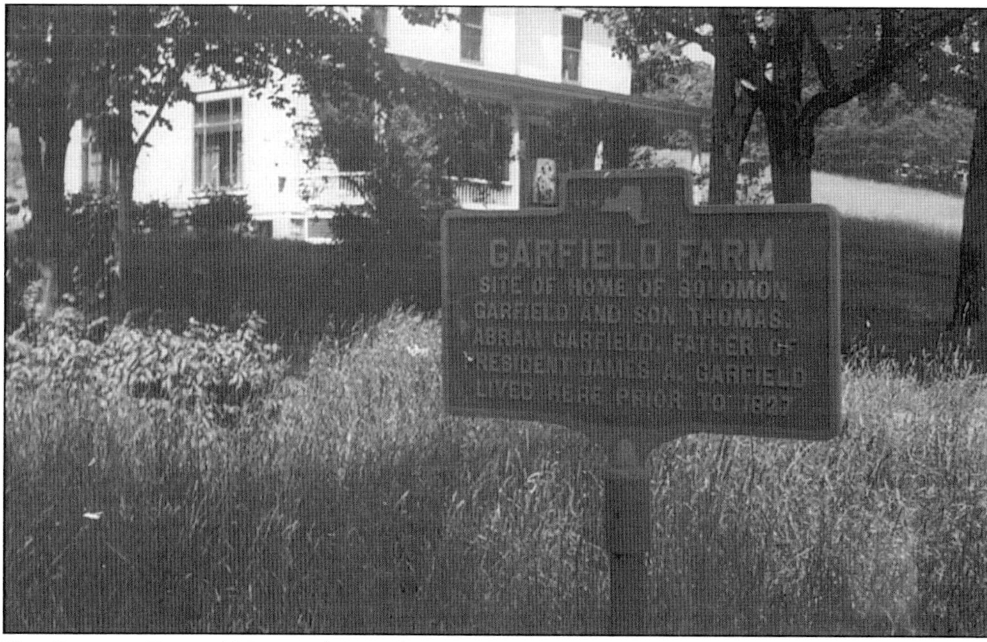

THE GARFIELD FARM. A New York State historical marker stands near the site of the log cabin where Solomon Garfield and his son Thomas Abram Garfield (grandfather of Pres. James A. Garfield) lived before 1827. The Garfield men all had a grim destiny. President Garfield's father, Abram, died of burns sustained while fighting a forest fire, his grandfather Thomas died of smallpox, and his great-grandfather Solomon died when hit by a falling tree. Thomas and Solomon were buried in the Garfield plot where the bank is now located.

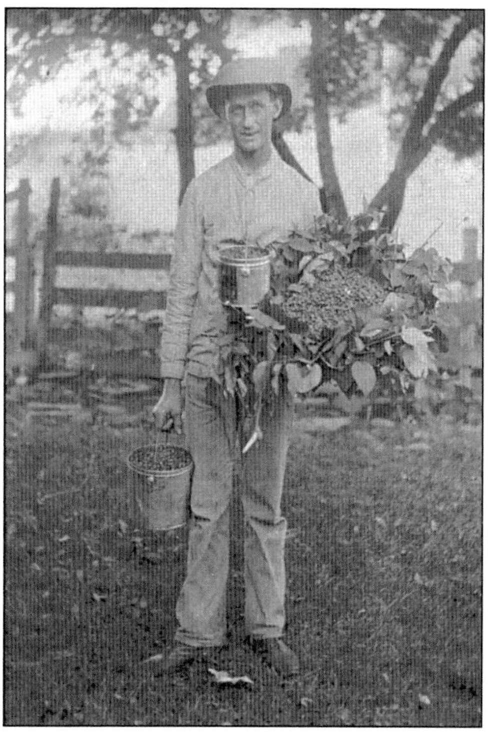

F.E. BOLLES. Frank E. Bolles was born in Birchardsville, Pennsylvania, on December 30, 1876. Bolles was a traveling photographer in the early 1900s, going from town to town and farm to farm. Many times, a family portrait was just 25¢ and lunch. He was once a photographer for the *Binghamton Press* as well as Kodak. He took many local photographs. Postcard collectors look for the old scenes with the familiar F.E. Bolles on the card.

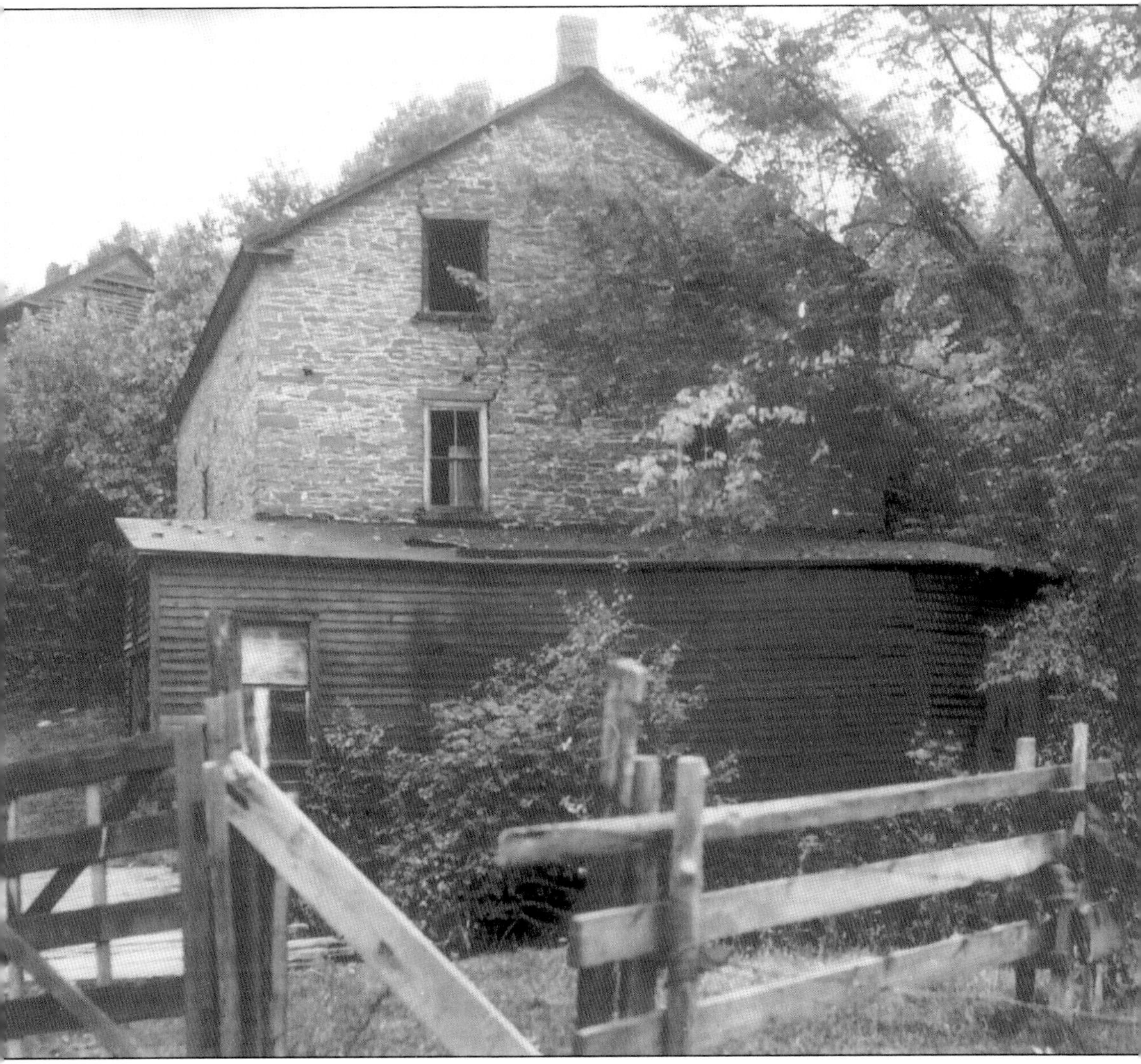

The Old Mill. Remains of the old stone mill still stand today. It is, however, severely damaged by weather, vandalism, and the ravages of time. When the leaves are off the trees, one can spot a glimpse of the mill from Interstate 88. The mill was part of the Electric Pond and is where the millstone and machinery were housed. Worcester homes were electrified in March 1899, but John VanBenthuysen (who worked night and day to bring Worcester electricity) died of pneumonia on May 8, 1899, at the age of 45. Several men died in connection with the management of the mill, and a shooting even took place there. These events led townspeople to believe that the plant was cursed.

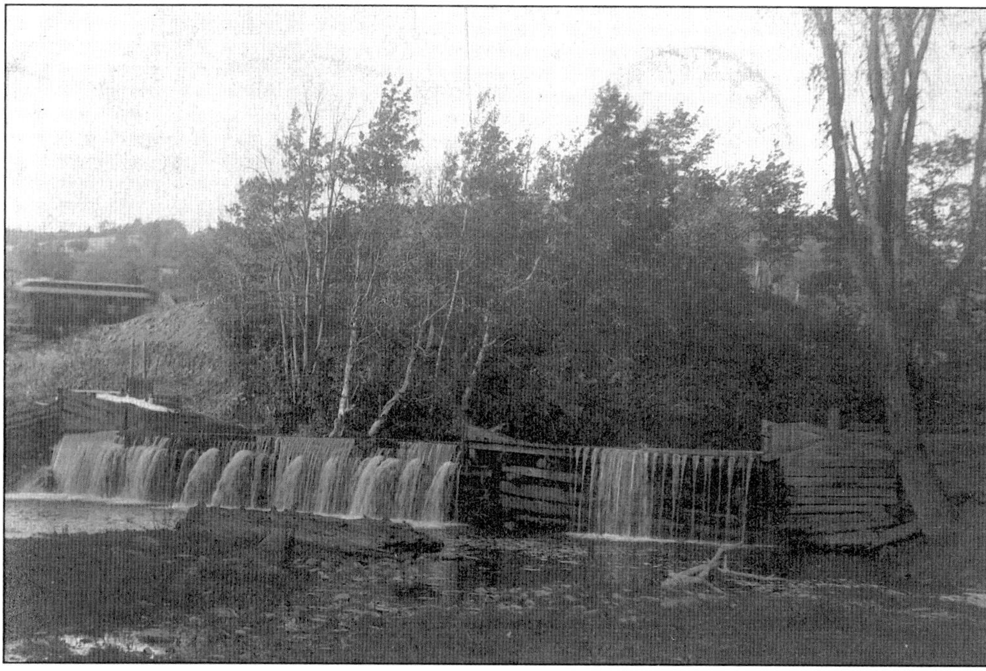

ELECTRIC LIGHT POND. The falls, although no longer there, played a significant part in the history of Worcester. In the wintertime when the pond froze over, the ice was used to stock local icehouses for use in the summer months. Area children enjoyed skating on the pond in the winter.

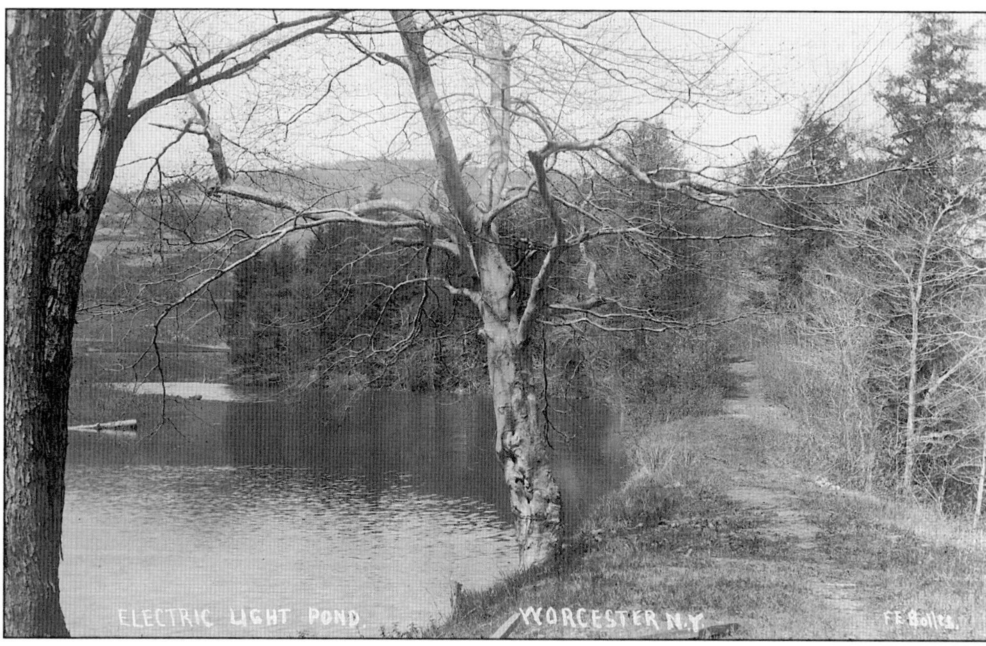

HOG'S BACK. In the early 1900s, young couples used the area called Hog's Back as a picnic spot. The unusual name came about because its shape probably reminded people of a hog. On the left is the Electric Light Pond. The pond, which is no longer there, was used as a town dump in the 1940s and 1950s. This is an F.E. Bolles real photo postcard.

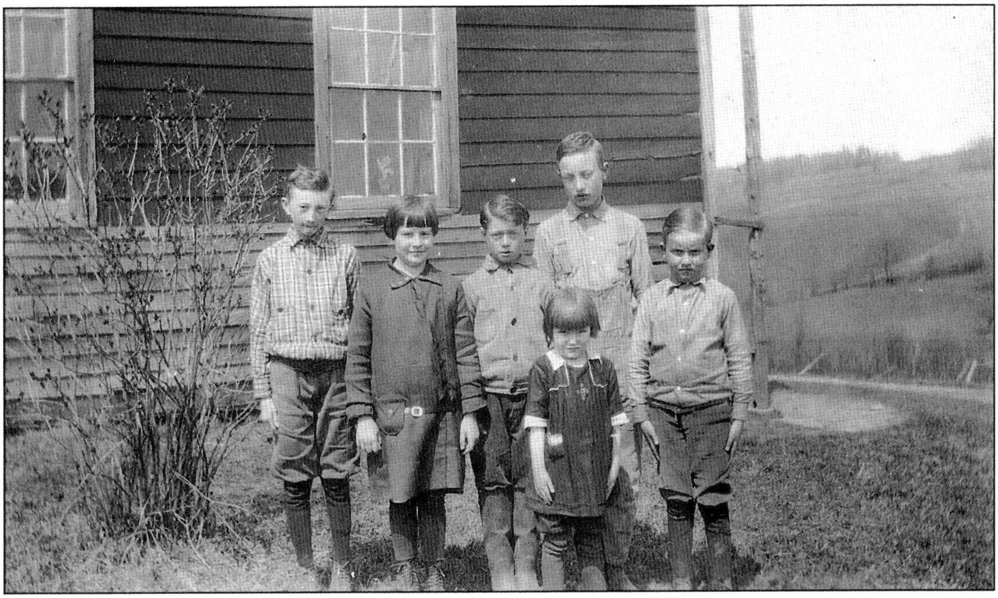

DISTRICT SCHOOL. This school was several miles from Worcester on South America Road.

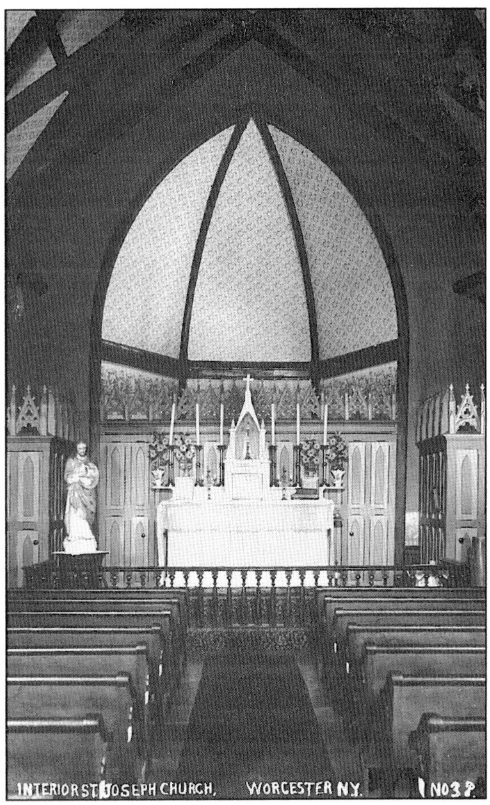

ST. JOSEPH'S CHURCH. This is the interior of St. Joseph's Catholic Church after it was built in 1875 for $1,900. In the early years, the church was a mission church, with priests coming from Cobleskill. The first ordained priest, Fr. Edward Reilly, came to the church in 1921. In 1922, the rectory, to the west of the church, was built.

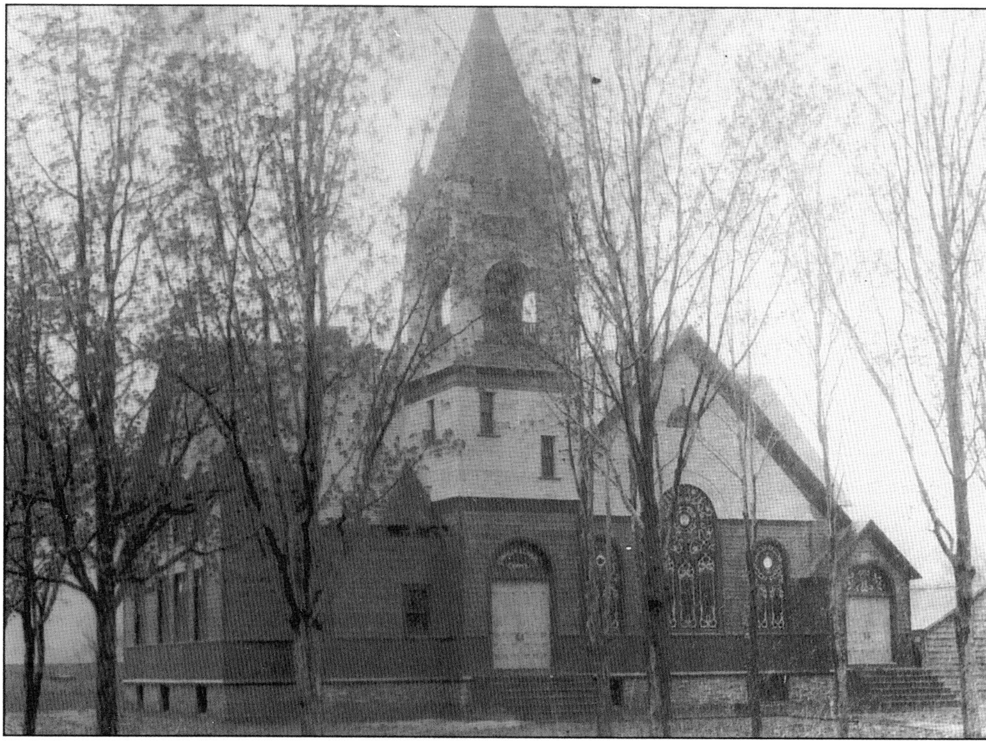

The First Presbyterian Church. This early photograph was taken shortly after the church was built in 1892. It was originally known as the Congregational church but, in 1917, it was changed to First Presbyterian. Note the different shades of paint decorating the exterior of the church in the Victorian style.

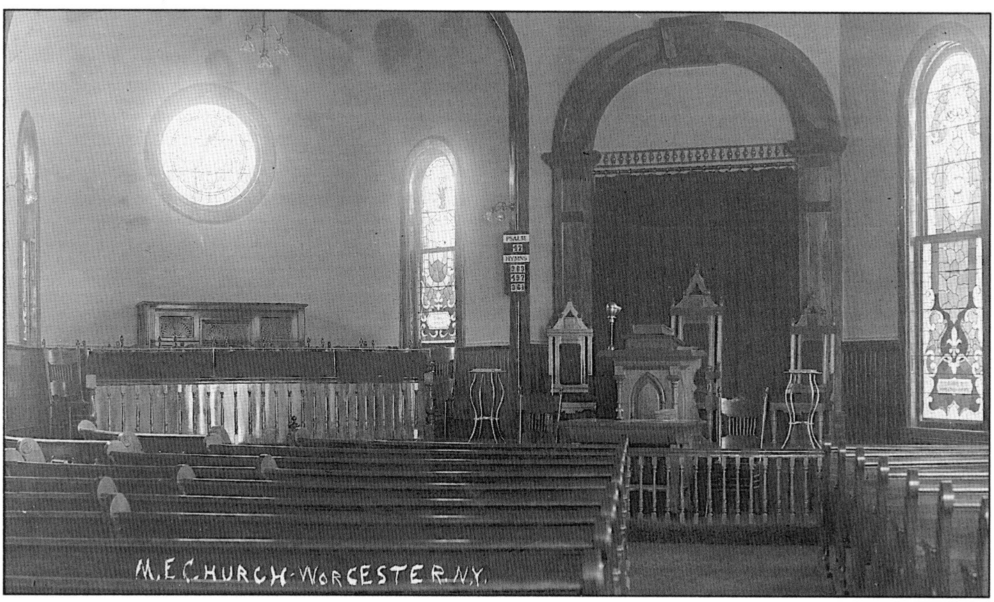

The Methodist Episcopal Church. Several changes have taken place in this church's interior since this 1910 photograph. The organ against the back wall was moved, and the round stained-glass window was moved to the right of the organ loft. The church is now Methodist.

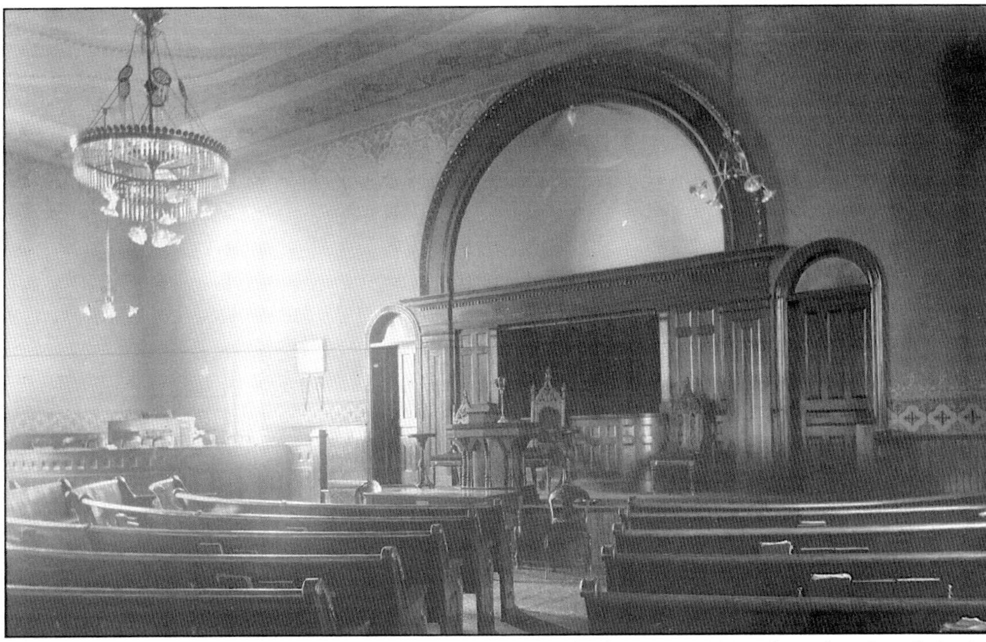

The Second Baptist Church. This interior photograph dates to 1920, when the church had a reed organ. The organ loft was enlarged in 1930 to accommodate a new organ. Note the beautiful stenciling on the walls and the fresco ceiling. Several years ago, Sidney Chase and Martha Cloughly decorated the walls and some ceilings with stencils in keeping with the early days of the church.

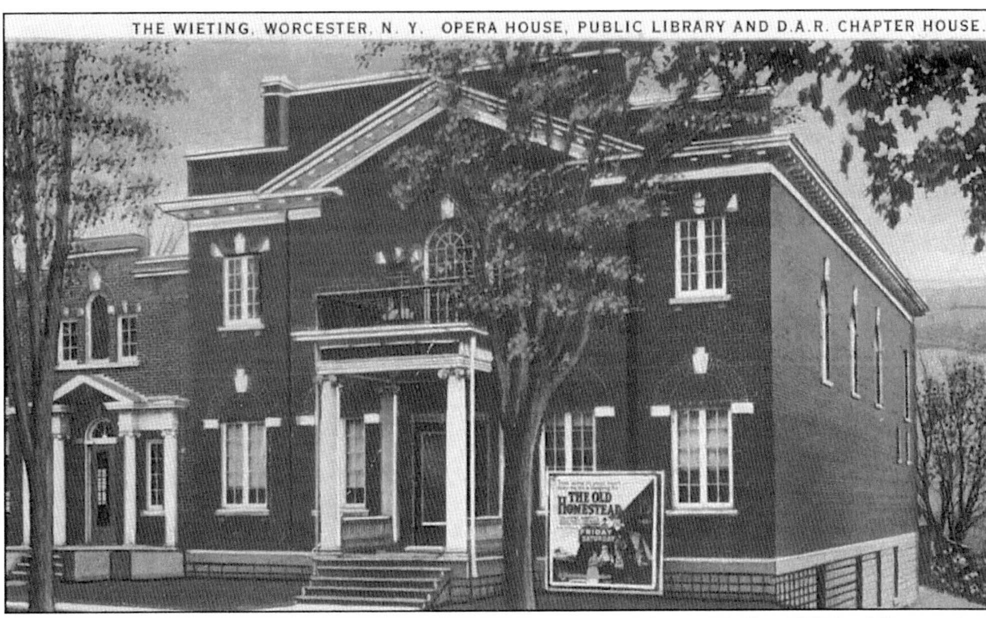

The Wieting. This building is known as the Wieting Opera House. Hellen Wilder Wieting had the brick structure erected in 1910 in memory of her late husband, Philip G. Wieting. She gave the building to the Worcester community along with a trust fund to help maintain it. The New York State Iroquois Chapter of the Daughters of the American Revolution and the Worcester Free Library also have rooms on the left side of the building.

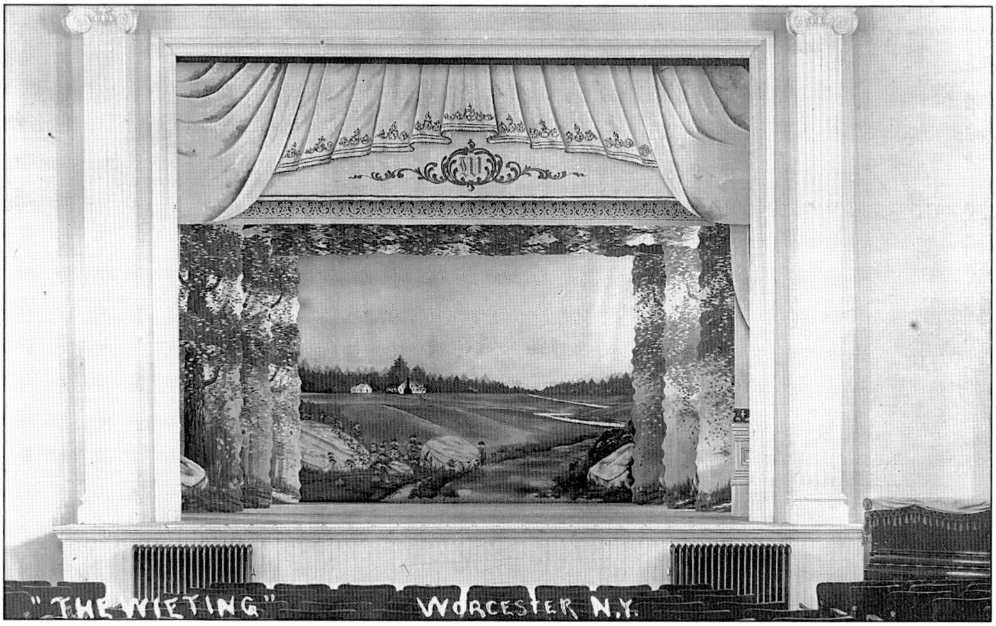

THE INTERIOR OF THE WIETING. This country scene is featured on one of the drop curtains in the theater. Dating from 1910, the theater was once known as a vaudeville stop between Albany and Binghamton. Plays, minstrel shows, concerts, and other community events took place here. With grant assistance, the building is being restored, with the addition of a new projector and sound system. Movies are now shown here in the summer.

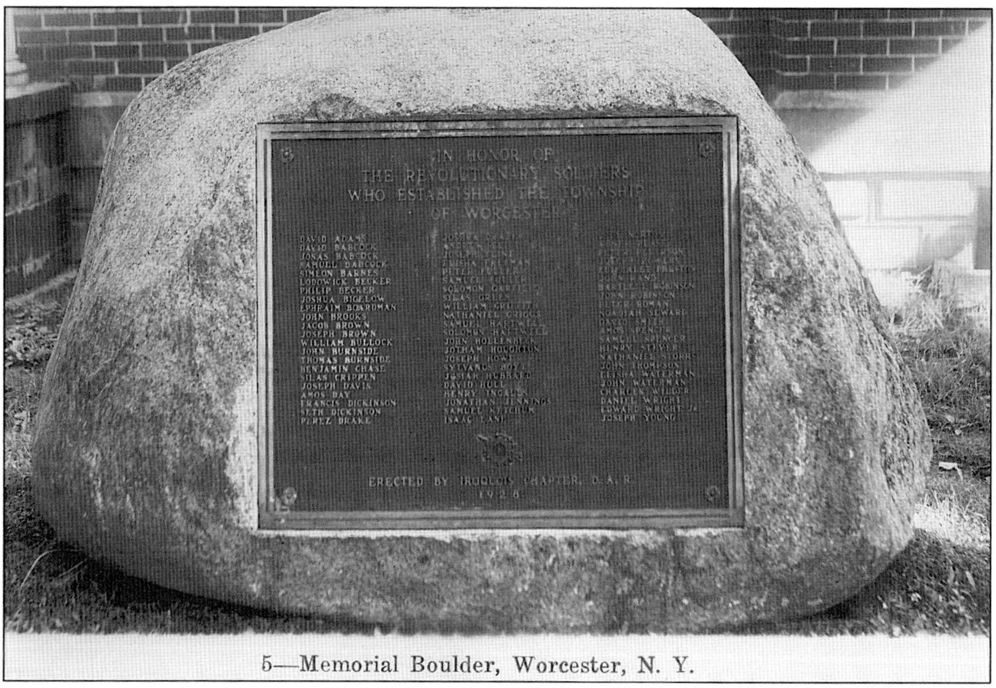

MEMORIAL BOULDER. Erected in front of the Wieting in 1928 by the New York State Iroquois Chapter of the Daughters of the American Revolution, the metal plaque honors 66 Revolutionary War soldiers who established the Township of Worcester in 1797.

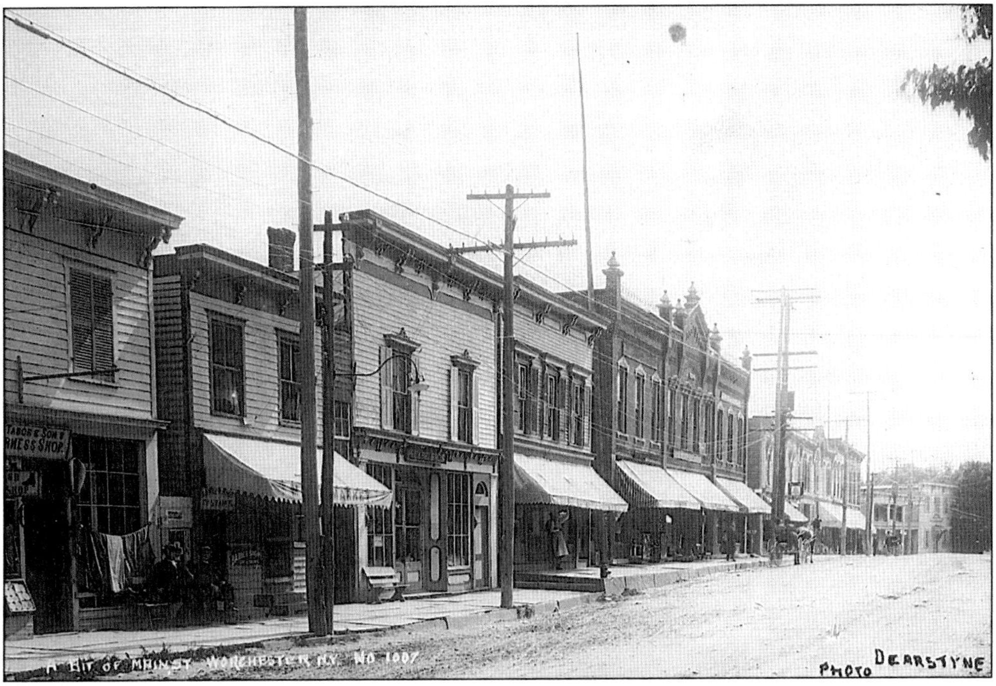

Main Street, Worcester. This photograph, taken in 1905 by William H. French, shows the south side of Main Street. On the left is the old harness shop next to a meat market. The building in the distance is the Worcester House.

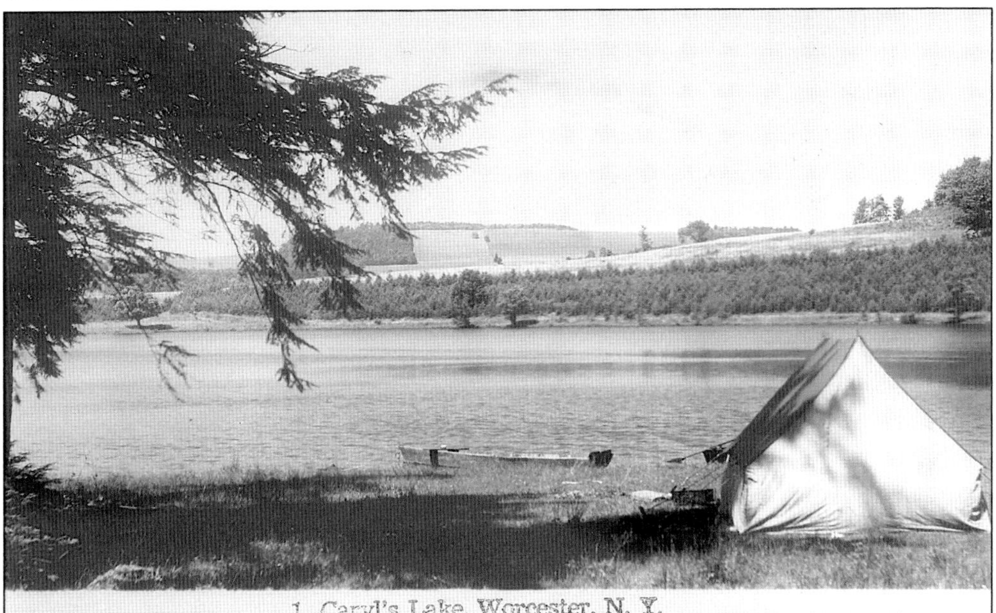

Camping at Caryl's Lake. In the 1920s, Van Wright borrowed a tent and other camping equipment and hired a farmer with a hay wagon and a team of horses to pull the load up the steep hill to the fence on the west side of the lake. He and his family carried the equipment about 300 feet to a spot near the water. Two tents were set up and the week was spent camping and fishing. Every day, Wright walked the mile to town to get perishables.

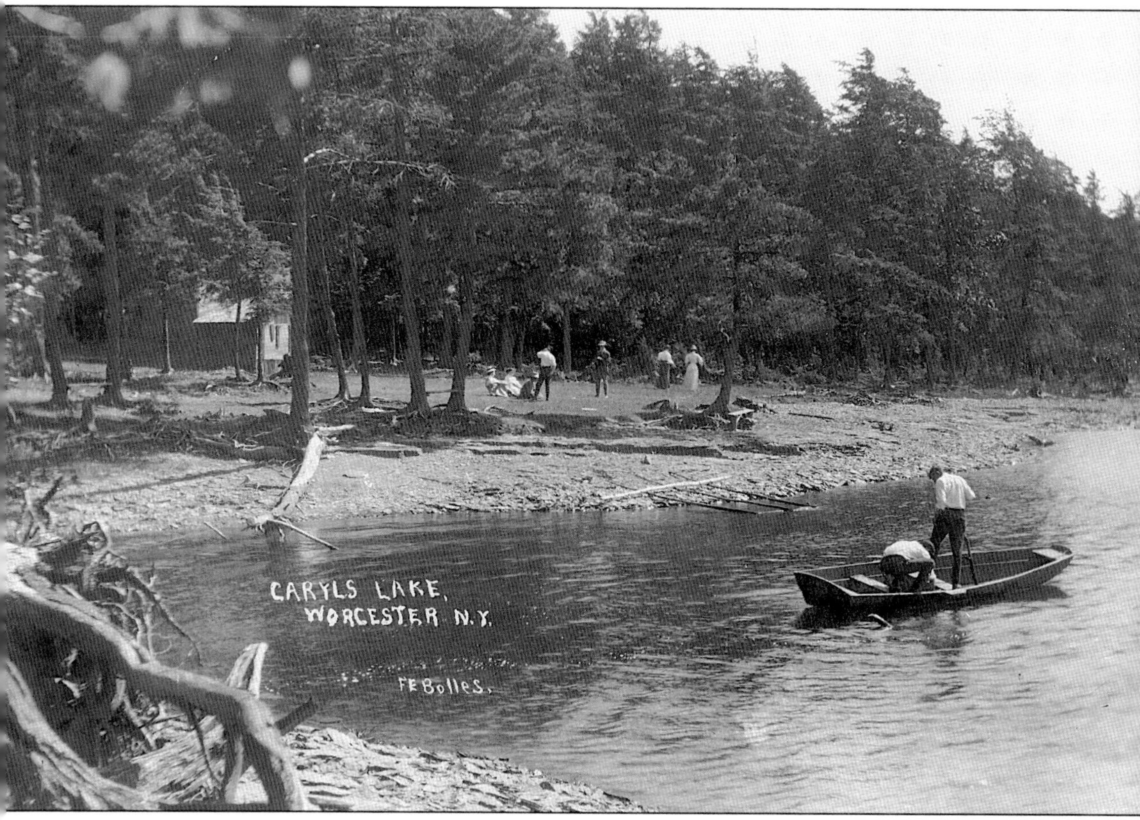

CARYL'S LAKE. Once Worcester's water supply, Caryl's Lake is located at the top of Lake Hill at an elevation of 1,800 feet. The water company was formed in 1887, and historical accounts say that 100 Italian laborers were hired to dig the trench down the hill and through the town. Stories from the late 1800s indicate that the lake is "consistently inconsistent." When the surrounding countryside is parched by drought, the level of the lake is the highest; in periods of abundant rainfall, so the story goes, the lake is at its lowest. This strange phenomenon has persisted over a period of many years.

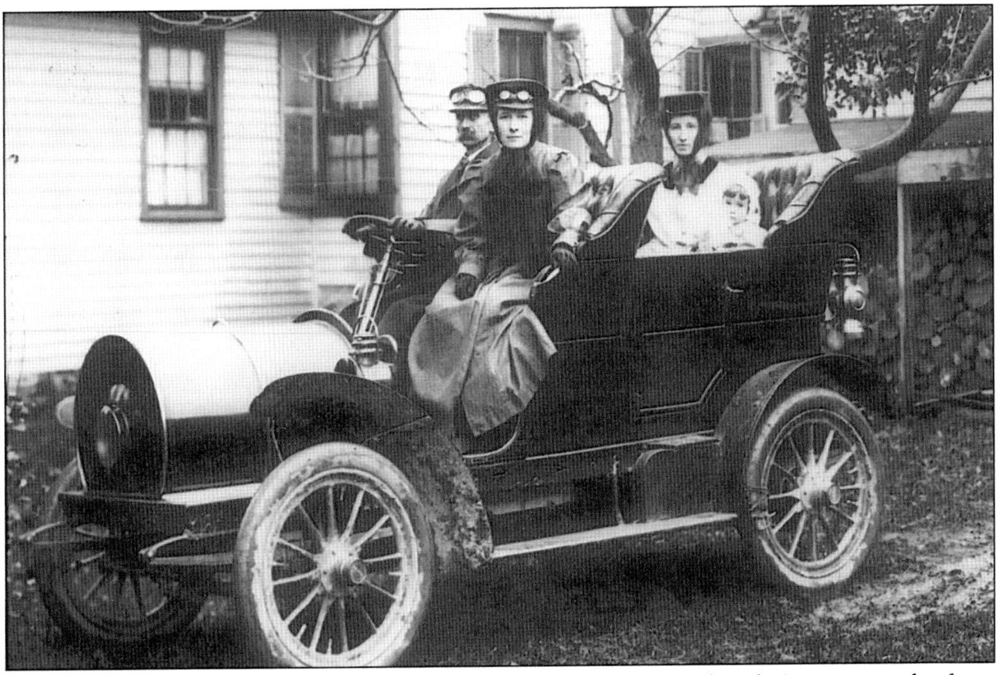

AN EARLY VEHICLE. Frank Rockefeller, a local mechanic of South Church Street, is in the front seat with his wife. In 1906, the town board considered limiting the speed through town to six miles per hour. Farmers complained of automobiles dashing through the town at 30 miles per hour, causing runaways and startling horses. The boiler in the front of the car contained water that was heated by a kerosene burner. Parts for the motor were kept under the seat.

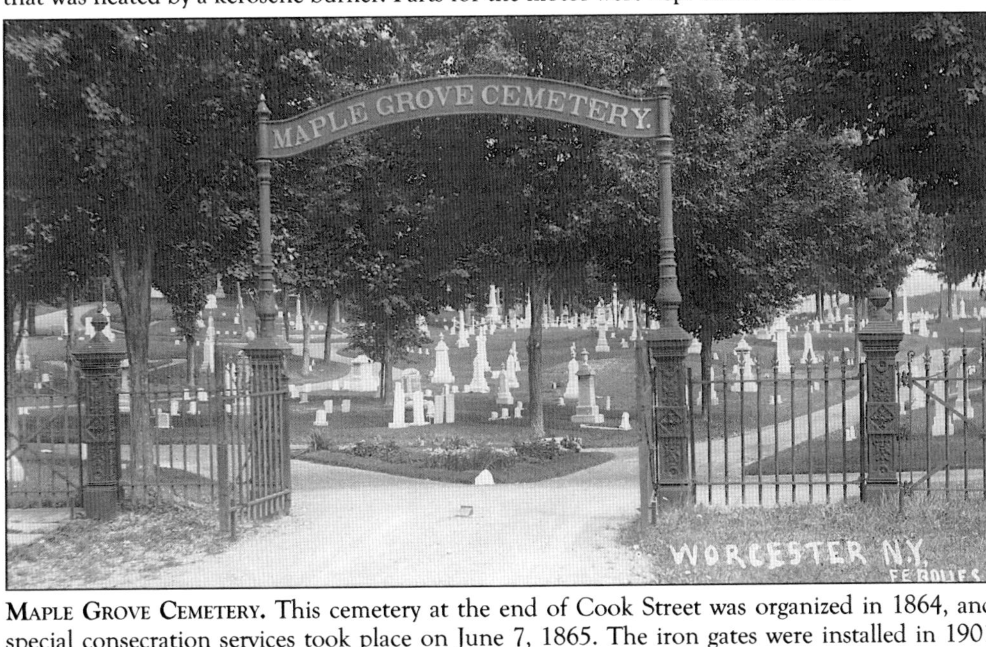

MAPLE GROVE CEMETERY. This cemetery at the end of Cook Street was organized in 1864, and special consecration services took place on June 7, 1865. The iron gates were installed in 1901 for $295.55. Many of the old gravestones from the Garfield plot on Main Street and the old Congregational burial grounds were removed and placed in a row toward the rear of the cemetery. This is an F.E. Bolles postcard.

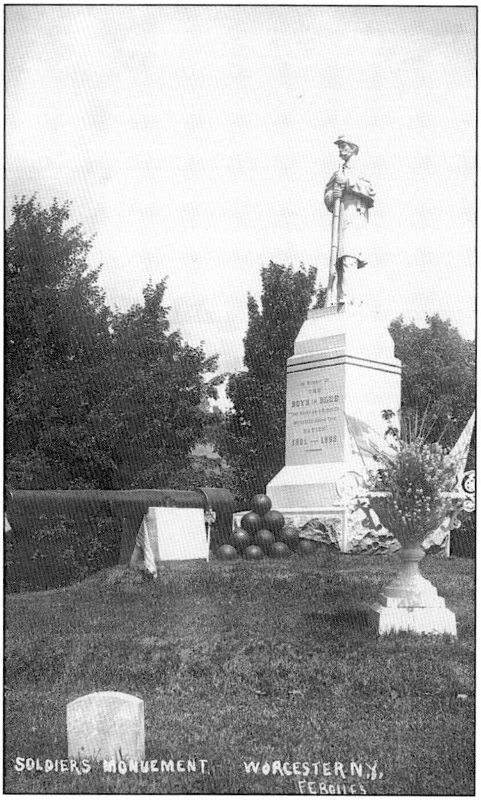

SOLDIER'S MONUMENT. This monument was erected in memory of "the Boys in Blue," with money being raised by the Women's Relief Corps, a group of wives of Civil War veterans. Bronze plaques were placed on the monument honoring veterans of the Civil War, World War I, the Spanish-American War, the Mexican War, and the War of 1812.

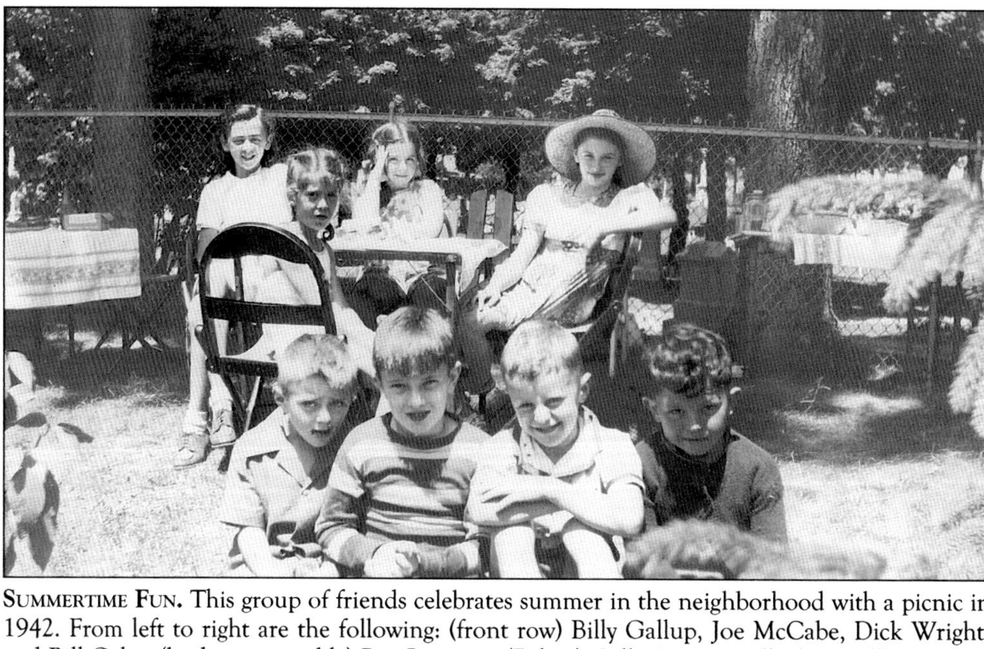

SUMMERTIME FUN. This group of friends celebrates summer in the neighborhood with a picnic in 1942. From left to right are the following: (front row) Billy Gallup, Joe McCabe, Dick Wright, and Bill Galer; (back row, at table) Pat Campion (Dilger), Sally Ann DeLello (Parshall), Lorraine Nichols (Sullivan), and Marilyn Wright (Dufresne).

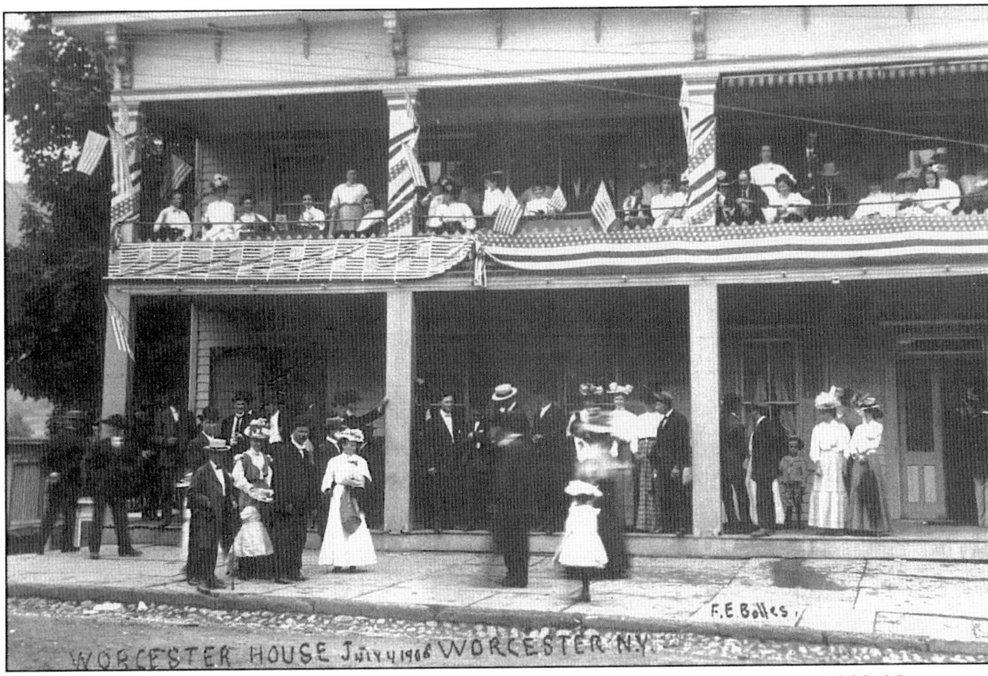

The Worcester House. John Eldredge built this structure at 68 Main Street in 1882. Newspaper reports state that 500 people enjoyed dancing there. In 1891, it was advertised as a "New Opera House." It was purchased by Joseph B. Nelson Sr. in 1921 and turned into a garage. This F.E. Bolles postcard shows people celebrating on the Fourth of July 1908.

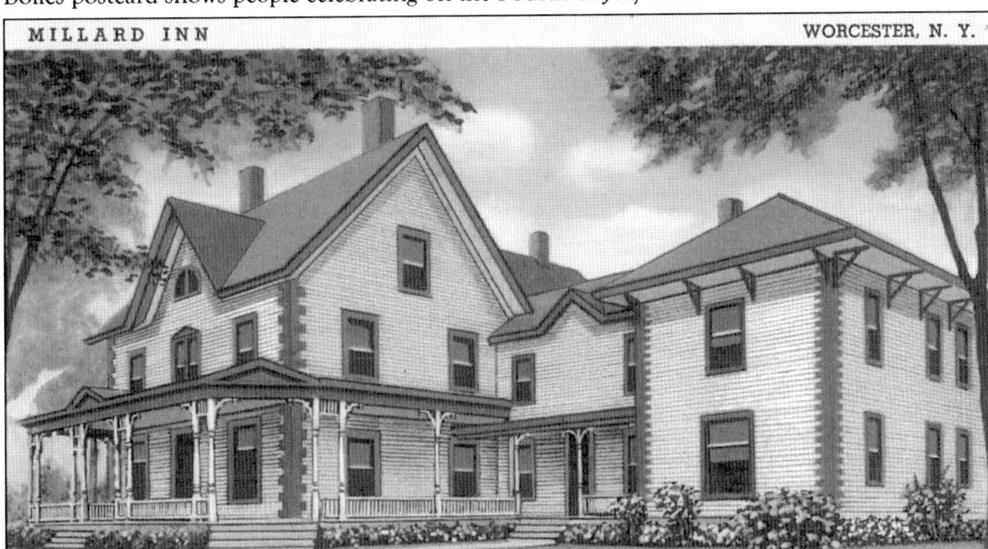

The Millard Inn. Jesse and Rena Millard purchased the John Trickey house in 1929. The property, located on Main Street next to the school, was a summer tourist destination for many years. George R. and Virginia Bruce purchased the home in 1981 and converted it into the John Trickey Bed and Breakfast.

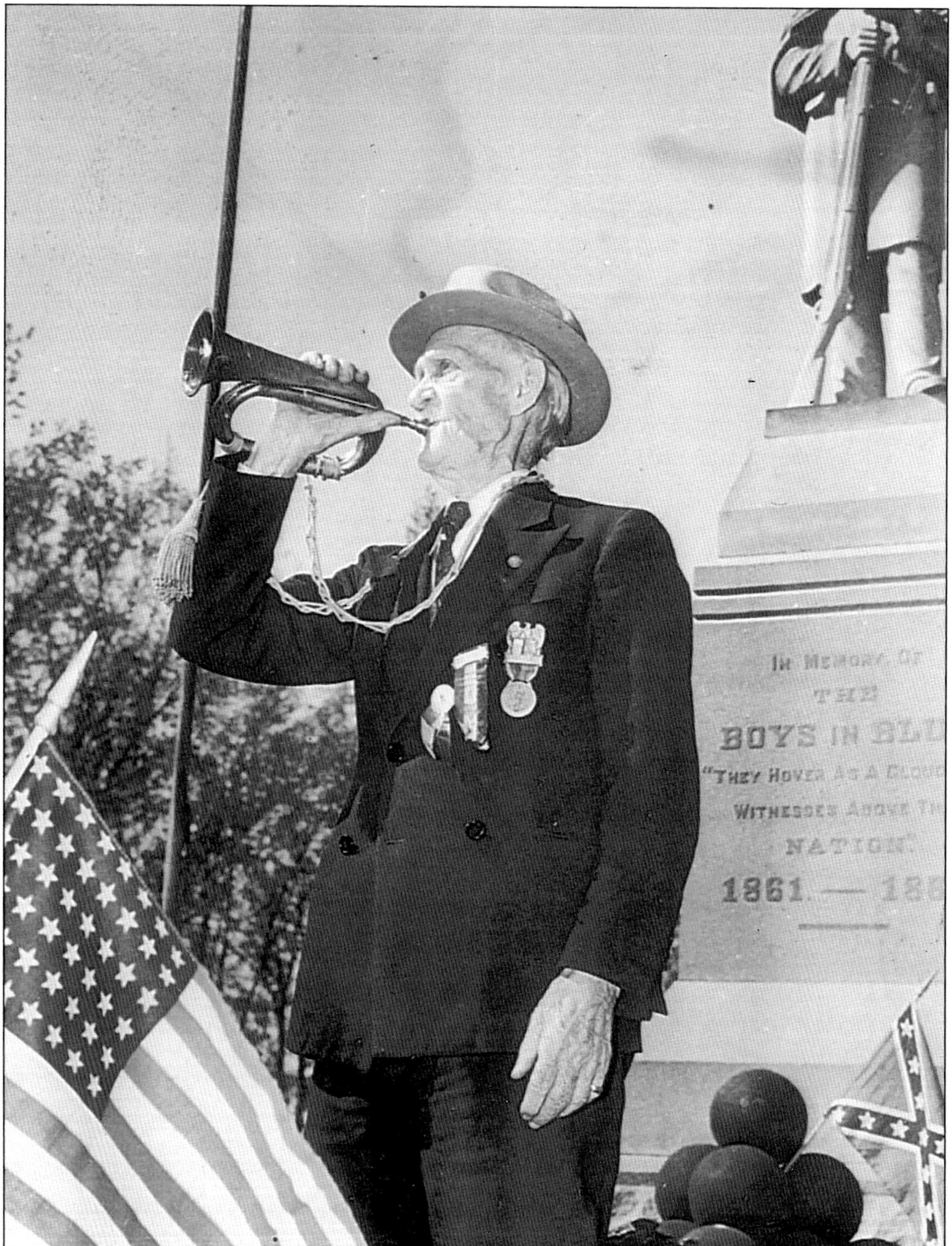

SETH FLINT. Born in Bern, New York, Seth Flint ran away from home, fearing his parents would object to his joining the service at the age of 15. He walked all the way to Albany to enlist in the U.S. Cavalry in June 1862. He changed his name to Charles M. Seaver, a name he used throughout the Civil War. Severe winters caused Flint to be hospitalized with arthritis, and he had a choice of discharge or becoming a member of Gen. Ulysses S. Grant's 5th Cavalry escort. He chose the latter. Seth Flint sounded the last call at Appomattox at the end of the Civil War, April 9, 1865.

BLOWING TAPS. Seth M. Flint returned to Worcester after the Civil War and established the Flint and Taylor clothing store. Flint always led the Decoration Day parade and blew taps on his Civil War bugle each year until his death in 1941 at the age of 94. At the time of his death, his home was located across from Worcester Central School. He summoned music teacher Carmen Caiazza and asked that his bugle be played at his deathbed. "I want to hear the old girl one more time," Flint said.

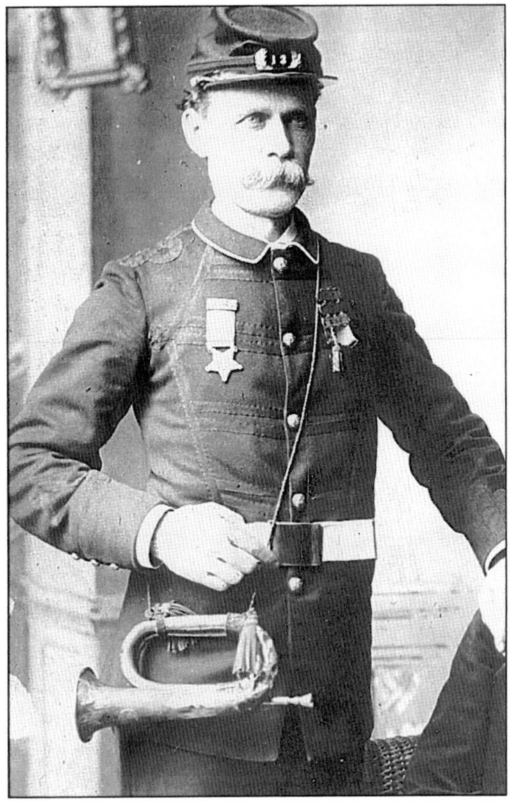

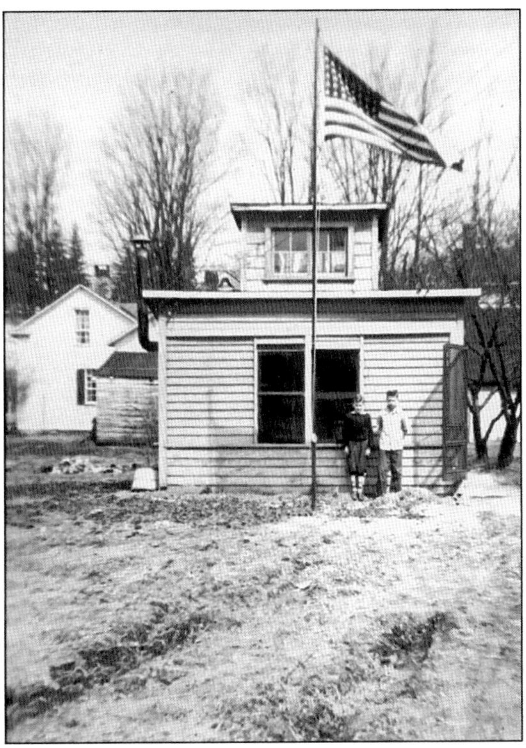

THE GROUND OBSERVATION POST. During World War II, community members took turns as plane spotters at the observation post, between Main and Maple Streets. Spotters had to familiarize themselves with a variety of planes, both domestic and foreign, and call in a report if a plane was observed in the sky. In this photograph, Morris G. France Jr. and Bill Tauzel stand in front of the post.

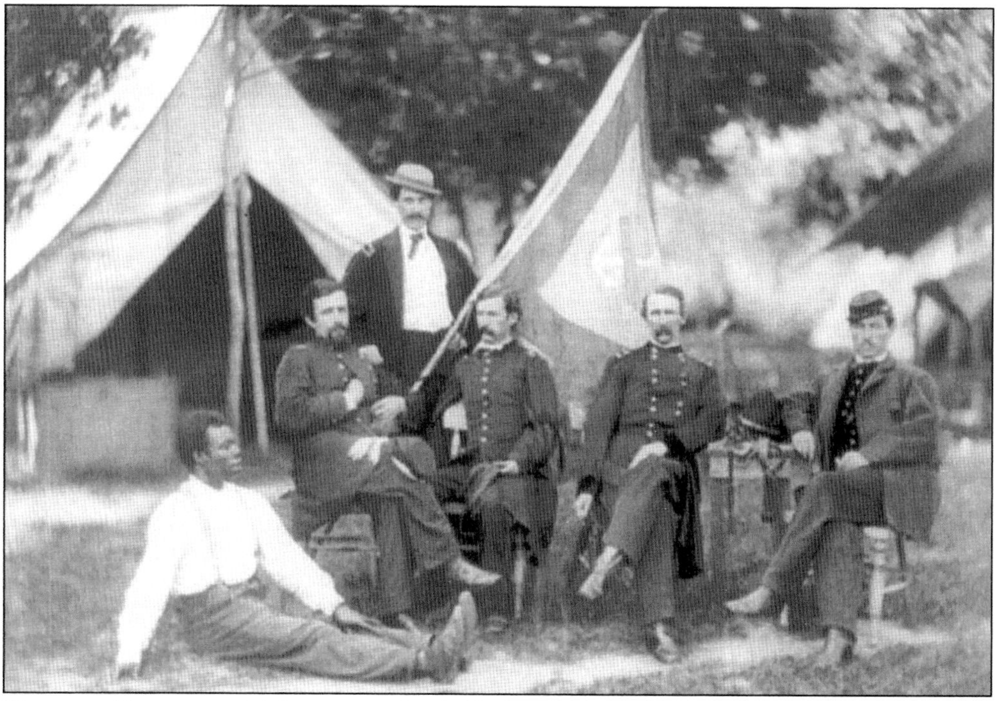

NAPOLEON BONAPARTE MCLAUGHLEN. In 1861, he was commissioned as a second lieutenant and joined the Union Army of Kentucky. He was later named colonel of the 1st Massachusetts Volunteers. McLaughlen fought in Chancellorsville and was in 11 battles, including Gettysburg and Bull Run. He achieved the rank of brevet brigadier general, was captured at Fort Stedman, and spent the rest of the war in Libby Prison. He retired to Worcester in 1882 and died in 1886.

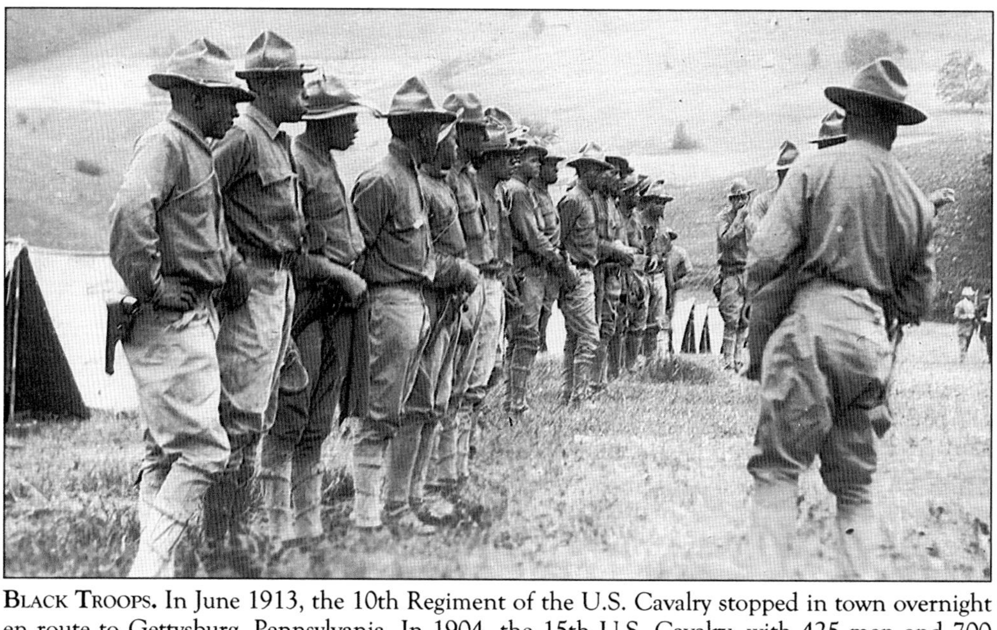

BLACK TROOPS. In June 1913, the 10th Regiment of the U.S. Cavalry stopped in town overnight en route to Gettysburg, Pennsylvania. In 1904, the 15th U.S. Cavalry—with 425 men and 700 horses and mules from Fort Ethan Allen—were on their way to maneuvers at the Civil War's Bull Run battlefield.

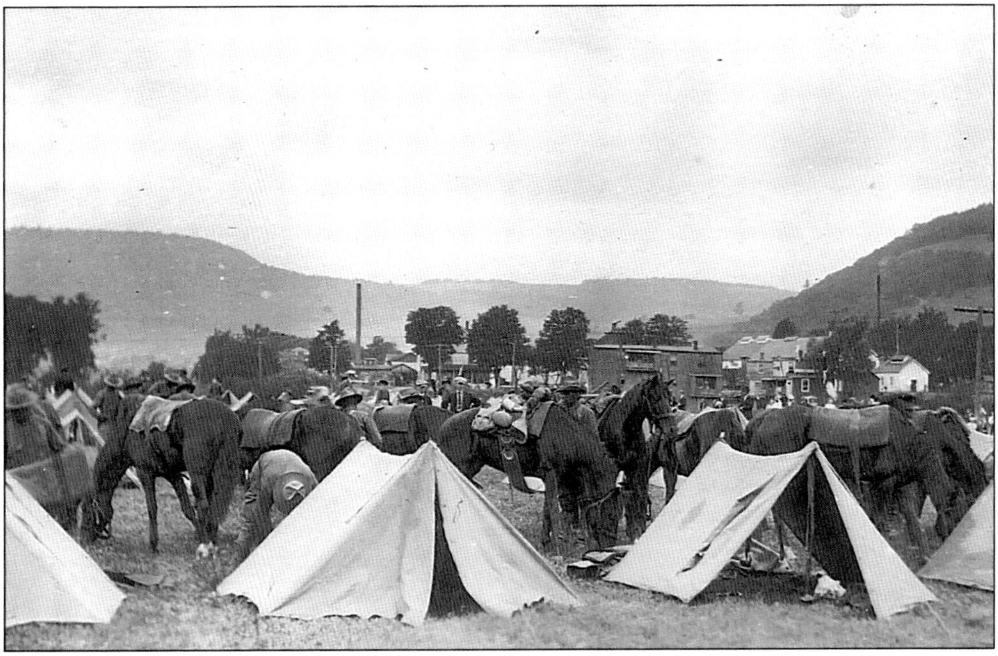

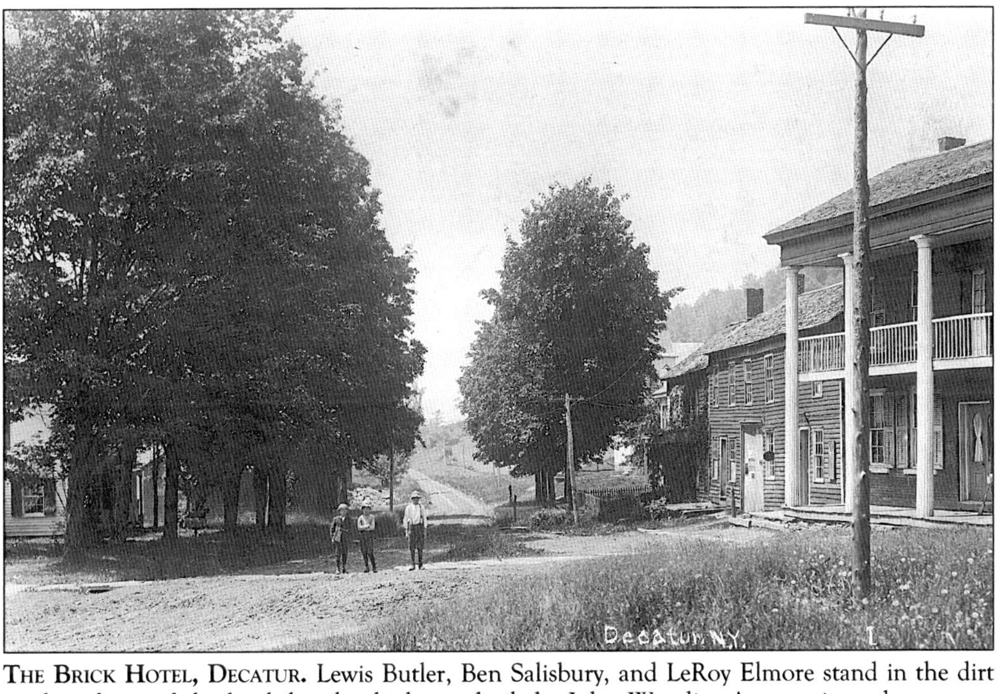

SETTING UP CAMP. Troops camped overnight on Goodell's flats, south of the railroad track. They planned to leave the next day for Gettysburg. Tents were pitched and the horses grazed in the field.

THE BRICK HOTEL, DECATUR. Lewis Butler, Ben Salisbury, and LeRoy Elmore stand in the dirt road in front of the brick hotel, which was built by John Woodin. At one time, there was a dentist's office on the second floor. The hotel, which closed in 1890, was a dwelling place for Mr. and Mrs. Sawyer F. Pearson and their son Eugene. Traveling medicine shows also provided entertainment on the second floor of this building.

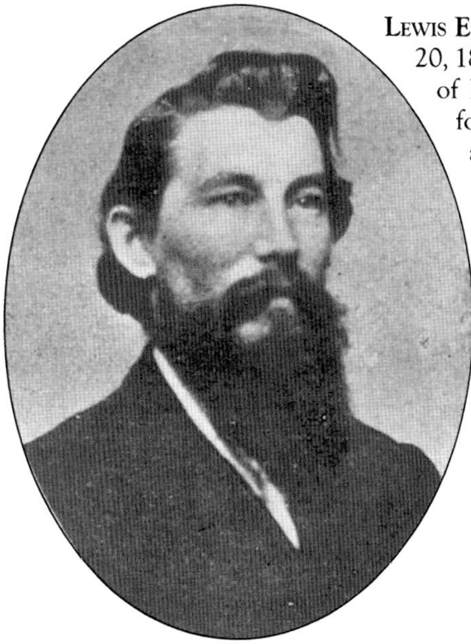

Lewis Edson Waterman. Waterman was born on November 20, 1837, about five miles from Worcester in the rural town of Decatur. Growing up, his fondness for books often found him reading by candlelight. Waterman accepted a job with the Aetna Insurance Company and moved to Boston in 1864. He lost a large insurance contract as the result of an ink spill on the document, which the customer refused to sign. He left the insurance company and designed a pen that used capillary action—the Waterman practical fountain pen. Waterman died in 1901, and Bic of Paris, France, purchased the pen company.

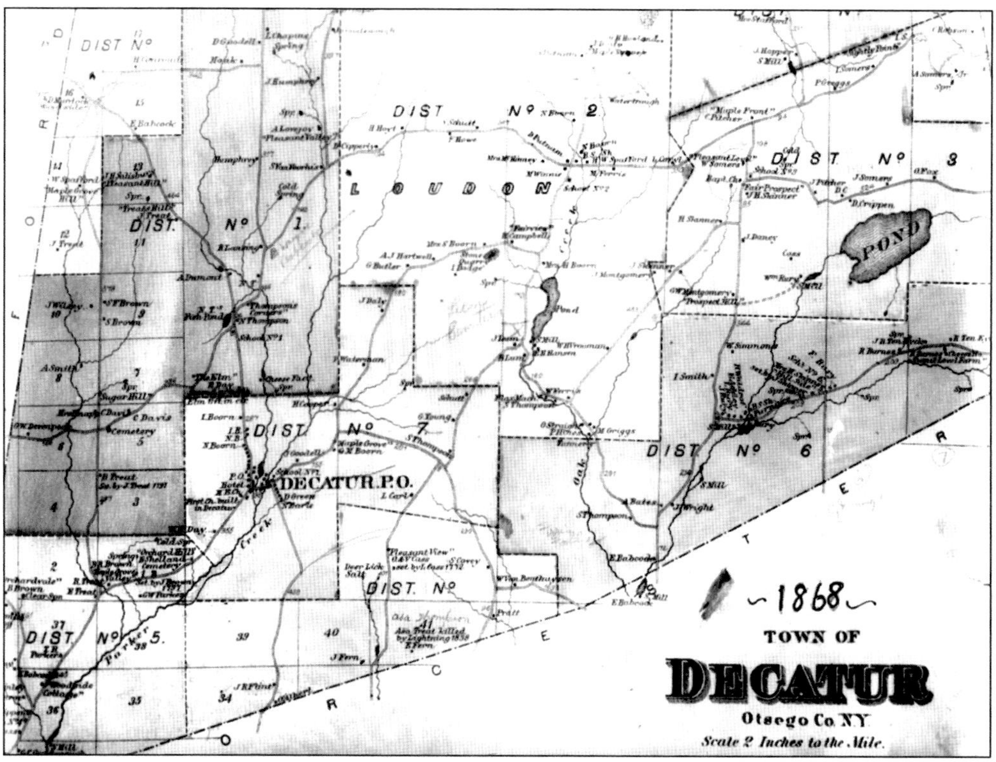

The Town of Decatur. Decatur, named in honor of naval hero Commo. Stephen Decatur, was formed from Worcester on March 25, 1808. The surface is hilly and broken by the narrow valleys and Oak and Parker Creeks. It is alleged that after the Albany & Susquehanna Railroad was completed, Decatur folks moved the five miles to Worcester, contributing to the town's growth.

"WATERMAN'S IDEAL FOUNTAIN PEN." This is an early Waterman's fountain pen advertisement. Various styles of Waterman pens still are sold today.

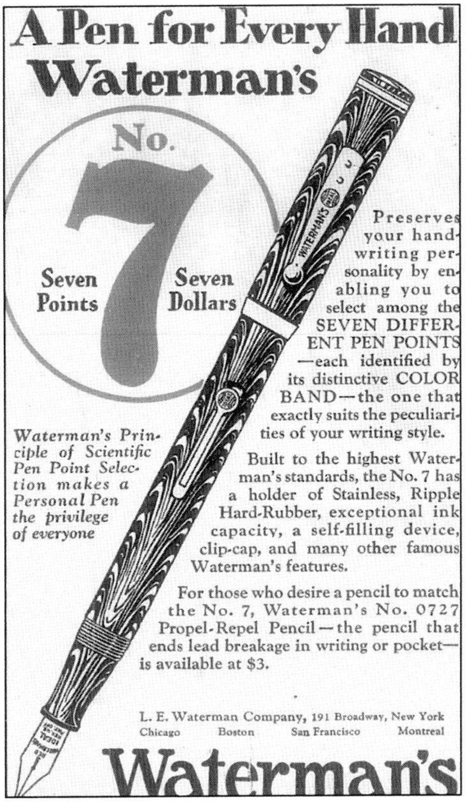

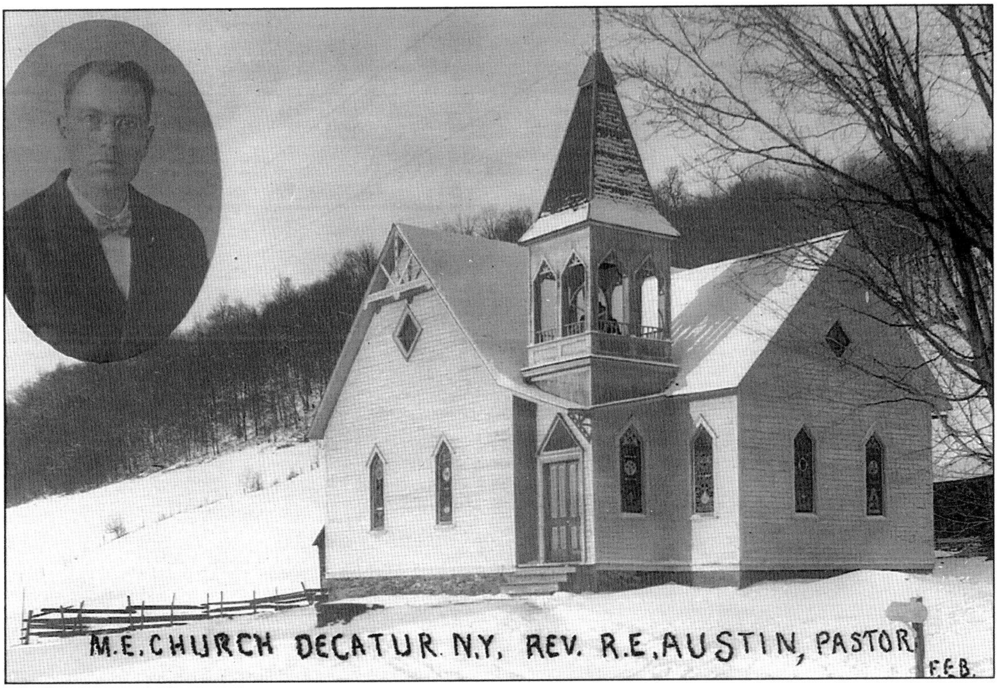

THE DECATUR METHODIST EPISCOPAL CHURCH. The inset shows Rev. R.E. Austin, who was pastor of this country church in 1908. The church was torn down several years ago.

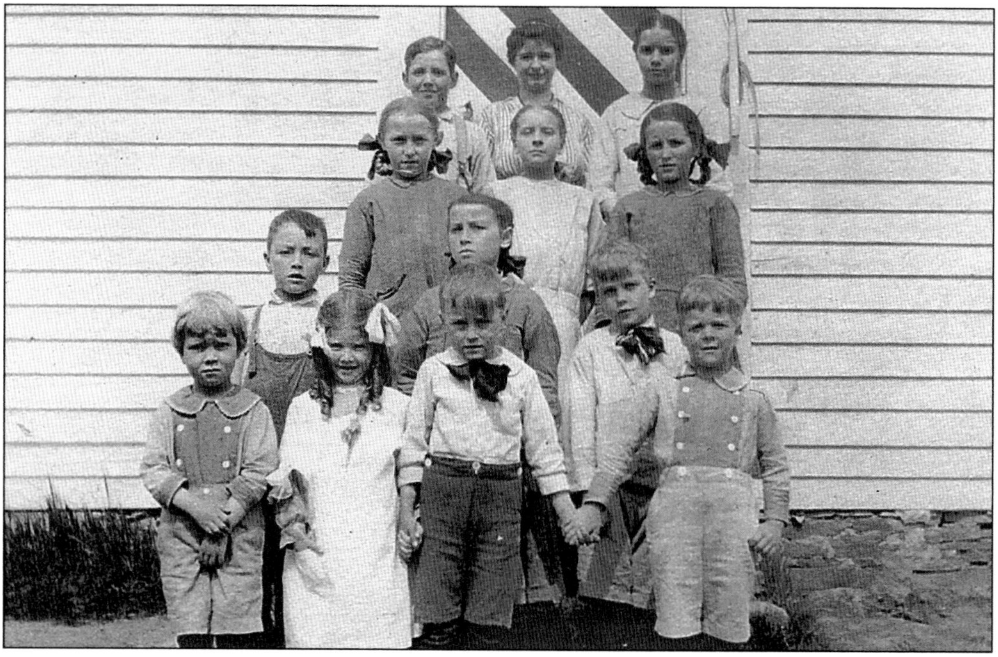

Winnie District No. 5. This district school, now used for storage, is located about three miles from Worcester. The teacher, Leah Wade (Wright), often walked to the school and back. The students are, from left to right, as follows: (first row) Everett Bull, Lucy Brownell, Lucius Mowers, and Willis Rosenthal; (second row) Matt Kromer, Katie Kromer, and Jerald Rosenthal; (third row) Rosie Kromer, Ruth Clark, and Tillie Kromer; (fourth row) Laurence Brownell, Leah Wade, and Emma Clark.

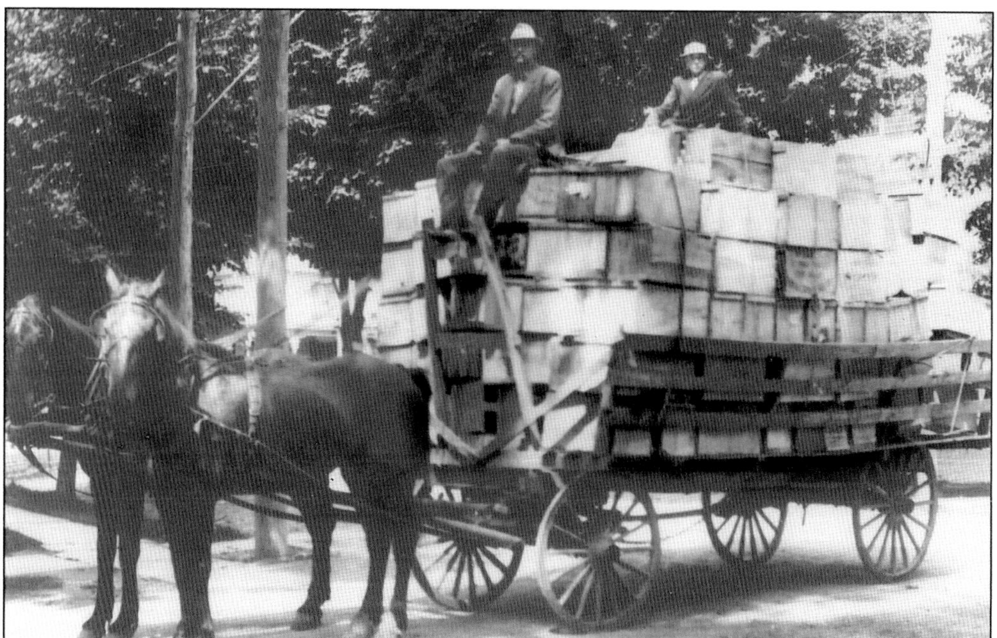

A Load of Eggs. This early-1900s photograph shows 250 cases of eggs headed for Mowers Grocery Store in Decatur. Perhaps some of the eggs were shipped out by train in Worcester.

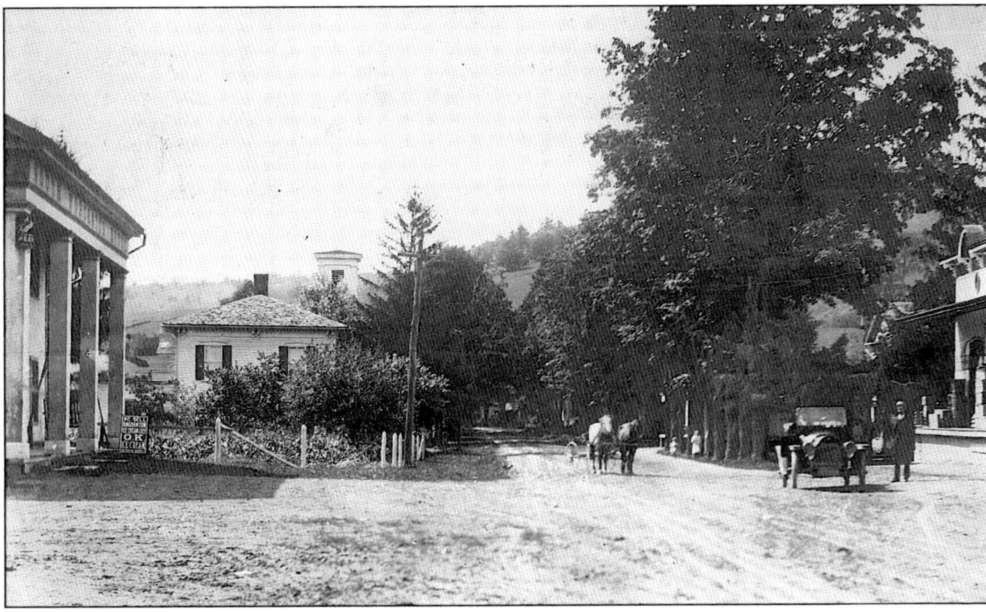

SOUTH WORCESTER'S MAIN STREET. The hotel on the left was built *c.* 1832. Several rooms were used as a tavern, and the innkeeper's family lived in another part of the building. Sherburn Becker purchased the hotel for use as a private home in the 1900s. Mr. and Mrs. Lawrence Kosciusko now operate a bed-and-breakfast there. The postcard was mailed in 1918.

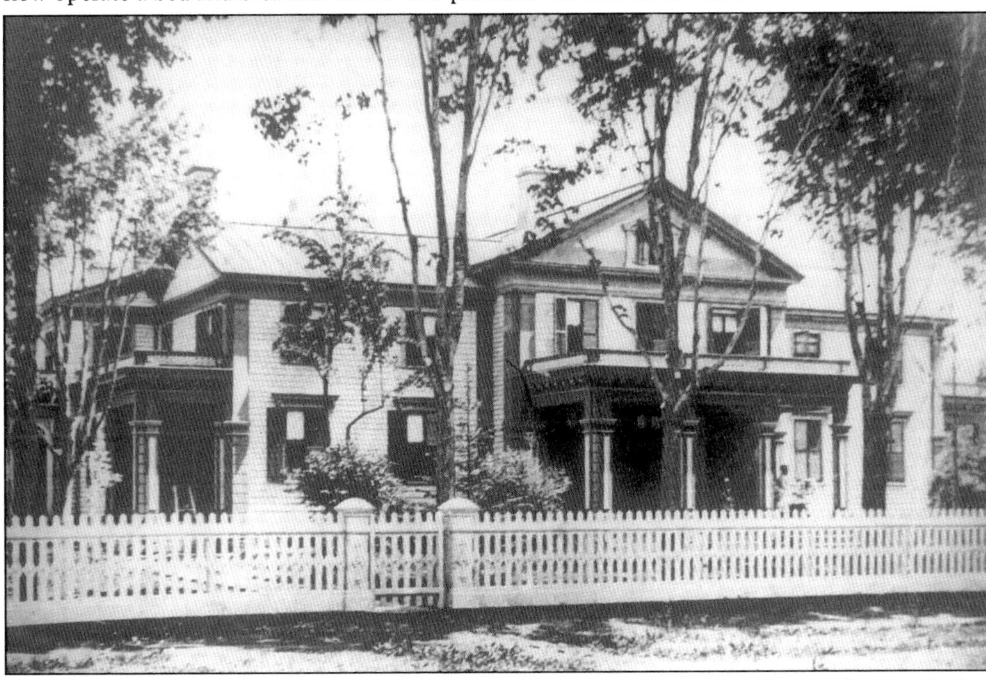

THE BECKER MANSION. Lindenwood, the 60-room house built by Abraham Becker in the late 1800s, was destroyed by fire in 1905. It is alleged that the fire was started when a servant placed a coal scuttle filled with hot coals on the wooden back porch. Abraham Becker, who became one of the most famous lawyers in Otsego County during his day, was the grandfather of Sherburn M. Becker, well known for his career as "the boy mayor of Milwaukee."

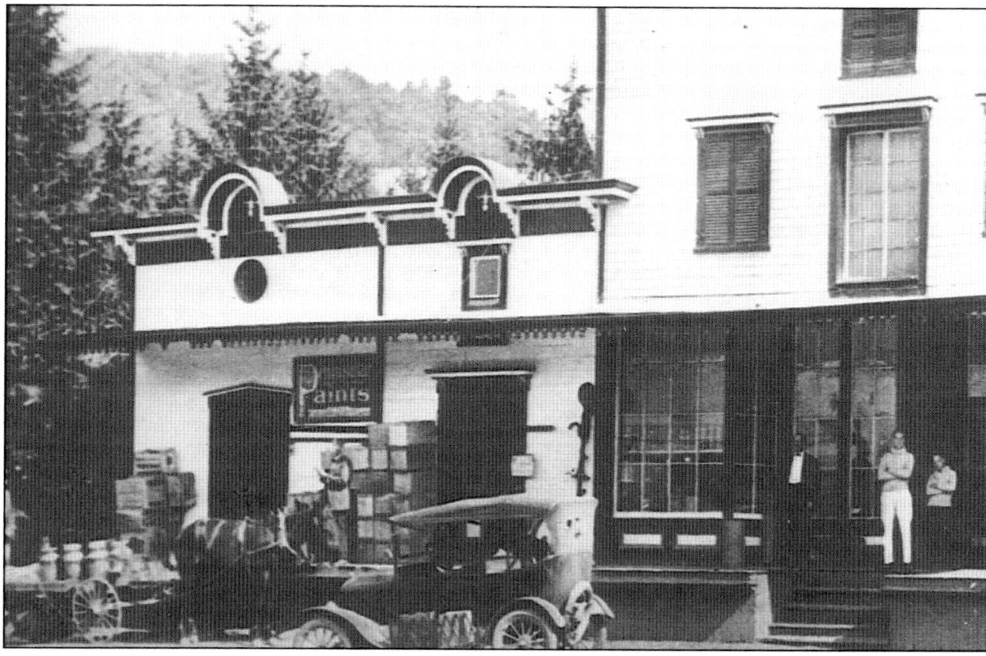

The Olmstead and Sturges Store. This country store continued to operate into the 1940s. Supermarkets and improved travel led to its demise. The railroad was important to the store at the height of its business. Two teams of horses were used to haul goods and feed over the hills every day from the railroad in Worcester. The trips took about two hours. In the early 1900s, farmers stopped at the store for goods on their return trip from hauling milk to the creamery.

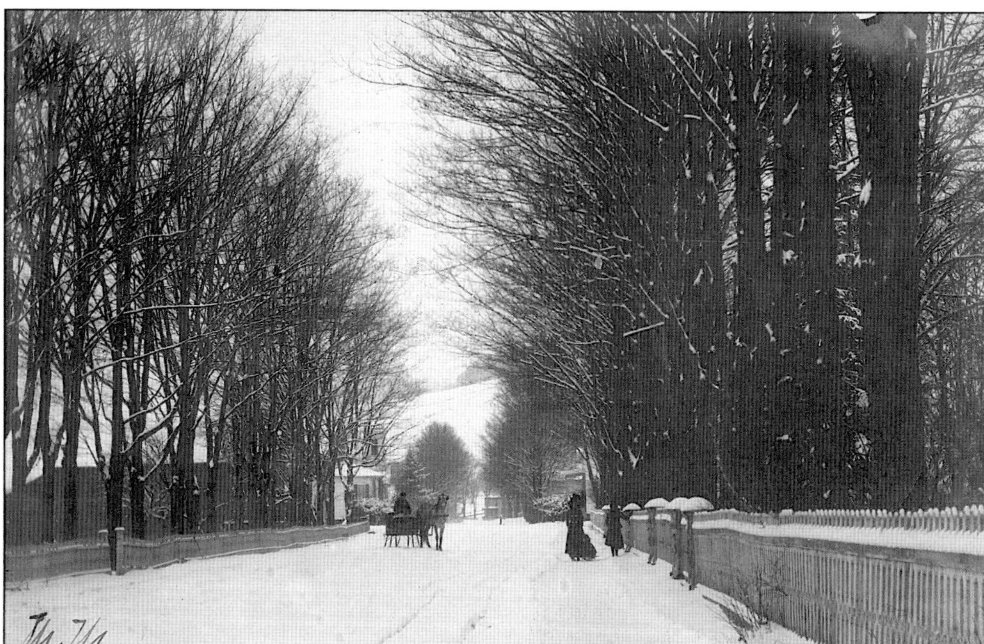

A Winter Scene, South Worcester. A horse and sleigh with driver travel down the snowy Main Street in 1906. The fence on the right is in front of the Becker mansion.

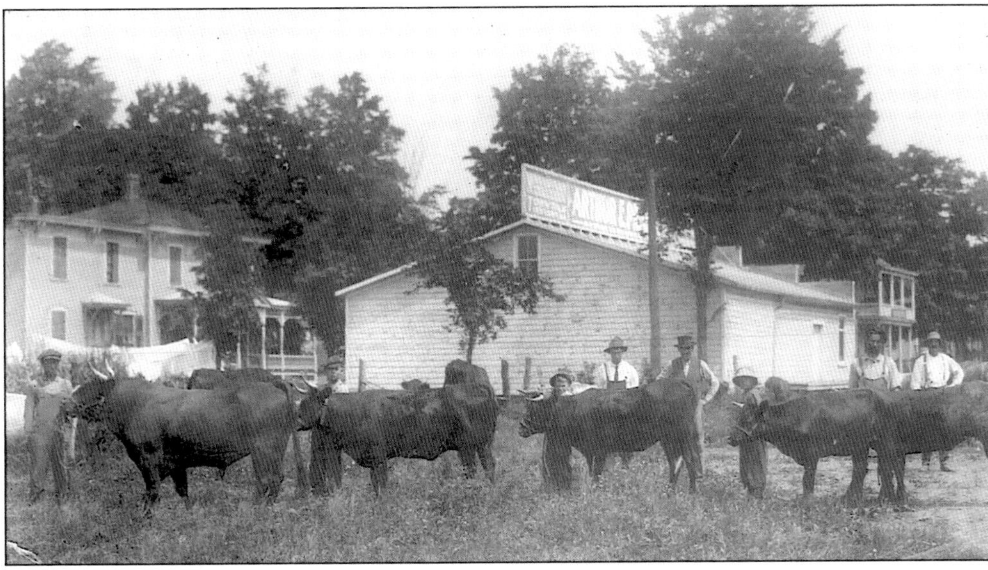

HILLIS'S PRIZE STOCK. Arthur Hillis, a grandfather of Ralph Hillis of South Worcester, traveled around the state by train with some of his prize stock. In the fall, Hillis took his cattle on a fair circuit where the animals won many blue ribbons. This photograph was taken near the Delaware & Hudson station at Worcester. The steer were to be shipped by train to the many fairgrounds for judging.

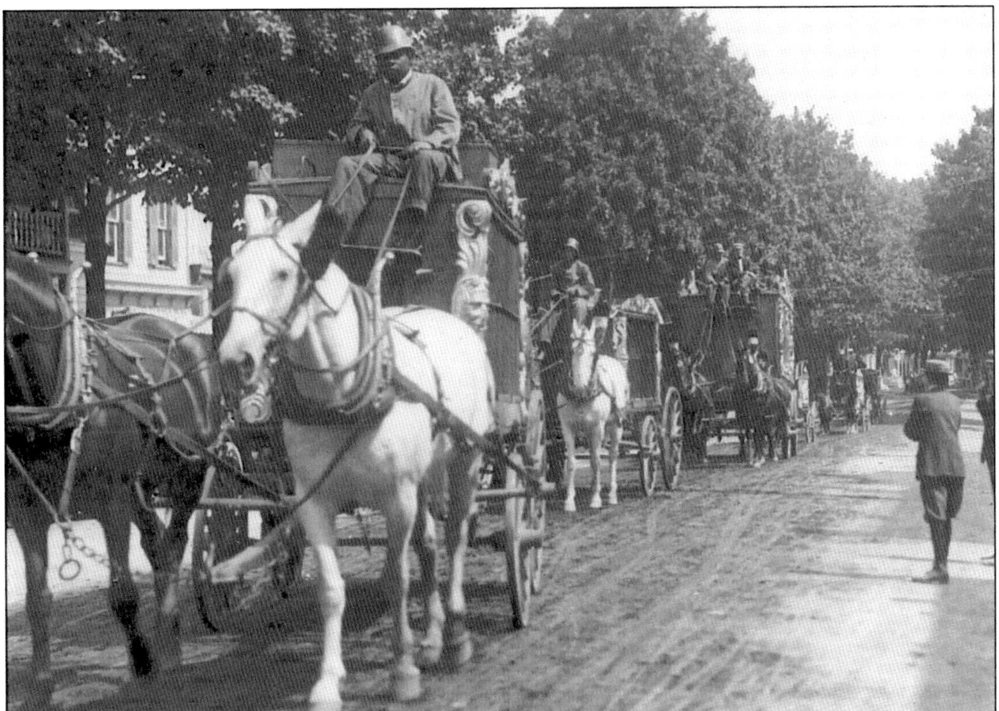

THE CIRCUS COMES TO TOWN. In 1910, the circus moved from town to town by horse and wagon. Early in the morning, these circus wagons moved along Main Street on their way to set up on Goodell's flats for several shows later that day.

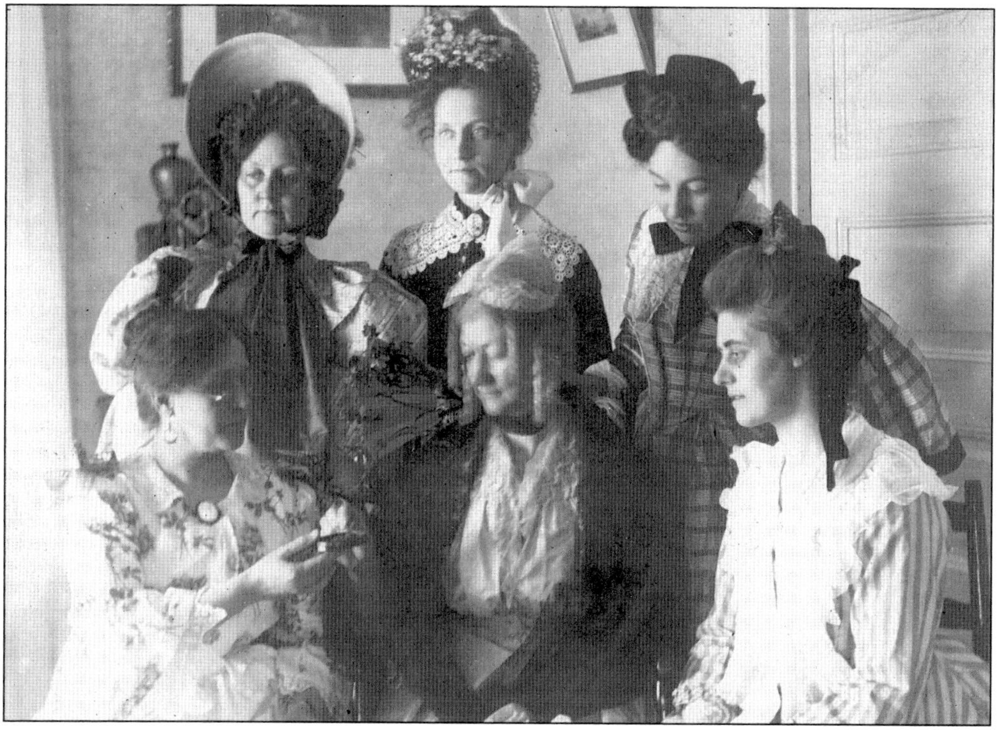

HOUSEWARMING. In March 1907, friends and neighbors attended a housewarming at the new home of George B. and Caroline Crippen on Cook Street. Several women took part in the Old Maid's Tea Party. From left to right are the following: (front row) Mary Callender, Grace Lehman, and Madge Wrigley; (back row) Katherine Bulson, Emma Wilson, and Anna Nichols.

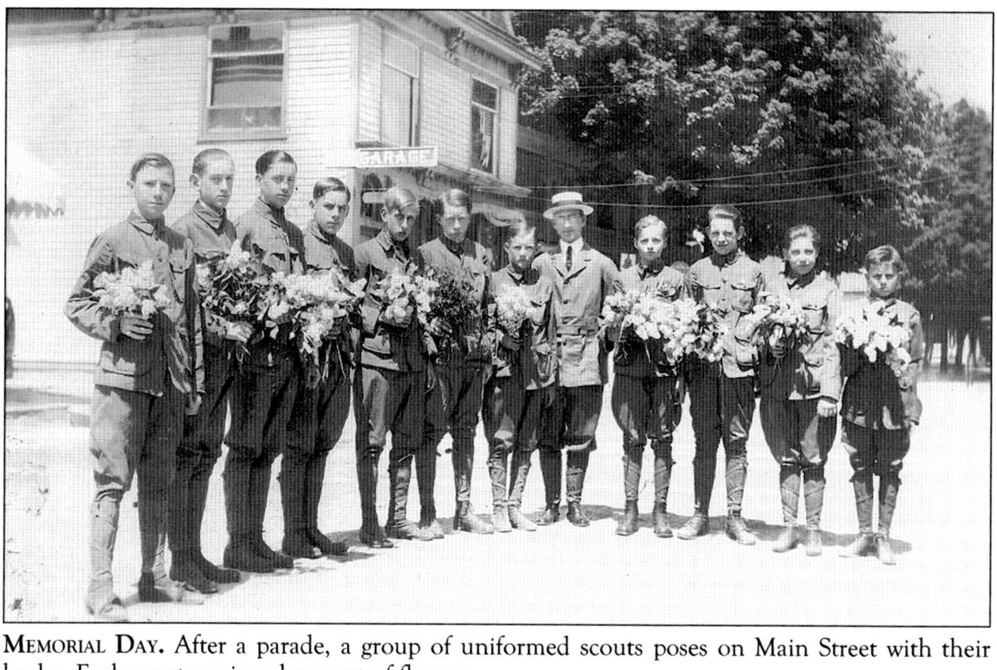

MEMORIAL DAY. After a parade, a group of uniformed scouts poses on Main Street with their leader. Each scout carries a bouquet of flowers.

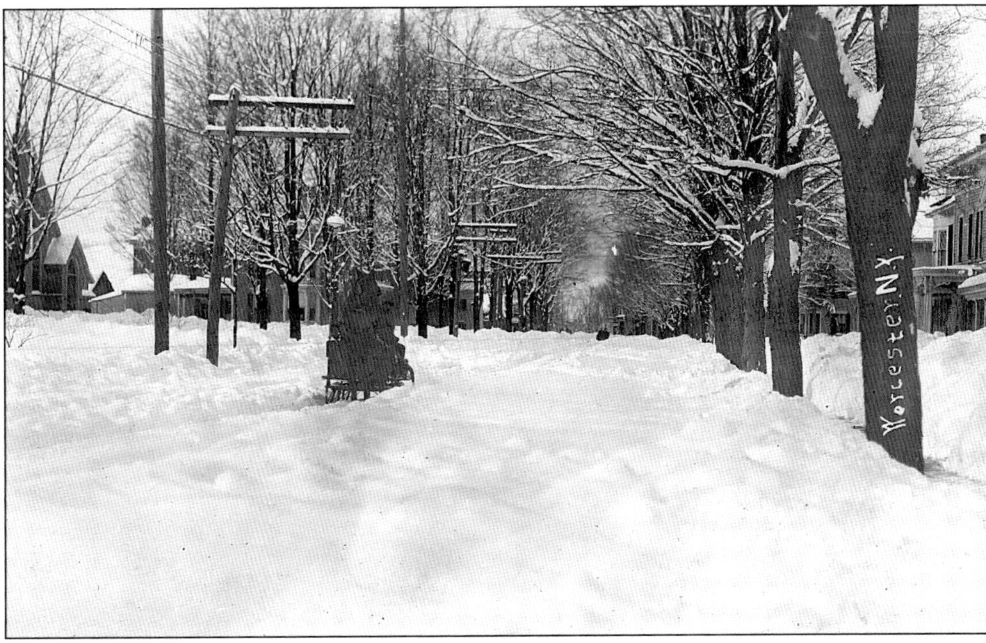

WINTER IN 1913. A horse with sleigh traverses Main Street in Worcester after a snowfall. In those days, travelers had to make their own way through the snow. The writer's message says that this photograph was taken after a blizzard.

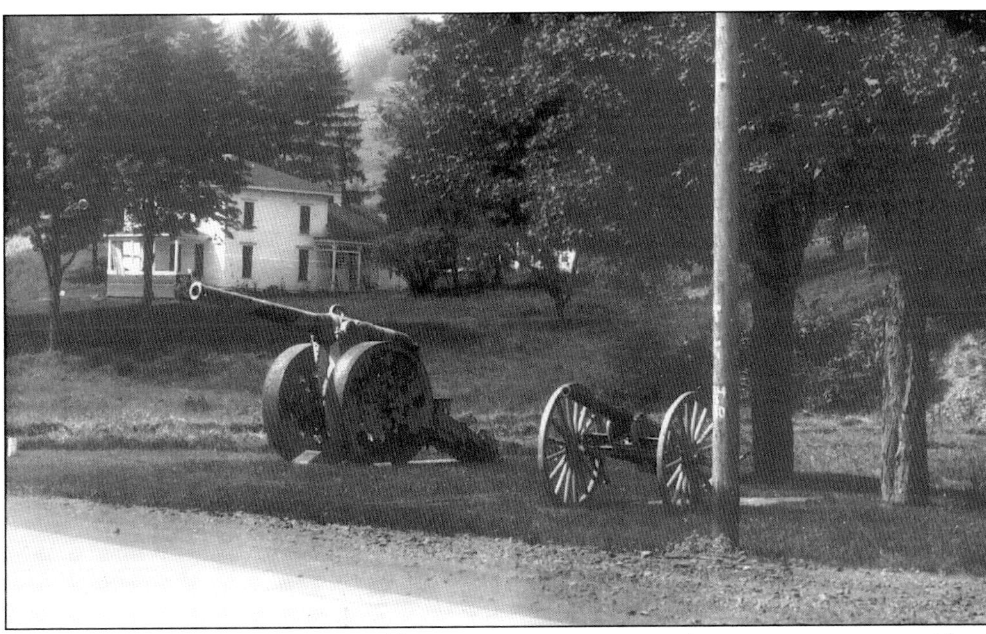

CANNONS IN TOWN. These two World War I–era cannons were kept at a rest area outside of town until World War II, when they were given to the government for the war effort. When the cannons were first received, they were placed on the lawn of Worcester High School.

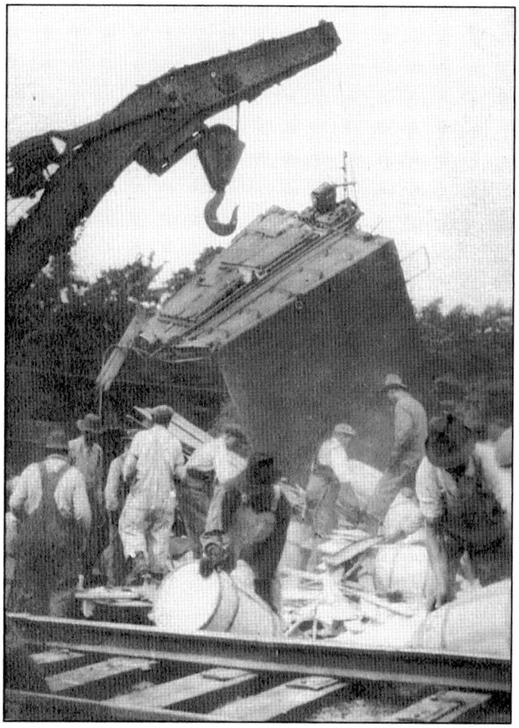

A Delaware & Hudson Wreck. A Delaware & Hudson crane was brought in to help following a derailment several yards from the station. Barrels of flour were smashed and dumped out during the crash.

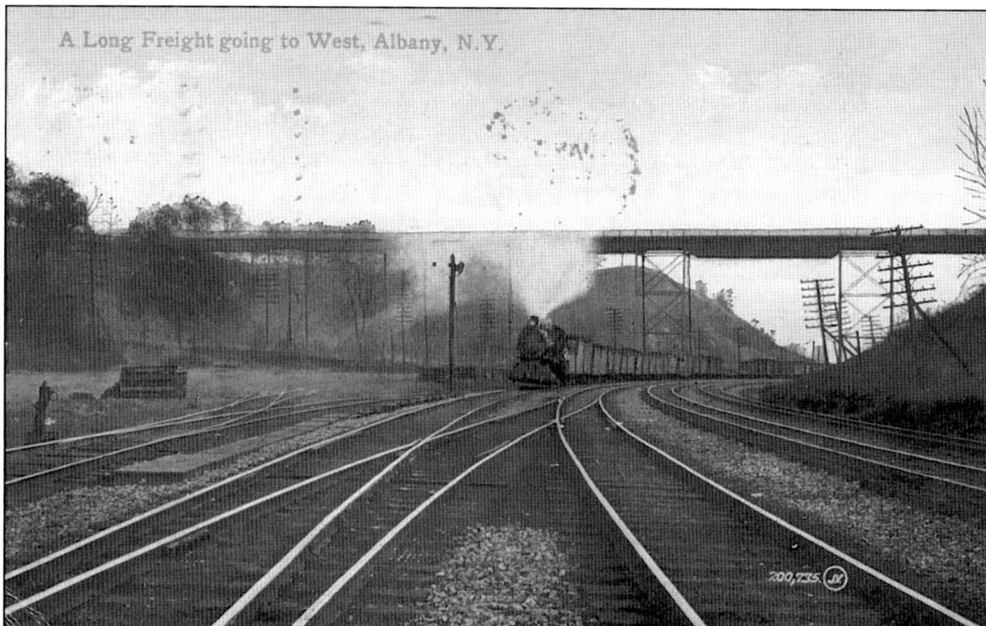

Long Freight. This 1909 freight train is headed toward the Albany area. At least four freight trains a day still use the old Delaware & Hudson tracks through the Tri Valley. In the 1920s, there were at least four or five passenger trains each day and numerous freights. If a farmer ordered baby chicks, trains shipped them. Children walking along the tracks were fascinated with the passing trains. Local boys would often arrange two nails like an X on the rails when a train approached so they would be squashed together.

Five

SCHENEVUS

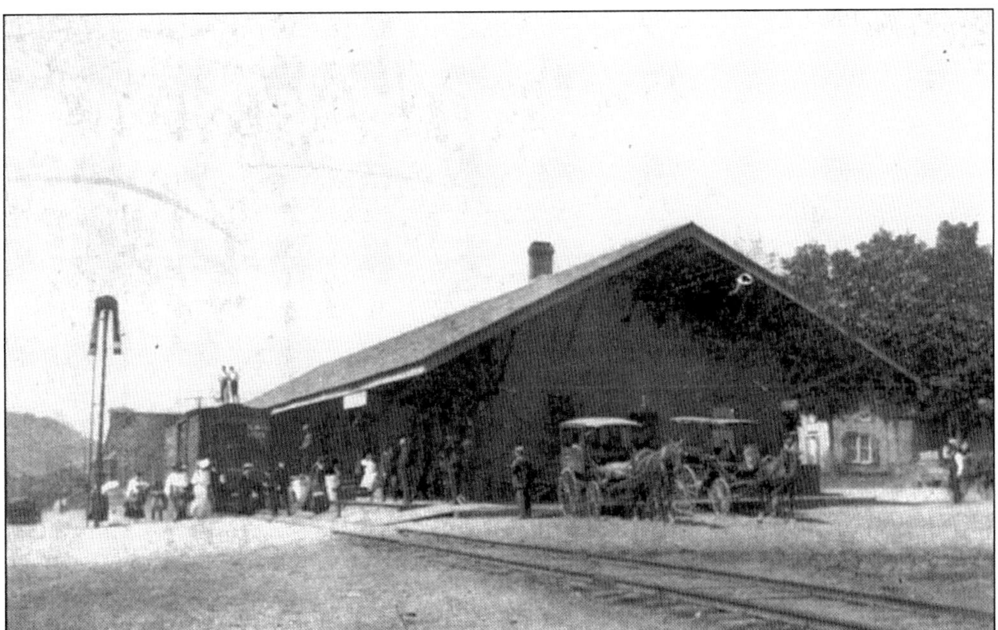

DELAWARE & HUDSON STATION. The station became a busy place after the railroad arrived, with operators working 24 hours a day. A news item from the *Worcester Times* dated January 28, 1909, stated: "3 masked men armed with revolvers held up the telegraph operator in the Schenevus Station on Saturday at 10:45 p.m. H.N. Bronk was reading a magazine when ordered to hold up his hands. The masked men took $17.75 and left. There were no clews [*sic*]."

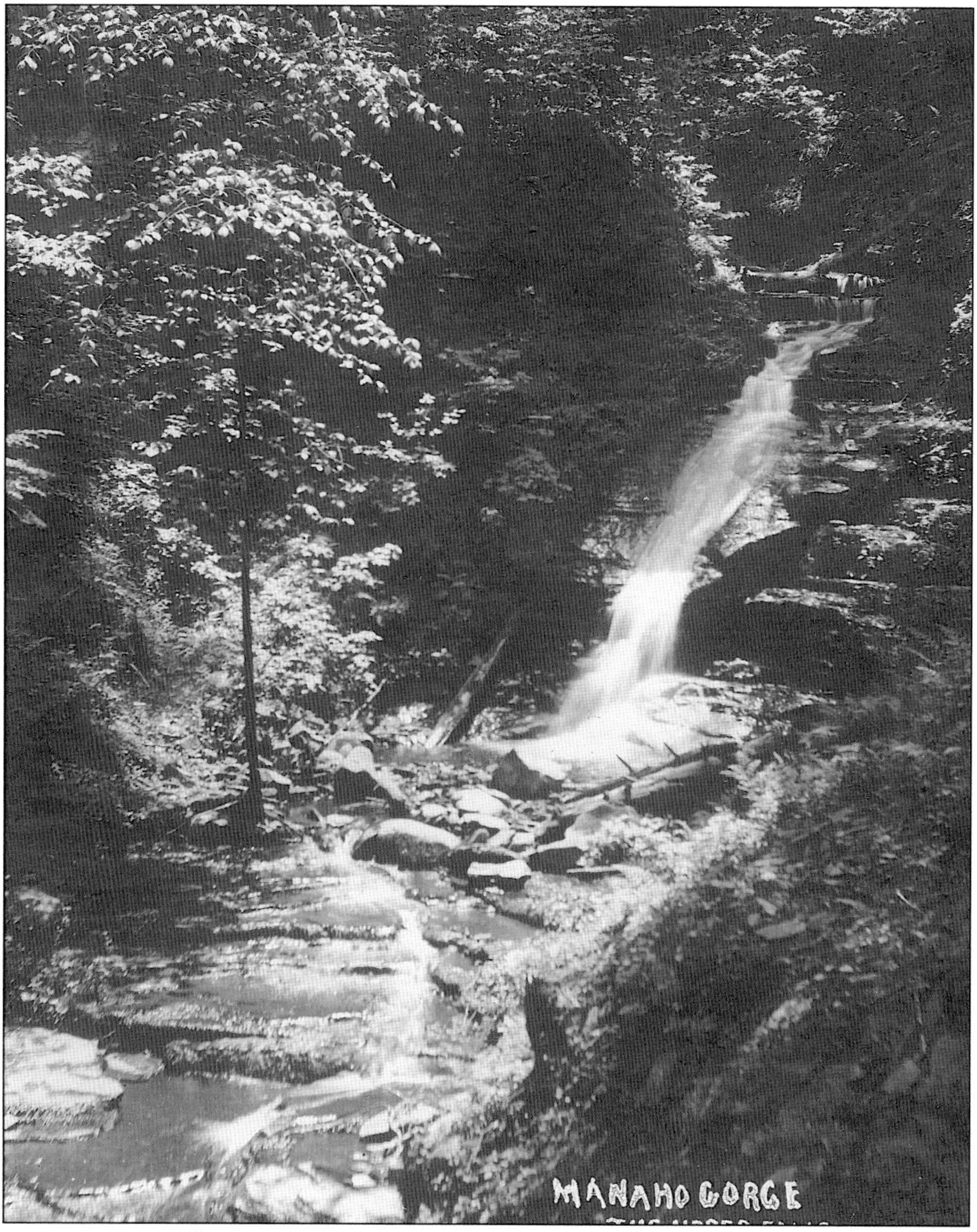

MANAHO GORGE. There is a romantic local folktale about the young woman whom the gorge is named after. Manaho, the lovely daughter of Chief Schenevus, loved the gallant Manatee. They frequently met at the foot of the falls and often gazed into the mirrored ponds. Manatee said, "Look, we are there in the water together." Another Indian, Changu, also loved Manaho. He thought to himself, "I will kill Manatee someday." One day, as the braves went on a hunt, Manatee took the trail to the gorge. Changu followed and snuck up behind Manatee, killing him. Manatee fell into the pool. In the evening, Manaho told her father that Manatee must be at the pool. She saw two faces in the pool; one was the drowned Manatee. She then joined the face in the water. Chief Schenevus found them the next day, both faces turned toward the sky. It is said that at twilight you can hear voices emanating from the gorge.

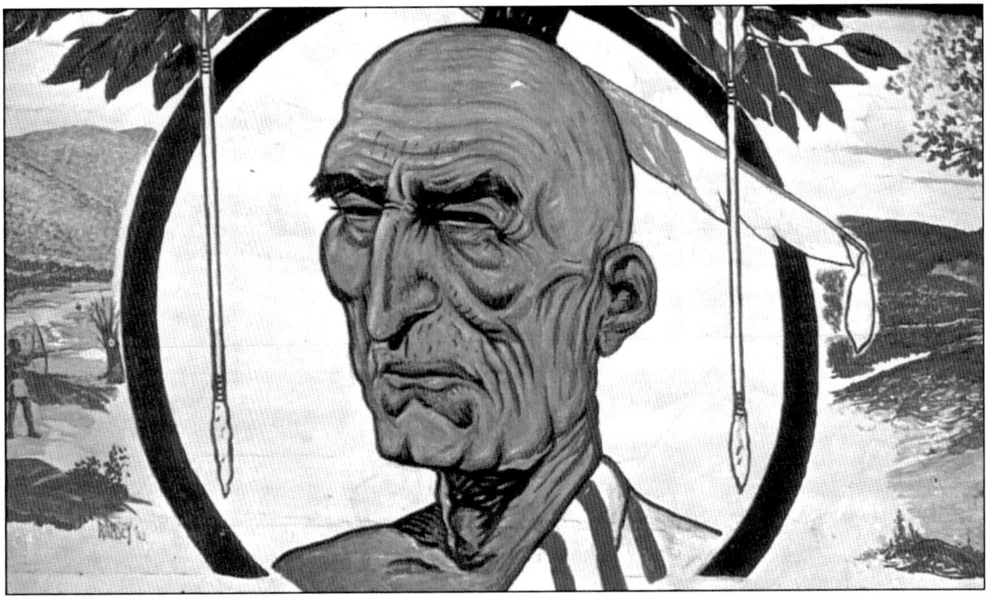

CHIEF SCHENEVUS. Legend has it that the chief, for whom the village was named, had great leadership abilities as well as hunting skills. He was well known in the Tri Valley area. This mural of the chief was painted on the side of a store by an itinerant artist known only as Ramsey. The present owners had the painting restored and named their restaurant Chief Schenevus Coffee Shop and Bakery.

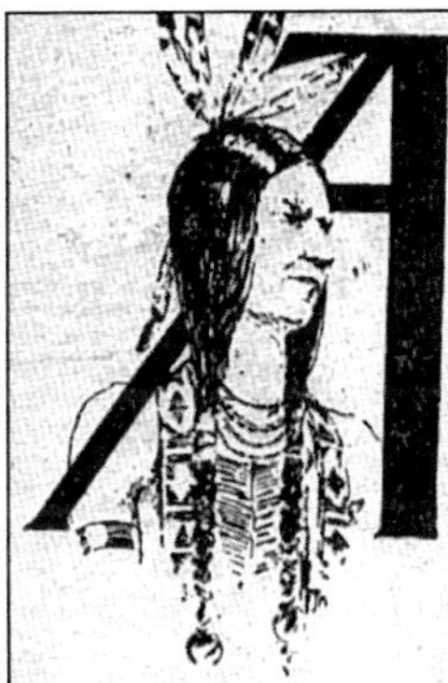

AT THE GRAVE OF CHIEF SCHENEVUS.

"Beneath these pines, Schenevus lies,
Chief of his tribe—the 'Speckled Trout'."

* * * * * *

So runs the legend; and the place,
Thick-sown with arrow-heads, keeps trace
And memory of his warrior-race.

Killed by his sons at his behest—
Helpless and blind he longed for rest—
Each pressed the spear which pierced his breast.

No more the feasting and the shout,
No more the war-dance and the rout,
Victor and vanquished as "Speckled Trout."

Yet, peacefully the stream flows by,
And beautiful the woods and sky,
Where old Schenevus chose to lie.

THE DEATH OF THE CHIEF. It is said that after the death of his daughter Manaho, Chief Schenevus aged rapidly. He summoned four of his braves and instructed them to ride with him to the hunting ground, where he commanded them to shoot him with their bows and arrows. It was his wish to die in a way that no one brave would be responsible for his death. After the chief's death, the tribe deeply mourned its loss.

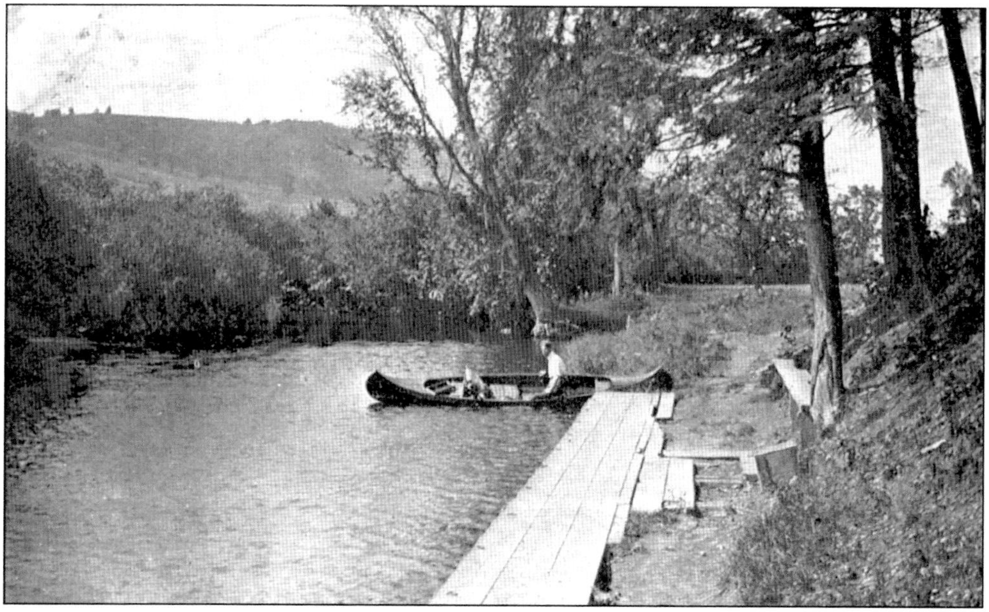

The Pines. At one time, there was a dam at the Race Street area of Schenevus Creek. This made the water deep enough for canoeing and boating. A small island with a picnic spot was located about a mile east of the village where there was a dense stand of pines, hence the name, the Pines.

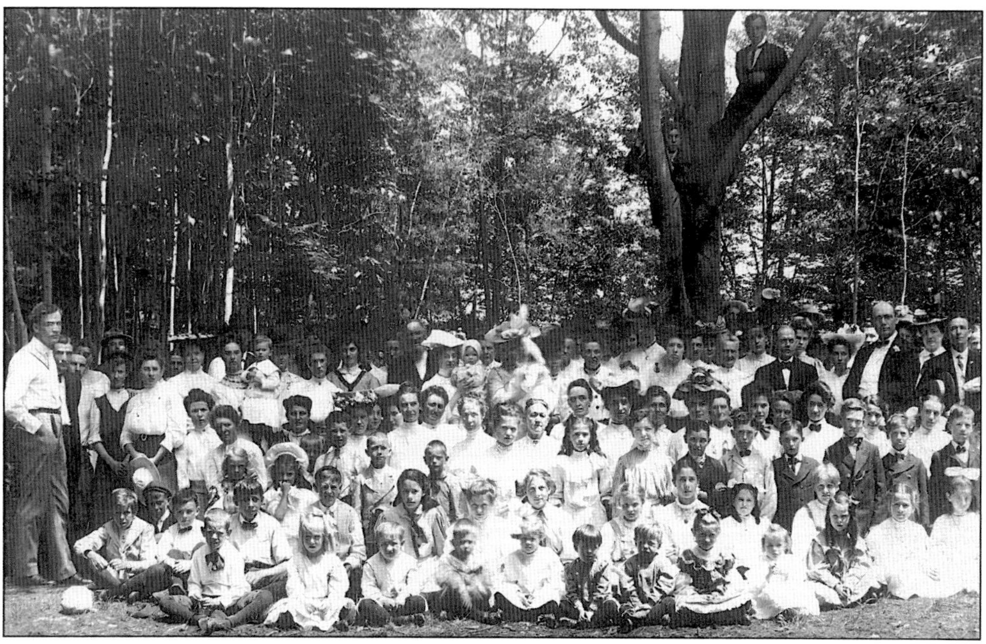

A Sunday School Picnic. This Sunday school picnic took place at the Pines in Schenevus in the early 1900s. Sunday school pupils and their teachers from Schenevus churches enjoyed the outing dressed in their Sunday best.

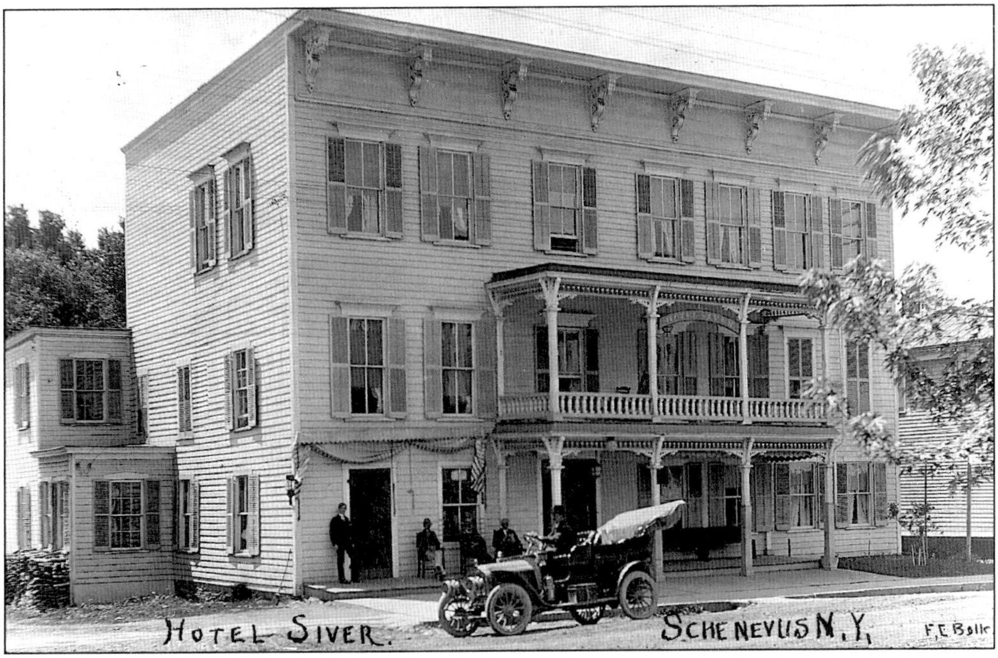

THE HOTEL SIVER. This was originally built as a two-story hotel. A third story was added on top of the old metal roof about 30 years later. In 1896, it had 30 rooms with rates of $1.50 per day. The business changed hands several times over the years. Everett and Beatrice Westcott became owners in 1945. They modernized the hotel and included an apartment for themselves. Their business was known as the Schenevus Hotel. The structure burned on March 28, 1954. This is an F.E. Bolles postcard.

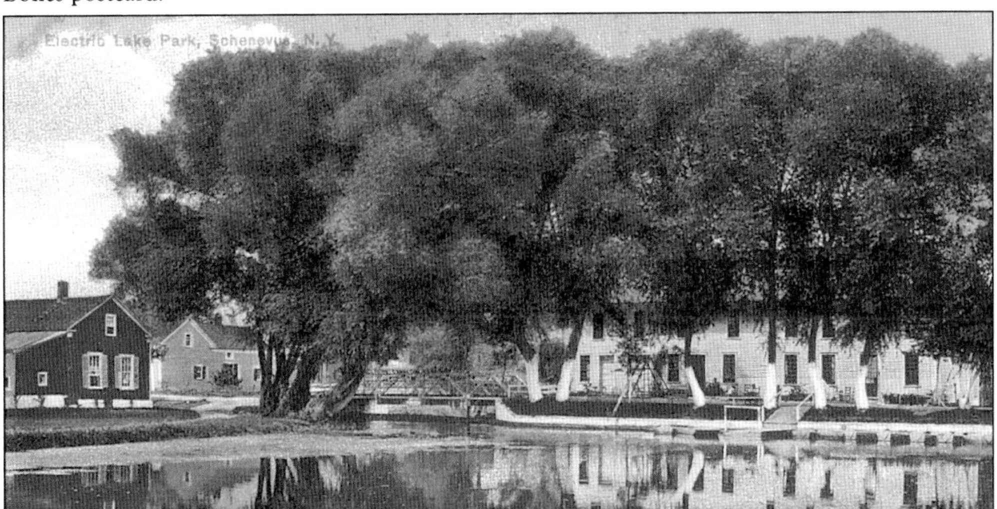

AN ELECTRIC LIGHT PLANT. At one time, Schenevus Creek provided power for an electric light plant. This was after the Great Bear Light and Power Plant. East Street crossed over the creek by the bridge. This area was used as a park and rental area for canoes. The long white building, which burned in 1912, was once a factory named White Mill and later housed the light plant. After it burned, the structure was rebuilt and was then used as a paint shop, dance hall, and chicken house.

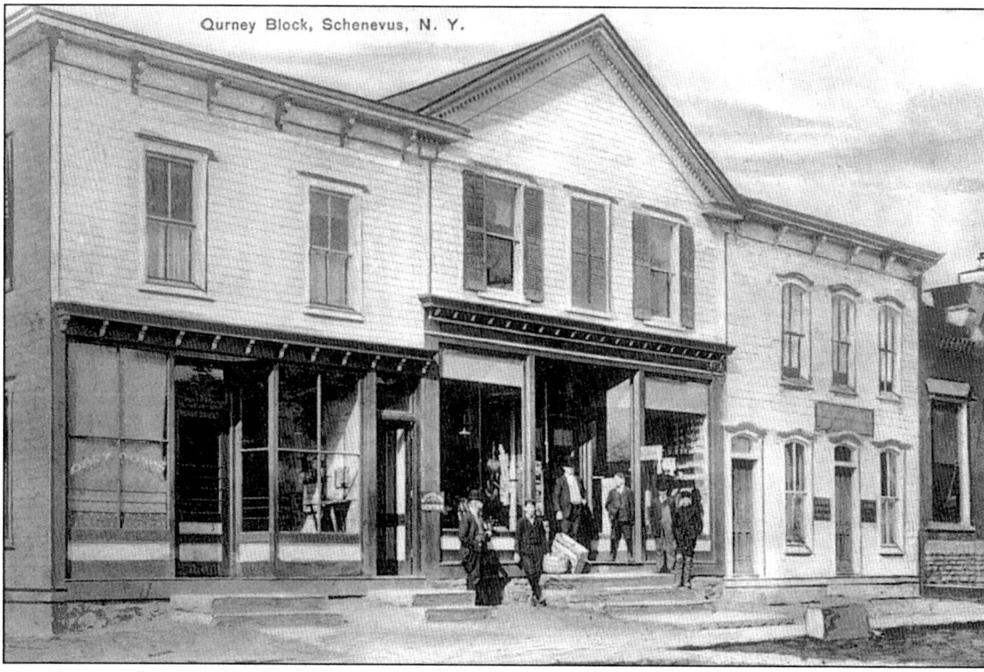

THE GURNEY BLOCK. In the early 1900s, Samuel Gurney had a dry goods store in the center of this complex, which is now occupied by the post office. Gurney had his living quarters upstairs. Members of the Grand Army of the Republic also used an upstairs room for meetings. The early post office occupied space on the left side of the building, while a dentist's office was upstairs. Orson Strail of Schenevus published this postcard.

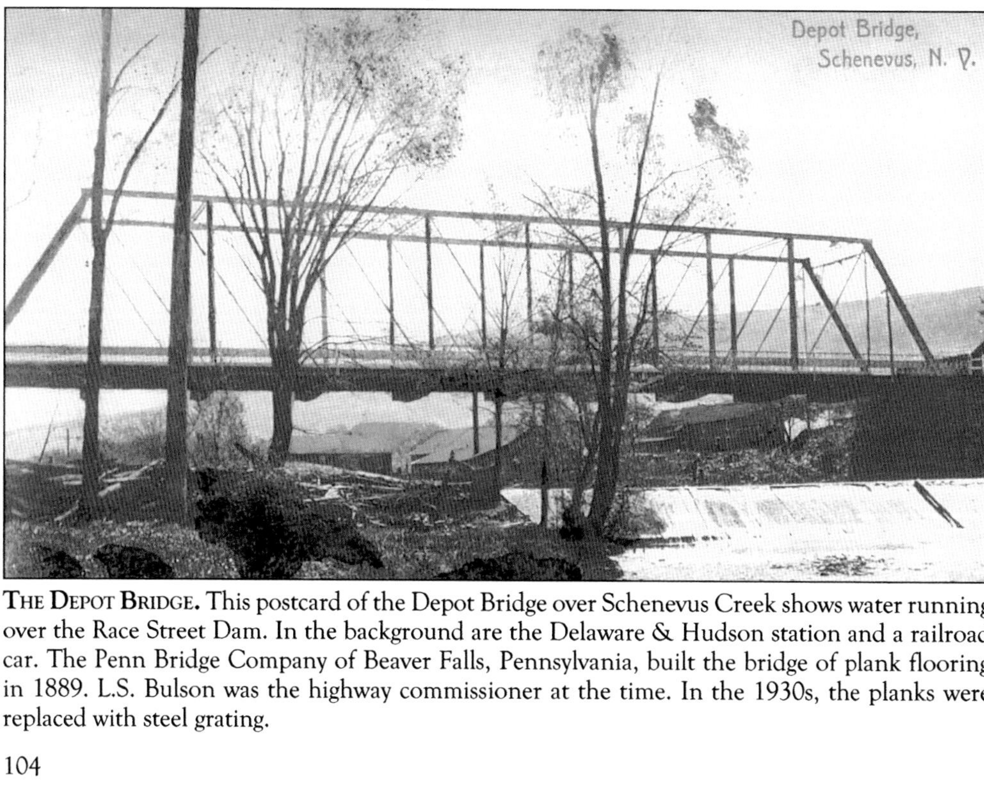

THE DEPOT BRIDGE. This postcard of the Depot Bridge over Schenevus Creek shows water running over the Race Street Dam. In the background are the Delaware & Hudson station and a railroad car. The Penn Bridge Company of Beaver Falls, Pennsylvania, built the bridge of plank flooring in 1889. L.S. Bulson was the highway commissioner at the time. In the 1930s, the planks were replaced with steel grating.

The Masonic Building. In 1883, the Masons purchased this lot on Main Street where they built their lodge. When this photograph was taken, there was a street-level hardware store on the left side of the building. Judge Melvin Baldwin, who had an office upstairs, stands in front with his partner, Charles H. Graham. The structure's foundation deteriorated and, in the 1950s, the building was jacked up, the foundation repaired, and the lodge was lowered one story.

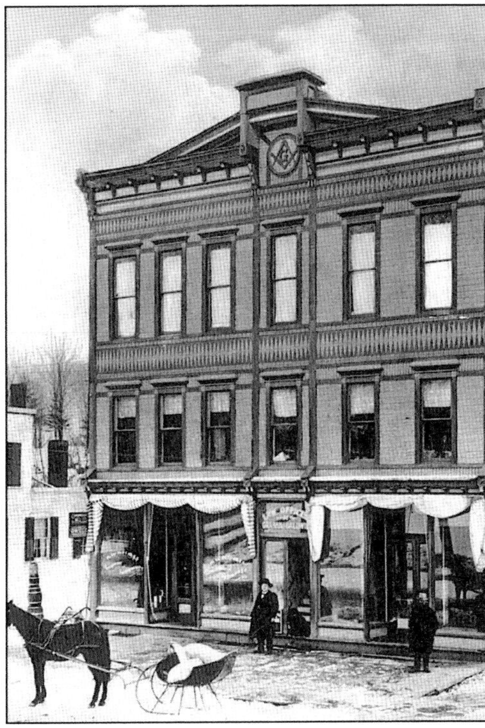

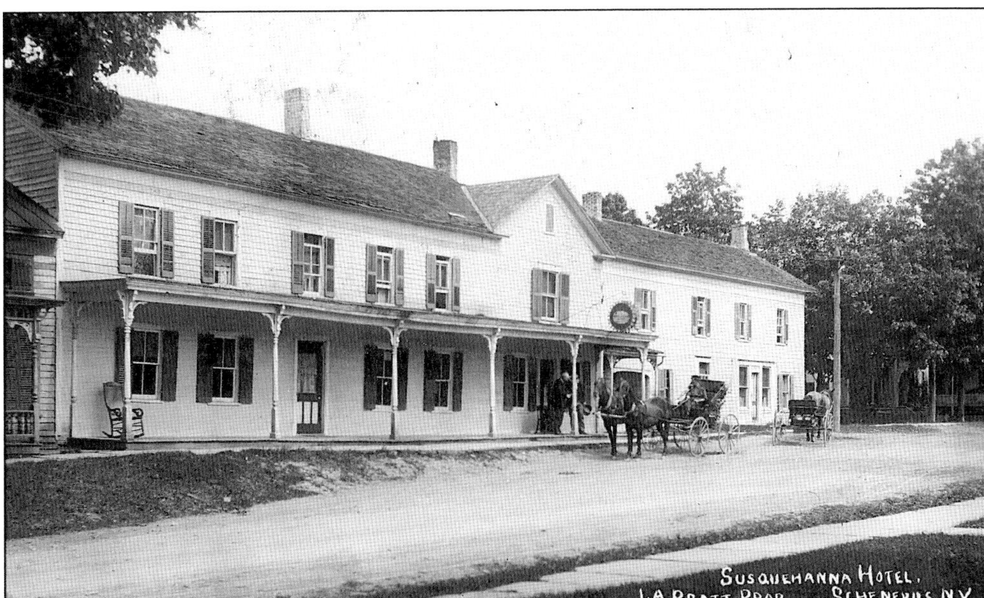

The Susquehanna House. This large hotel was once at the top of the hill on Main Street in Schenevus. L.A. Pratt was the proprietor in the early 1900s. It is said that some of the doors were built large enough to accommodate a team of horses, which were used to draw huge logs into the building for the central fireplace. The Susquehanna House burned down on April 28, 1910. It is rumored that a frequent patron's wife made good on a threat to burn down the place if her husband continued to spend so much time drinking in the tavern. The Susquehanna was one of the most popular hotels on the Delaware & Hudson Railroad from Albany to Binghamton.

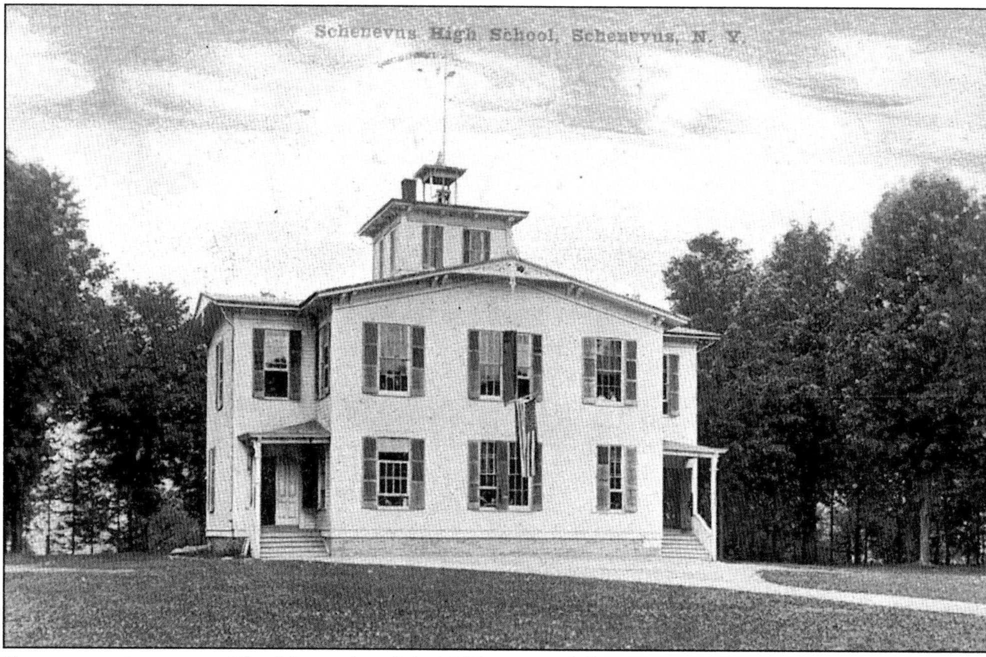

SCHENEVUS ACADEMY. The November 24, 1869 issue of the *Schenevus Monitor* announced that a special meeting would take place at the upper schoolhouse. "Opposition is giving way to reason and better judgement. We hope there will be a full attendance and a right spirit will prevail." Things must have worked out since the Arch Street School was built in 1872 when two school districts voted to consolidate and construct a new building.

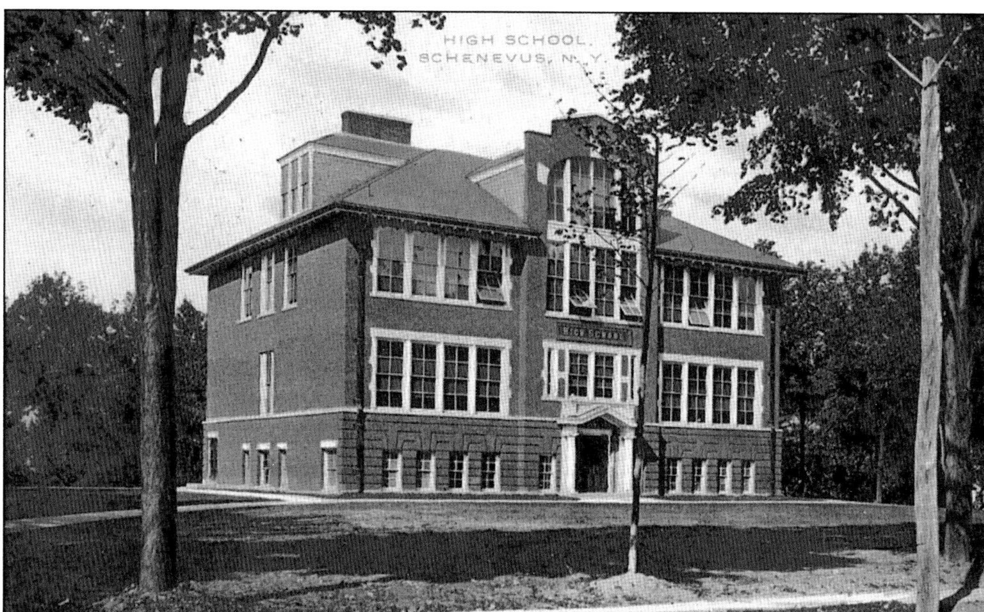

HIGH SCHOOL. This new brick high school was built in 1911, replacing the wooden Schenevus Academy building. After the present school was built in 1941, this building was a fire department and glove shop. In 1976, it was torn down and the Snyder Apartments were built on the site.

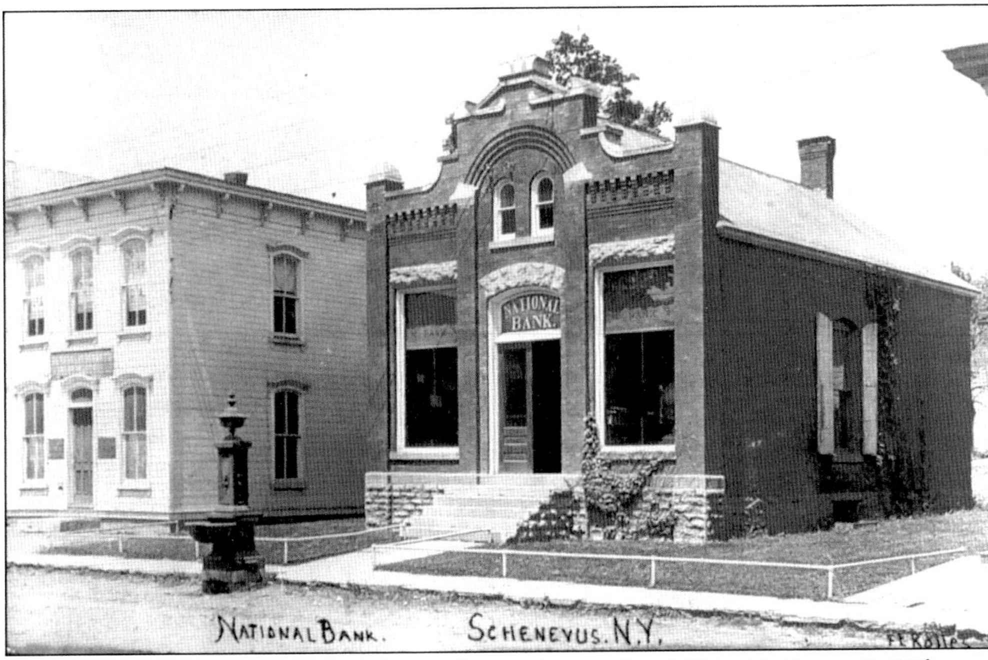

THE SCHENEVUS NATIONAL BANK. This bank was chartered in 1894 with Simon B. Wilson as the first president. The business is now known as the Schenevus branch of Wilber National Bank. The fountain in front of the bank was named in honor of C.H. Graham, a lawyer and prominent citizen. He was instrumental in the organization of the Schenevus Fire Department and Hose Company, which now bears his name. The fountain was sold for scrap during World War II.

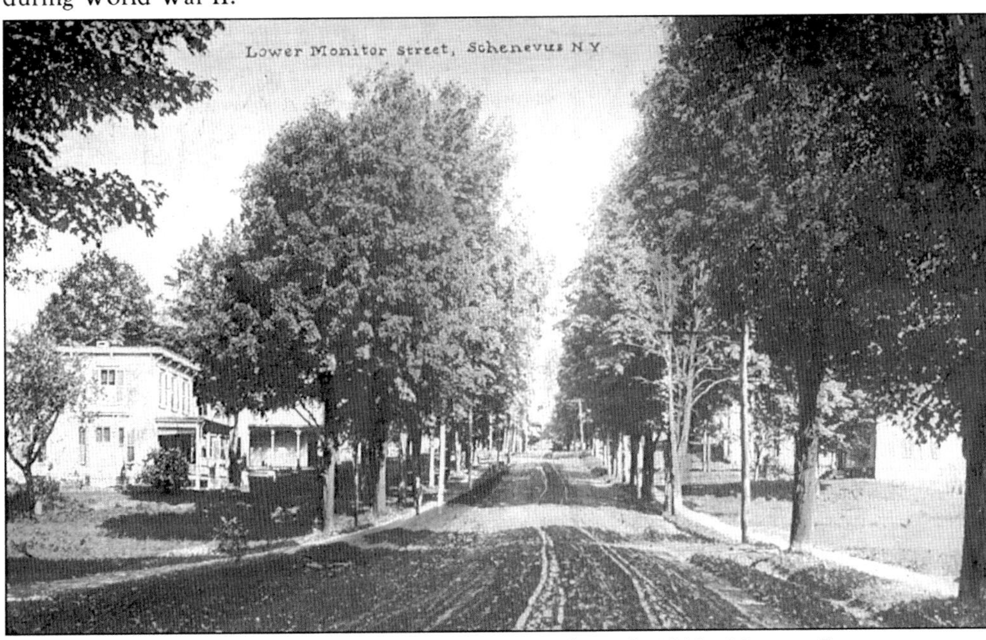

LOWER MONITOR STREET. A quaint, tree-lined street in the early 1900s, Monitor Street was named after the hometown *Schenevus Monitor* newspaper, which served the community for many years.

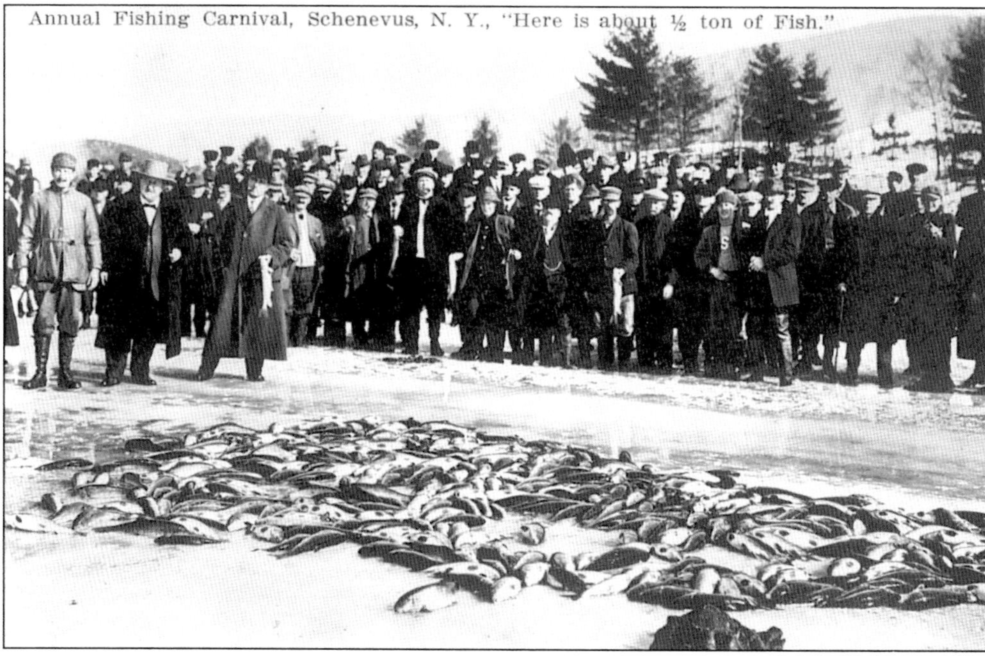

The Annual Fishing Carnival. Around 1910, Schenevus organized an annual fishing carnival, which took place on Schenevus Creek, behind the Hazen barn on Route 7. When the creek finally froze over in January or February, the event attracted a large group of men. While fishing through the ice, it was easy for the men to catch nearly half a ton of fish within the allotted time. The large man standing second from the left is Judge Melvin Baldwin.

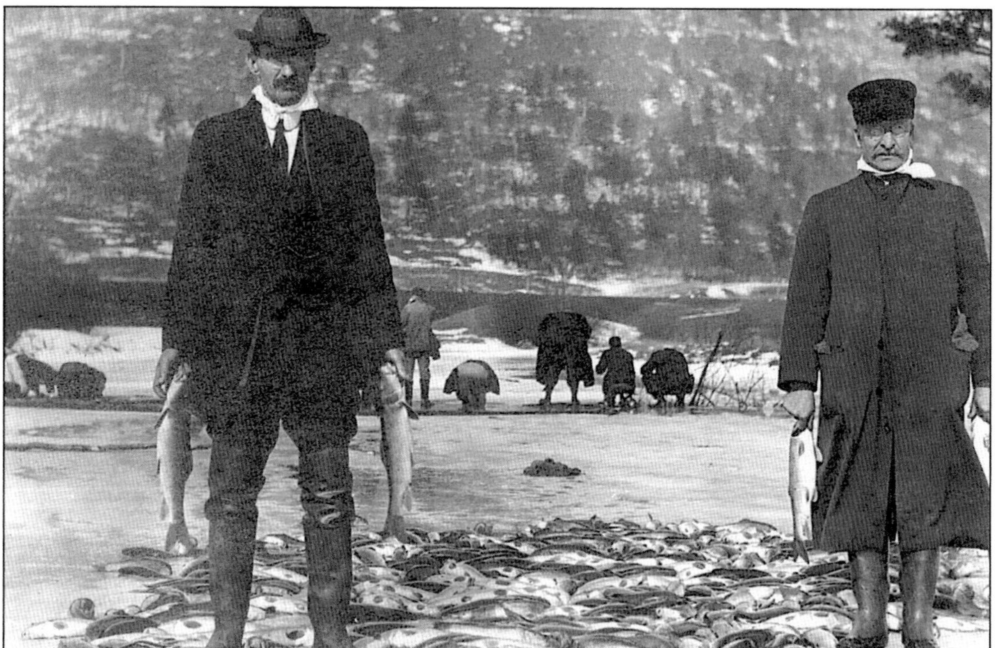

Inspecting Fish. Some men fish while others observe the suckers that were caught. Others pound on the ice with mallets to scare the fish and send them swimming toward those fishing.

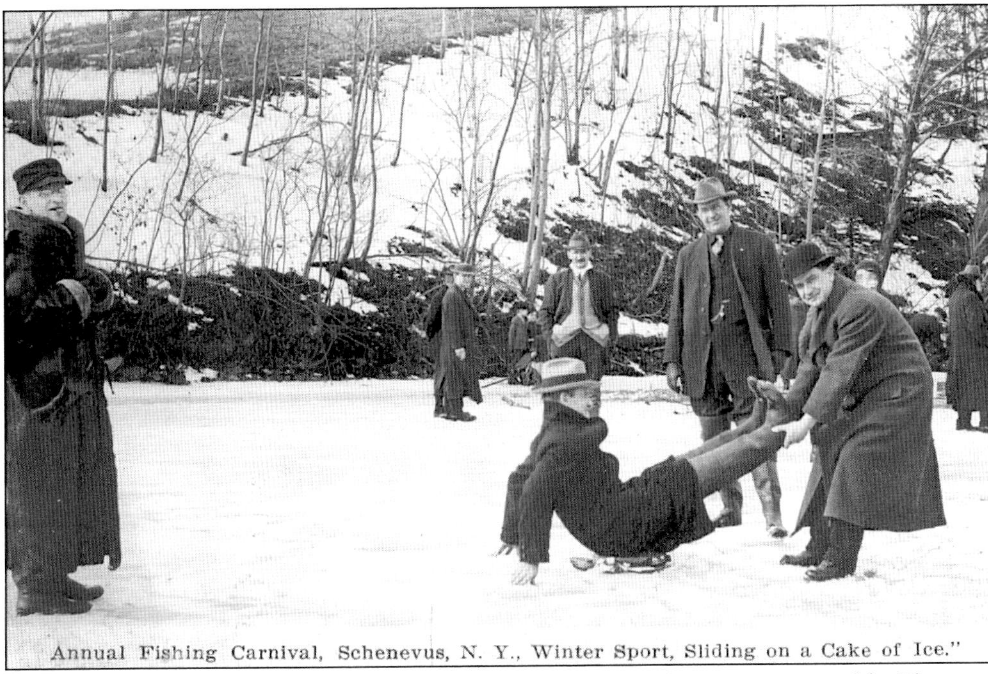

HORSING AROUND. During the fishing carnival, some antics on the ice were inevitable. This man sitting on a pair of skates is being pulled around the ice by another fisherman. One can only hope his boots did not come off in the process.

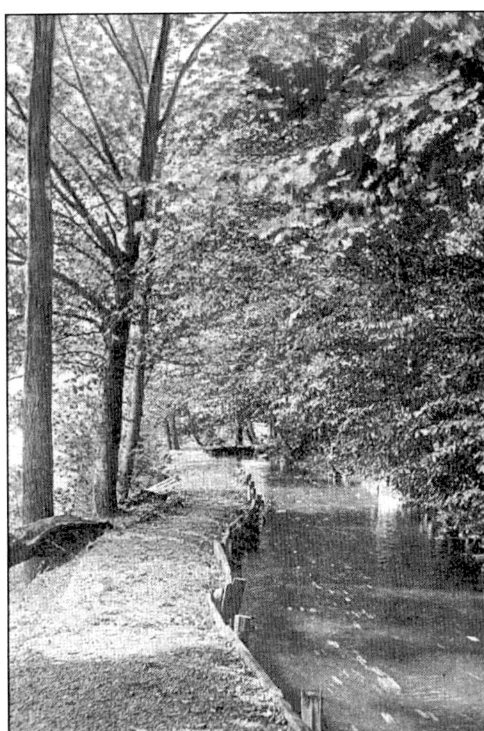

THE RACEWAY. The stream known as the Raceway flows beside Race Street and empties into the Schenevus Creek. In the 1880s, the stream was used as a source of power for mills.

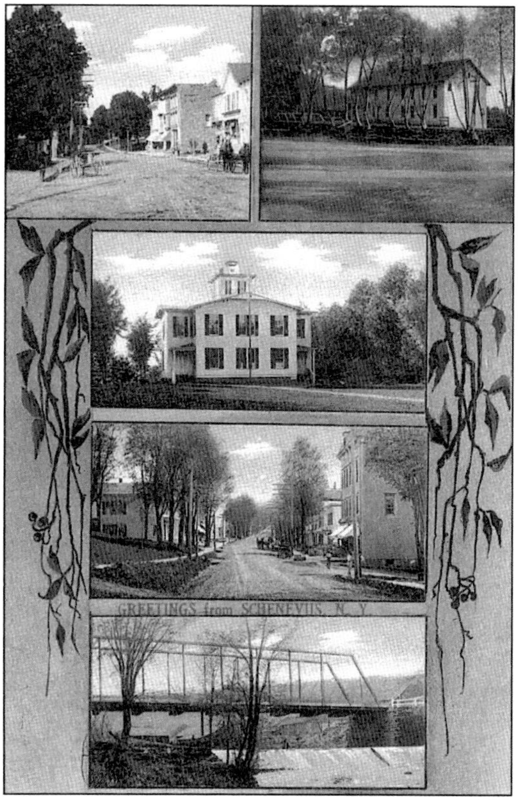

GREETINGS. These five views of Schenevus are on an early postcard that was printed in Germany. The writer lists the food she had for dinner: "beef stake [*sic*], sweet potatoes, grapes, rye bread, and bread pudding."

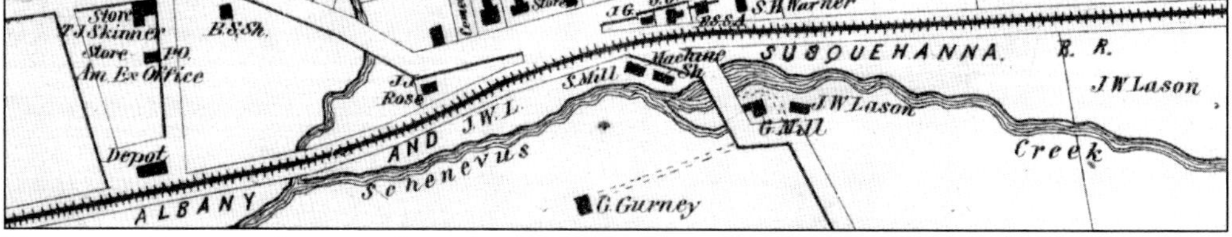

MARYLAND CENTRE. The Township of Maryland was formed in 1808. The settlement of the town took place in 1790, when Elisha Chamberlain and his three brothers—Israel, Elephas, and Phineas Spencer—moved to the area where the railroad station was later built. The map shows the railroad track area of the Albany & Susquehanna Railroad line.

Six

Colliersville and Surrounding Area

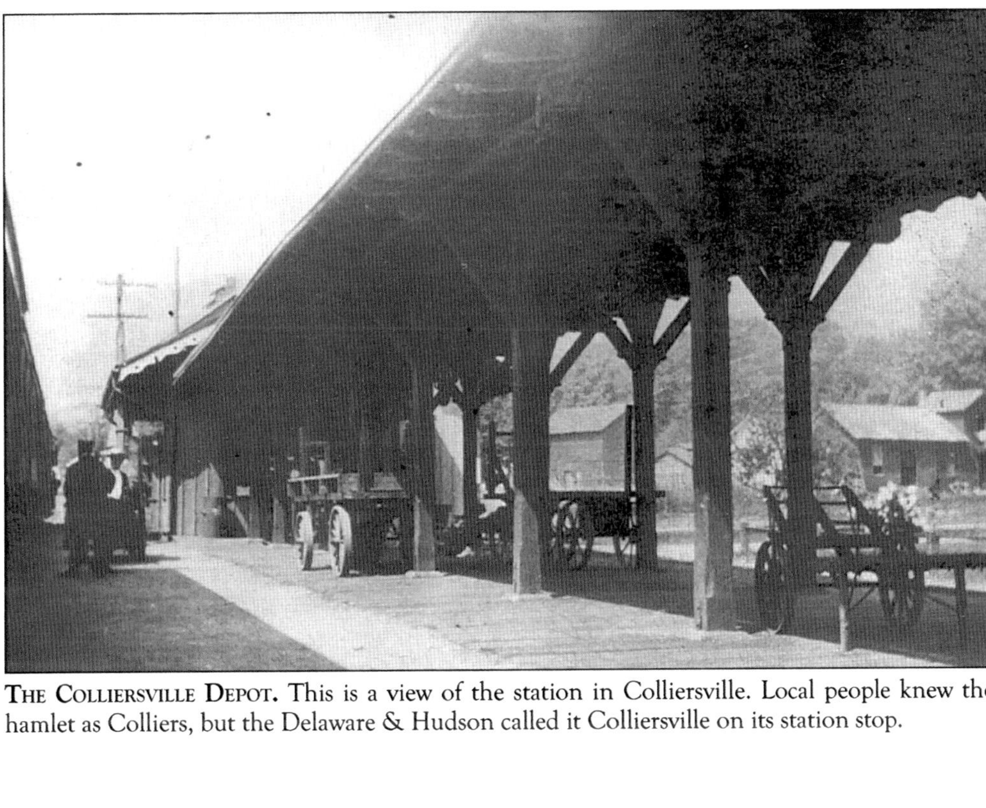

THE COLLIERSVILLE DEPOT. This is a view of the station in Colliersville. Local people knew the hamlet as Colliers, but the Delaware & Hudson called it Colliersville on its station stop.

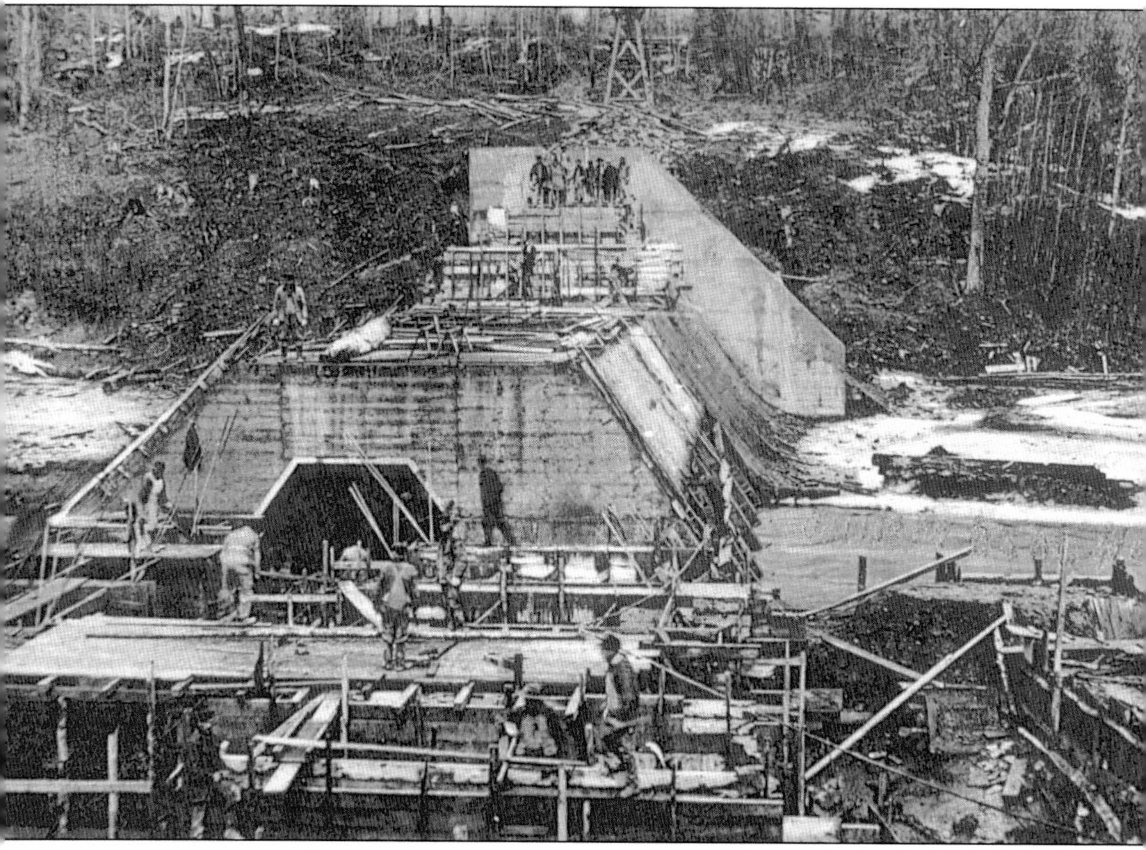

The Power Dam. This 1908 postcard features a photograph of the new power dam in Colliersville, near the Delaware & Hudson line. The Oneonta, Mohawk Valley Railroad (OMV) formed the Susquehanna River Power Company in 1908 and built a hydroelectric plant at Goodyear's Mills. The extra electricity was needed for private homes and the OMV, which operated an electric train. The freight line was kept buzzing because of the interchange with the Delaware & Hudson Railroad, made possible by connecting with the Broad Street line in Oneonta. Milk was hauled to creameries in Mohawk and Cooperstown on these lines.

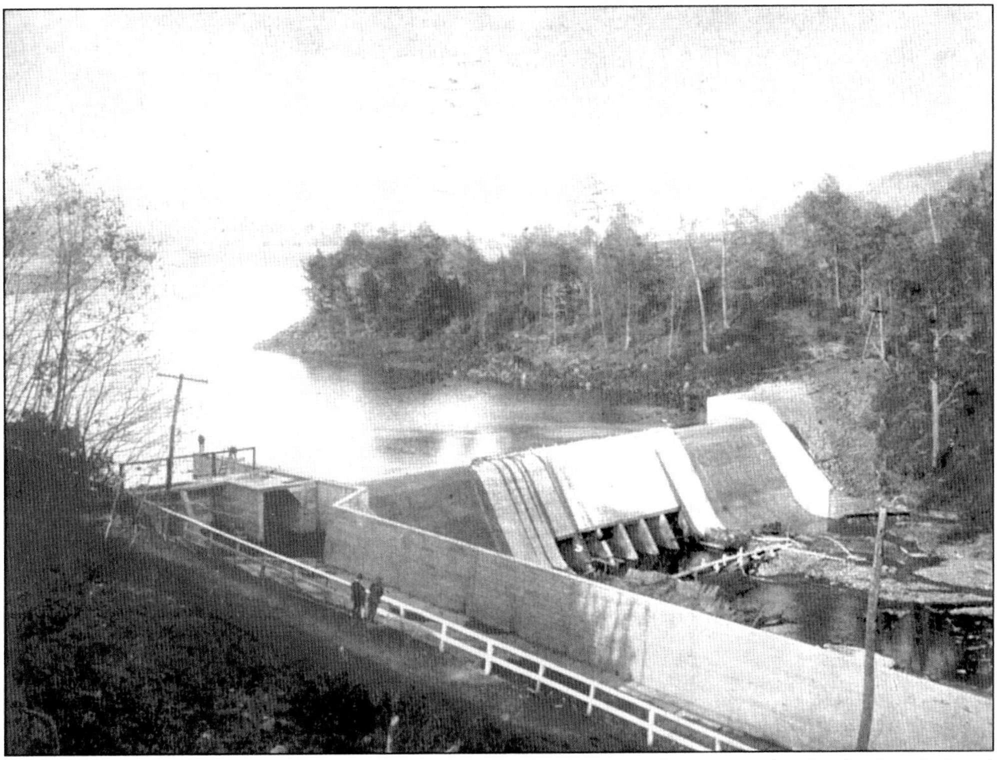

Colliers Dam. This is another view of the dam built in 1908. The waters that backed up behind the dam formed Goodyear Lake. The local people called the area Colliers, named after Isaac Collier, the first settler in the village.

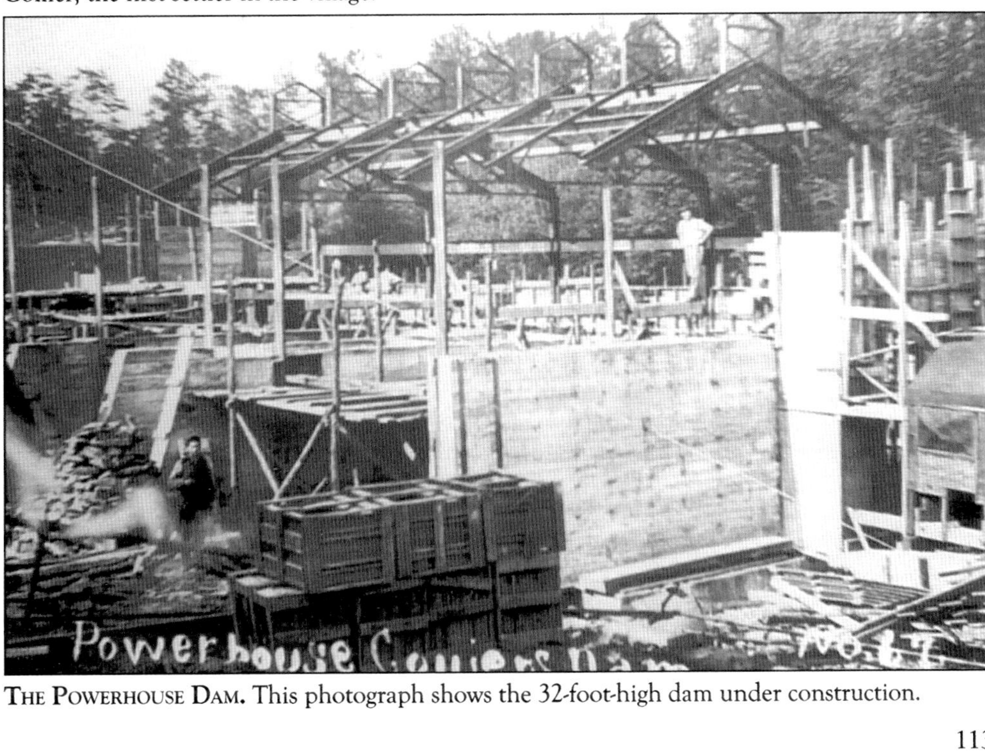

The Powerhouse Dam. This photograph shows the 32-foot-high dam under construction.

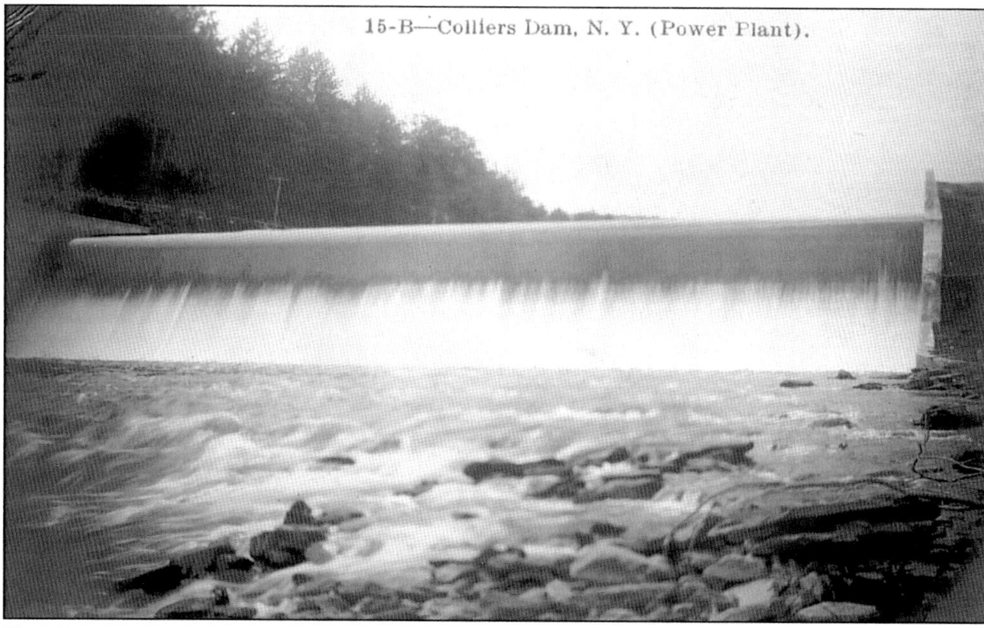

THE COMPLETED DAM. Water pours over the dam of this completed project. This area is rich in history, and one can imagine how it appeared during the American Revolution when many bateaux floated down the river in 1779. General Clinton's army joined General Sullivan in a campaign against the Indians. During the Revolutionary War, Col. Alexander Harper captured a Tory leading a band of Indians who were headed 20 miles south of Oneonta to destroy a settlement. Prisoners were led over the Schohanna Trail and through the Tri Valley to Albany.

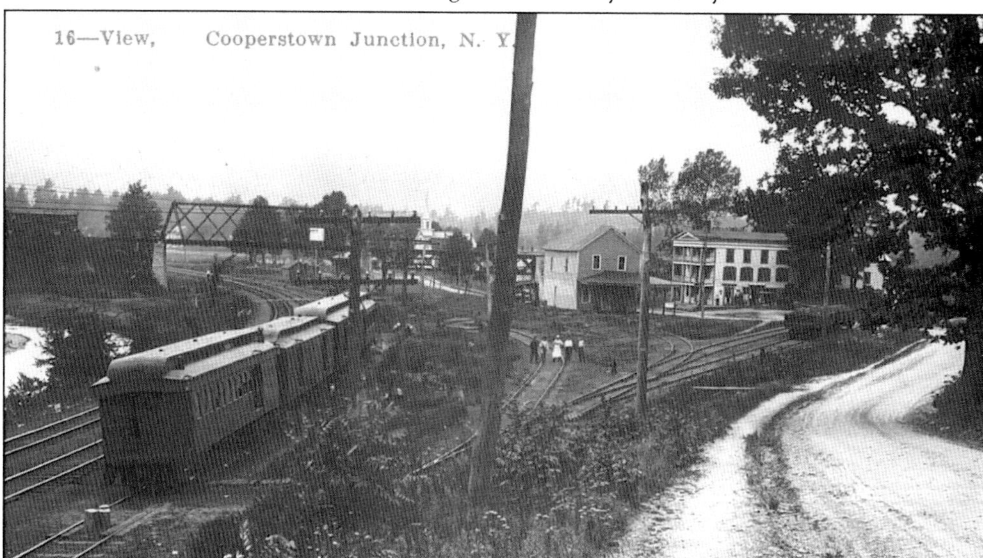

COOPERSTOWN JUNCTION. Not far from Colliersville is the area called Cooperstown Junction. In 1903, the Delaware & Hudson purchased the Cooperstown & Charlotte Valley Railroad, which crossed the Delaware & Hudson tracks at the junction. The dirt road passing under the trestle is now Route 7. The three tracks led from the junction into the Oneonta rail yard. This August 4, 1910 card shows a bustling junction; one train is on the track heading south while another is just passing over the trestle in the distance.

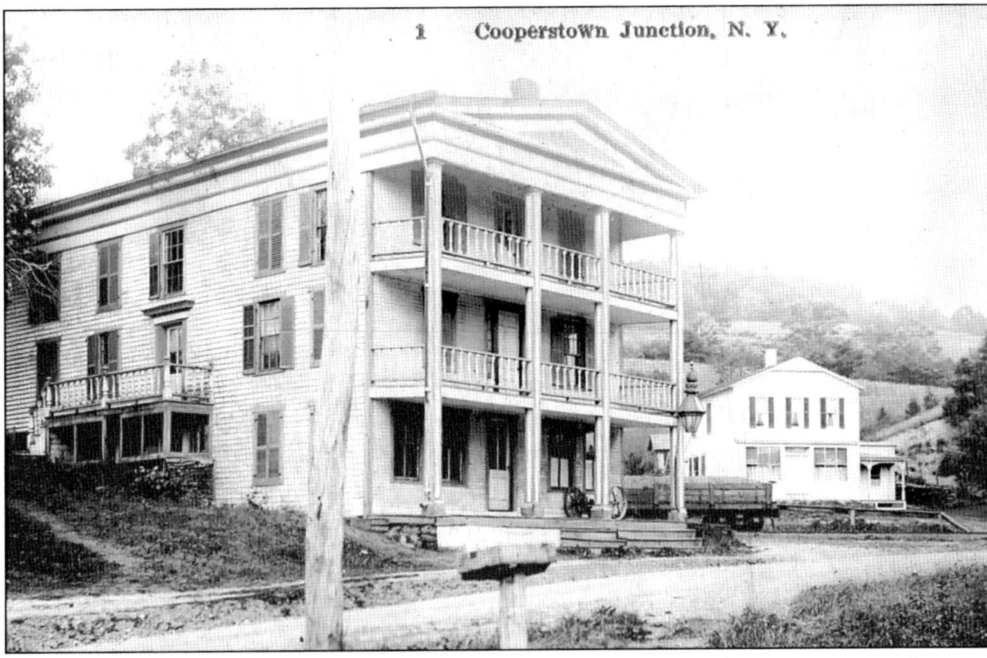

A JUNCTION LANDMARK. This three-story building, once known as the Cooperstown Junction Hotel, was located near the railroad tracks at the junction. The building burned to the ground in 1922. Austin's Auction Barn later replaced it.

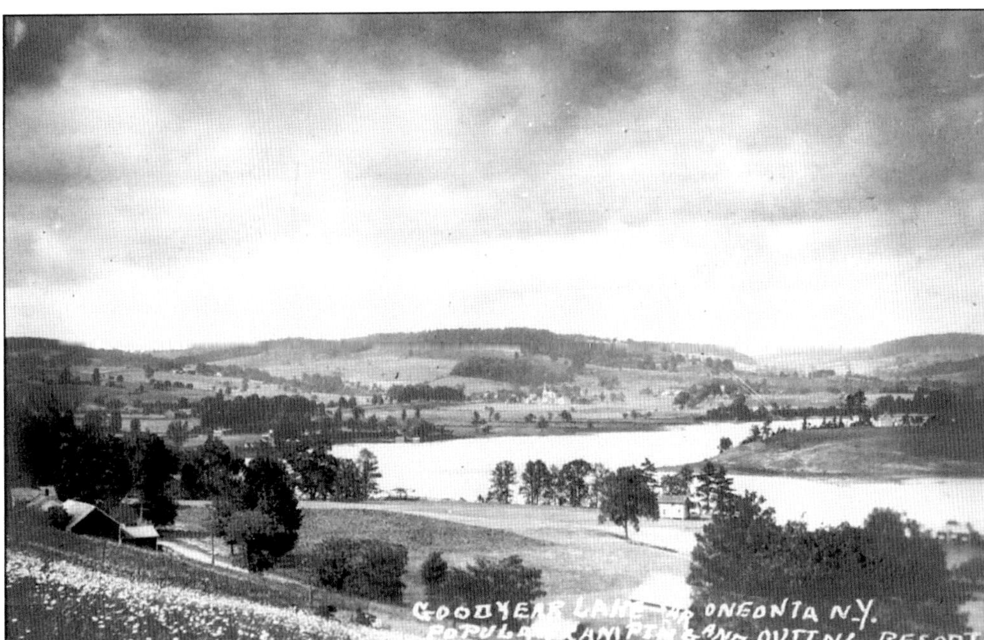

GOODYEAR LAKE. After the construction of the dam, Goodyear Lake was formed. It is a popular camping and fishing spot, and there are many seasonal camps and year-round homes around the lake.

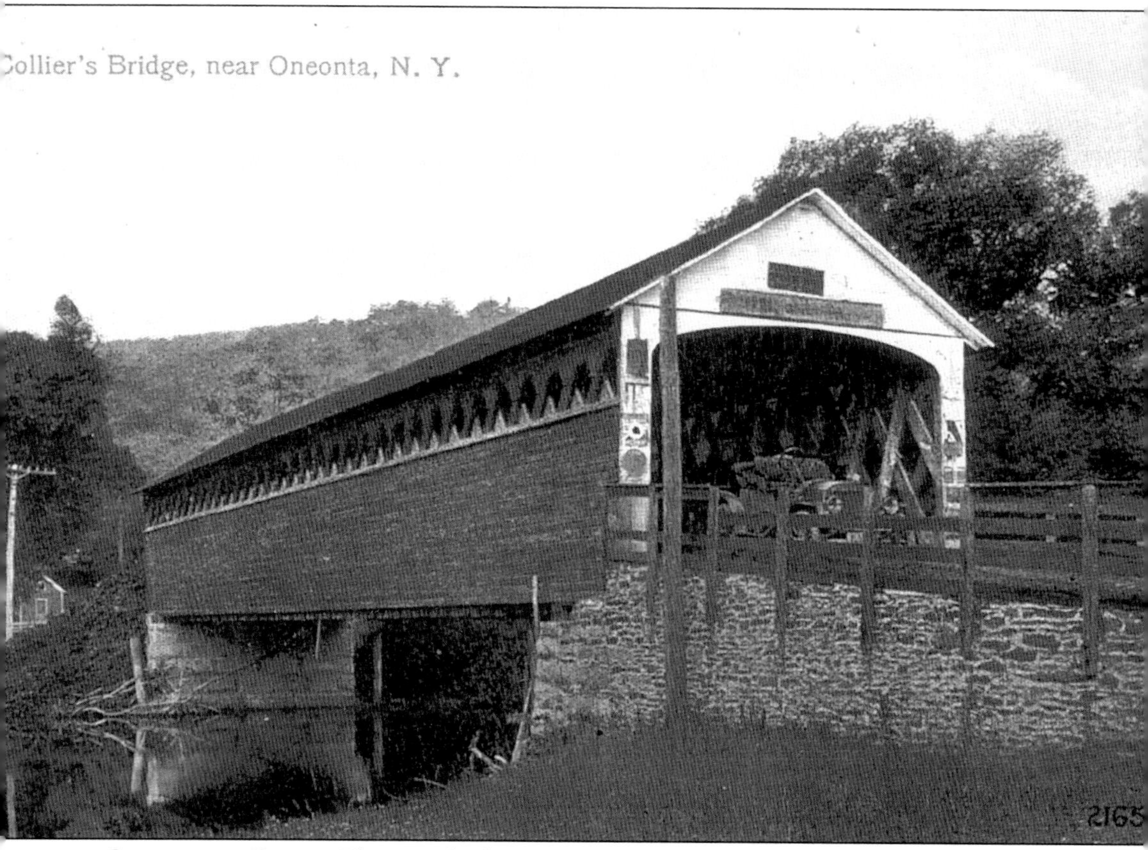

COLLIERSVILLE BRIDGE. This was the last remaining covered bridge over the Susquehanna River in New York State. The span was north of what is now Route 7. The bridge was built in 1832 with native hemlock timbers, which were sawed at the mill on the dam site. The lumber was then drawn to the covered bridge site by a team of oxen. The "up and down" sawmill was owned by Jared Goodyear who, at the time of his death on October 24, 1874, left behind the largest property estate ever accumulated in the county of Otsego up to that time. Goodyear and his father-in-law, Maj. Peter Collier, were instrumental in the settling of this area of Otsego County.

Seven

The Delaware & Hudson: Imprint on History

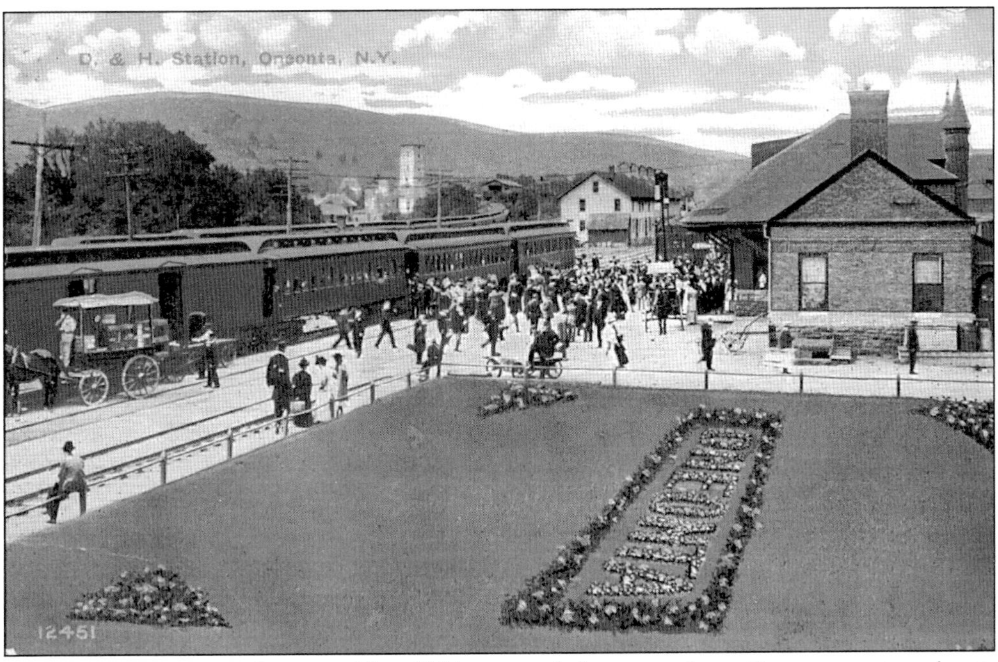

Delaware & Hudson Station. This 1911 postcard features a busy Oneonta station that is decorated with flowers. Great pride always was taken in this station's appearance. The blossoms in the flower bed even spell the city's name. Women disembarking at the station were presented with bouquets of flowers.

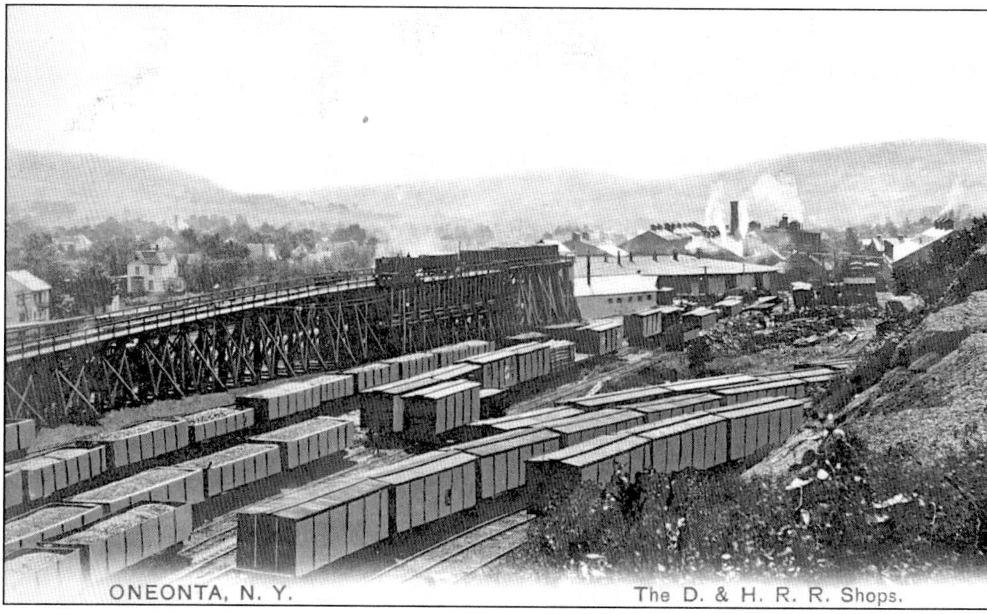

THE DELAWARE & HUDSON SHOPS. The Oneonta rail yard was a bustling hub of activity. The trestle on the left was for unloading coal cars into coal pockets. Sometimes there were more than 400 tons of coal in the cars and chute. In 1946, following a bad fire, the Delaware & Hudson replaced the old wooden structure with an electric coal plant. The roundhouse and smokestacks are visible in the distance. This photograph was taken in the late 1900s.

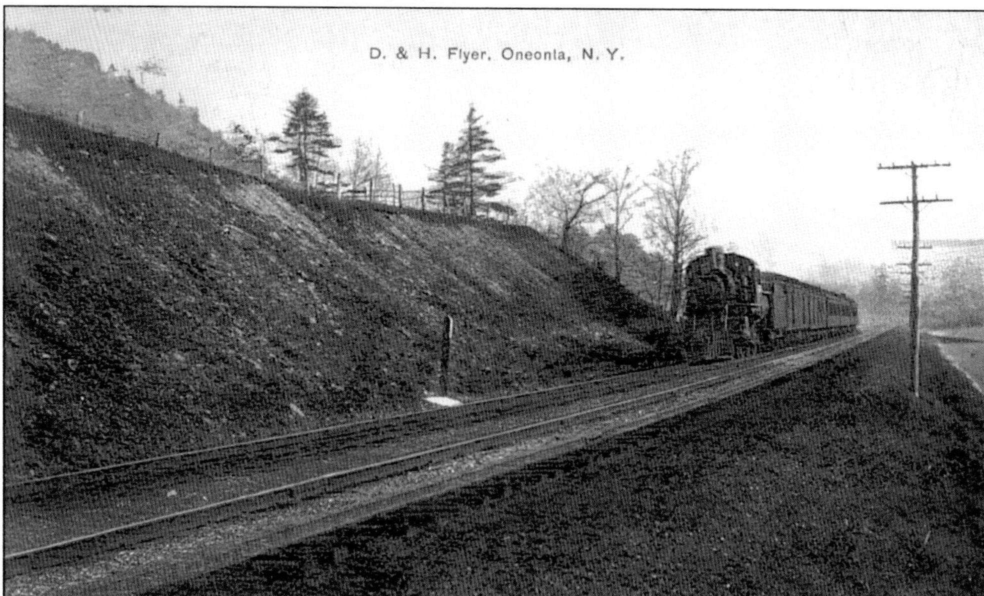

THE DELAWARE & HUDSON FLYER. A fast train whizzing past many of the small stations was able to make a mail pickup without stopping. Mailbags hanging outside stations on a contraption shaped like the letter F were snatched up as the train rolled by and placed inside the mail car. Mail clerks rode the line from Albany to Binghamton and back each day for a week and then had a week off. Replacements took over on the odd weeks. Clerks sorted the mail between stops, memorizing names, cities, and towns.

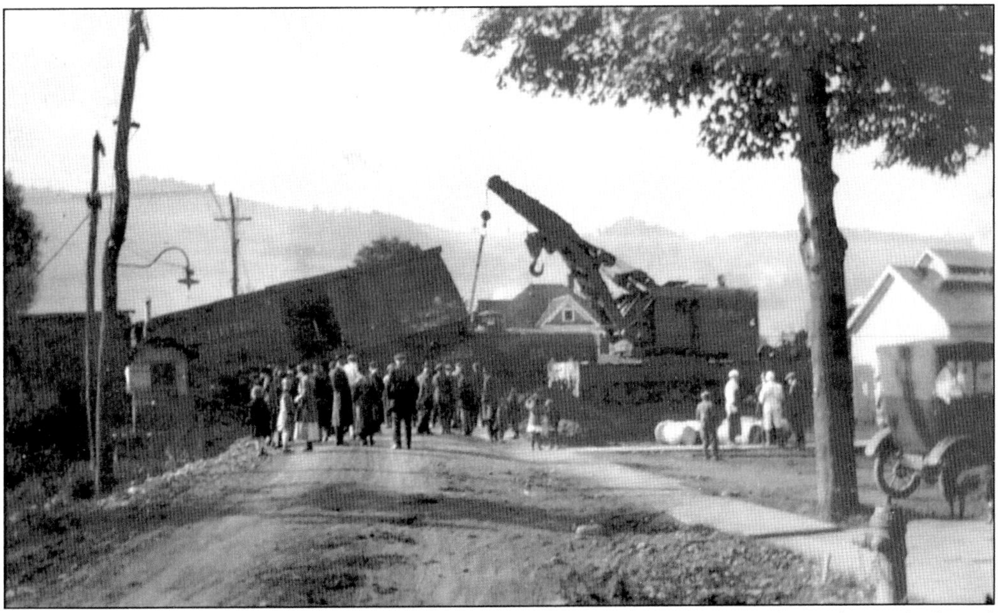

A CROSSING ACCIDENT. An accident at the Worcester railroad crossing in the early 1920s forced the road to be closed for hours. Bystanders picked up cans of sardines after boxes of them spilled during the derailment. Some folks ate sardine sandwiches for weeks after the wreck.

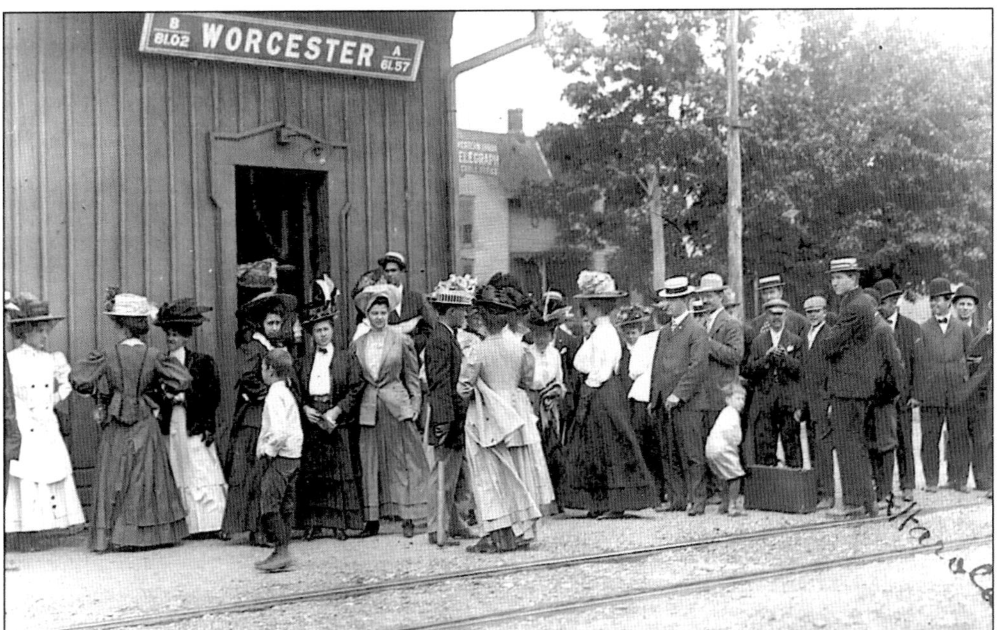

AT THE STATION. Men, women, and children wait in line to purchase train tickets at the Worcester Station for the next eastbound train to Cobleskill to see a baseball game between the local team and Cobleskill. It was common to travel by train in 1909 to see an event and return home later in the day.

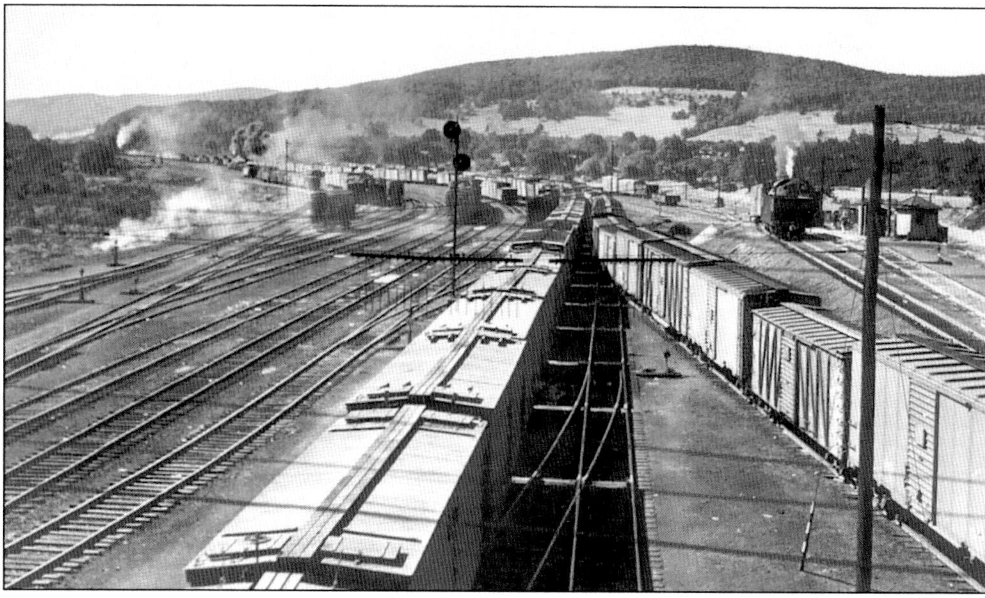

THE DELAWARE & HUDSON YARDS. Miles of track, engines spewing steam, and rows of boxcars all make up the giant rail yard in Oneonta.

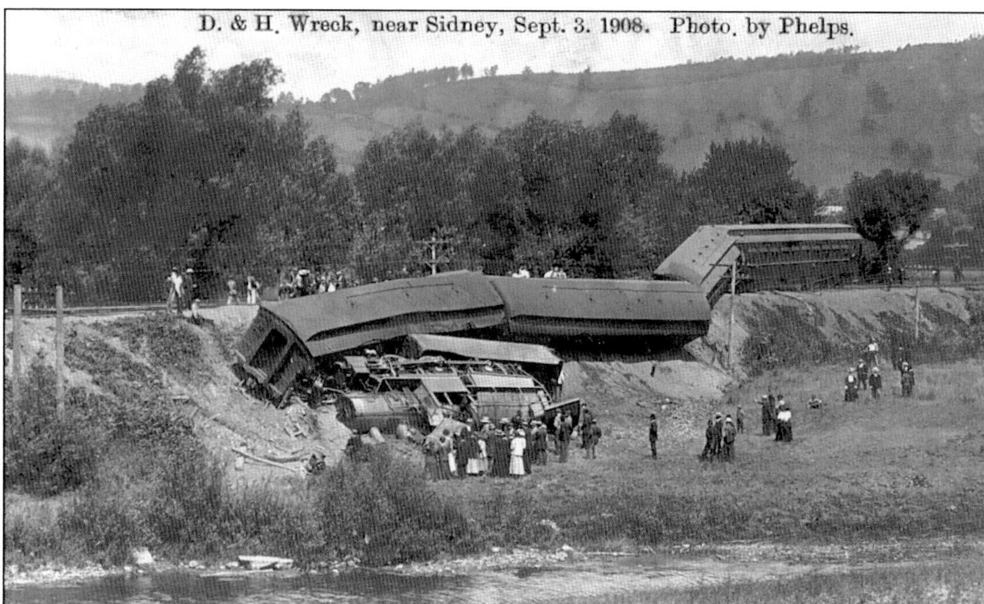

A DELAWARE & HUDSON WRECK. Mother Hubbard Engine No. 500, pulling the train from Albany, did not make it to the bridge outside Sidney, New York, on September 3, 1908. The engine, going 50 miles per hour at a temporary crossover where repairs were being made, went down the embankment, followed by three cars. The battered engine and cars were dragged back to the rails by wrecking crews. The engineer jumped from the train, and the baggage man (although not hurt) was pinned under a lot of baggage.

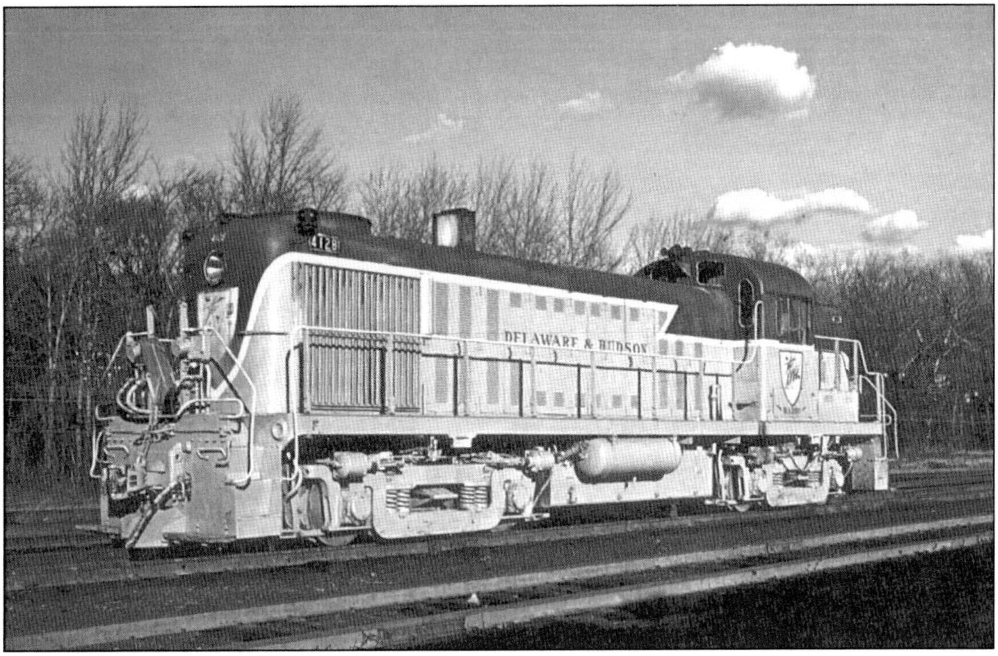

DELAWARE & HUDSON NO. 4128. The Alco road switcher is typical of one of the first generations of diesel engines. The 16,000-horsepower engine was built in August 1953. Jim Shaughnessy took this photograph.

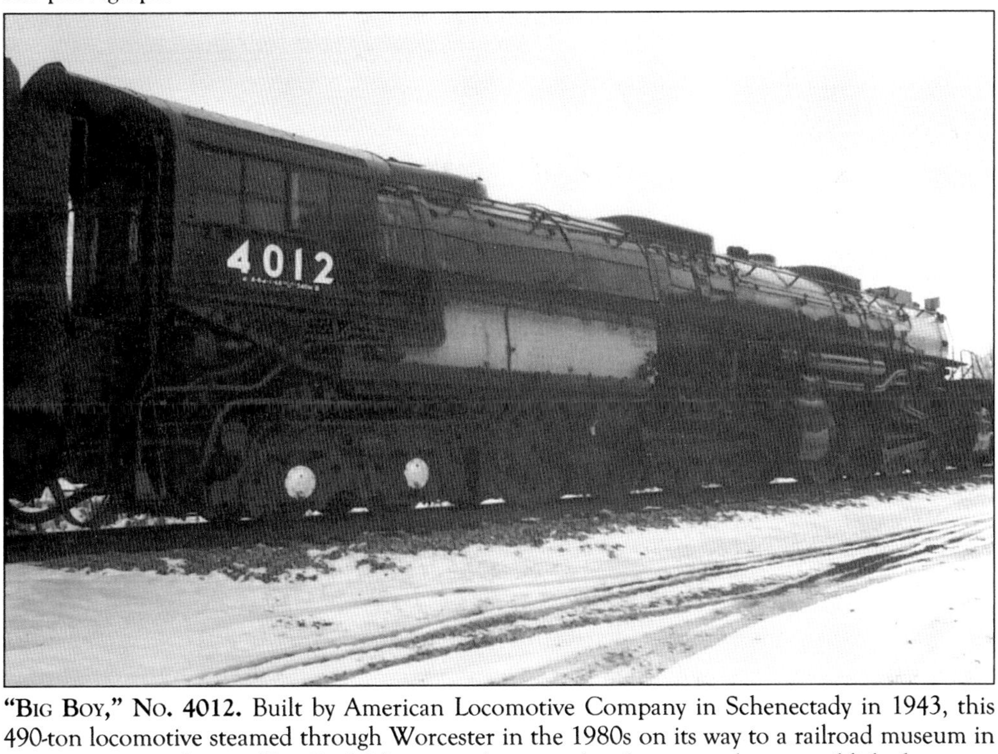

"BIG BOY," NO. 4012. Built by American Locomotive Company in Schenectady in 1943, this 490-ton locomotive steamed through Worcester in the 1980s on its way to a railroad museum in Scranton, Pennsylvania. "Big Boy's" huge combustion chamber, according to published reports, was one of the biggest in the world.

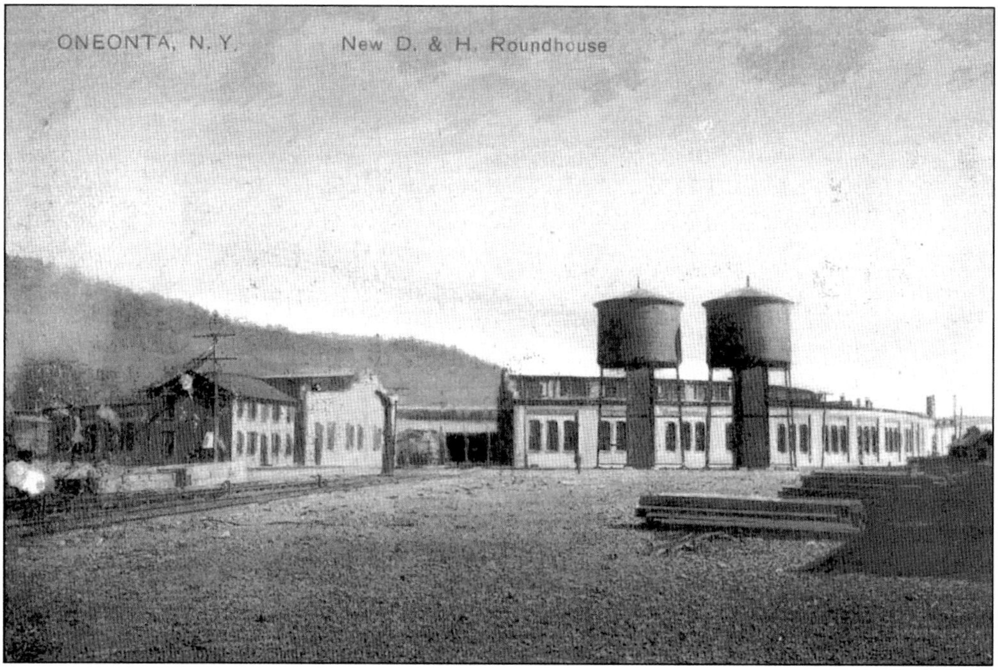

THE DELAWARE & HUDSON ROUNDHOUSE. This postcard features Oneonta's 52-stall roundhouse, built in 1906 and enlarged in 1921.

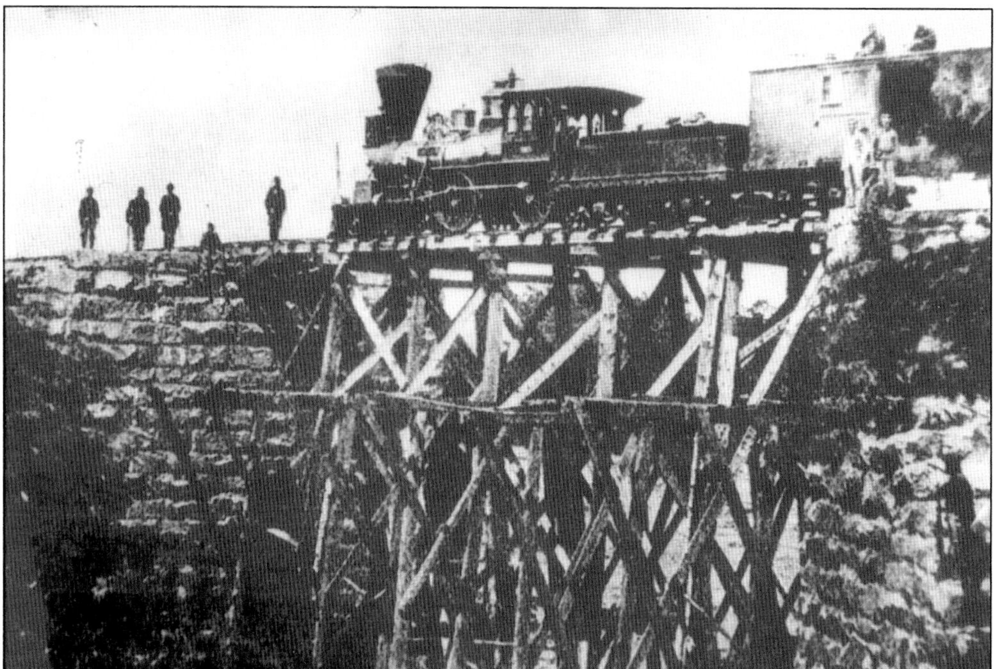

THE MILL STREET TRESTLE. The trestle in Richmondville was built entirely of timbers in the 1860s. This is a scene from the early Albany & Susquehanna Railroad. Civil War Union soldiers guard the bridge as the train goes over.

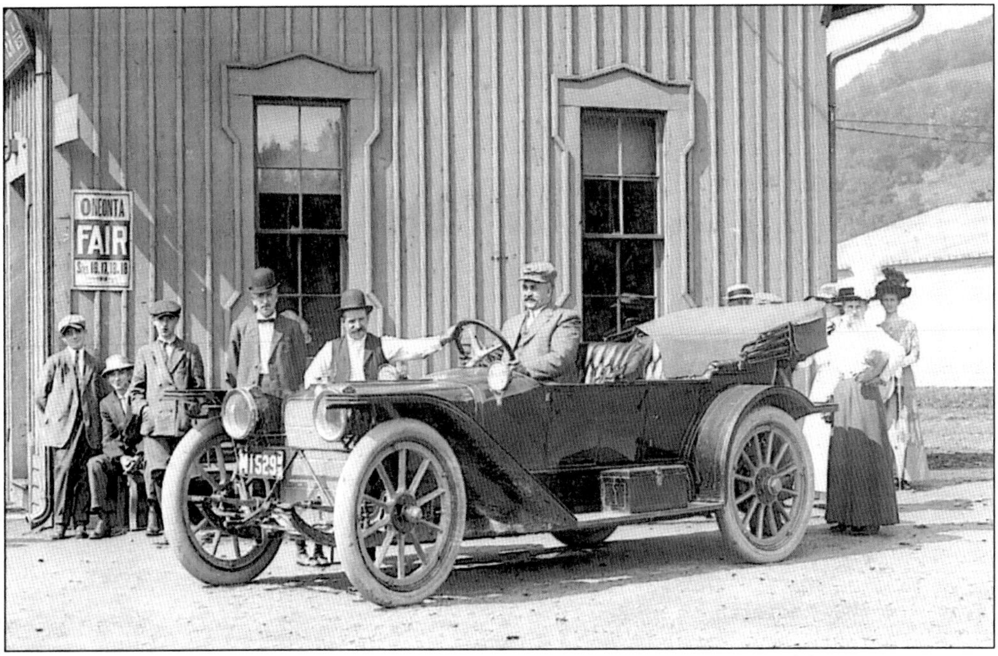

Delaware & Hudson Station, Worcester 1912. Omar Sloat, proprietor of the Worcester Inn, shows his new Buick to people waiting at the Delaware & Hudson station. From left to right are Fred Cannistra, Everett Galer, Ben Borst, Herman Judd, and A. Cannistra. Jennie Campbell and Mrs. Judd stand behind the vehicle. Note the poster advertising the Oneonta Fair tacked to the side of the station.

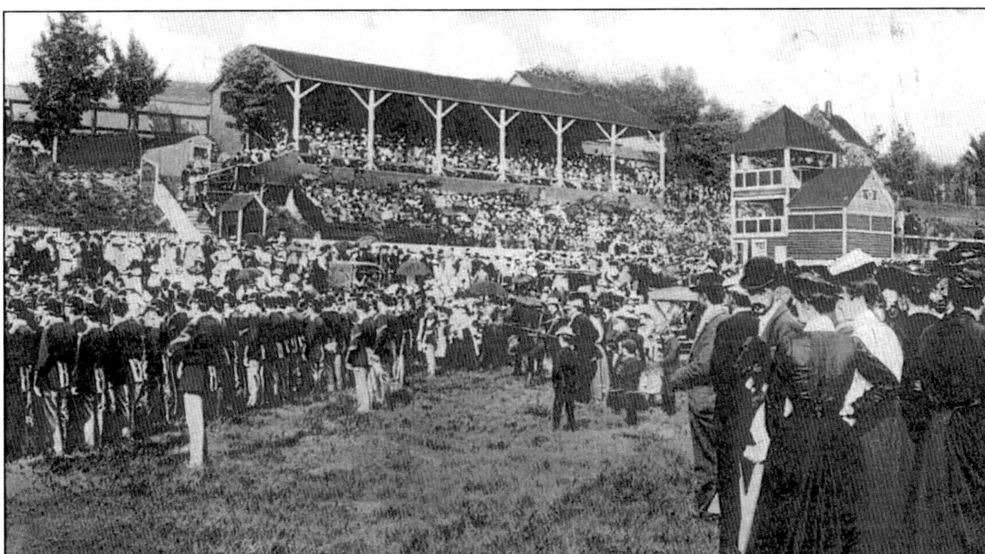

The Oneonta Fair. Crowds came by the thousands to the fair via the Delaware & Hudson Railroad. Special trains ran from the Albany, Troy, and Schenectady areas, bringing people from the cities and small towns along the way. The first fair was in 1874, and the last exhibition was in 1926. The fair, which occupied the area now known as Belmont Circle, was the event of the year for Otsego residents. Sometimes, as many as 30,000 people packed the fairgrounds on a special day.

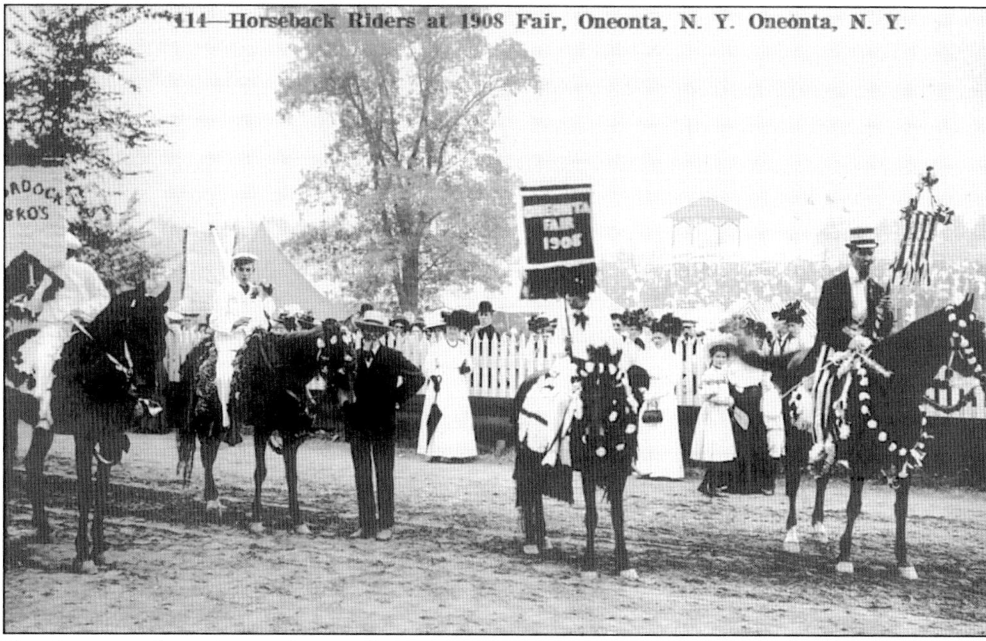

The Oneonta Fair. A special act at the Oneonta Fair in 1908 was the Burdock Brothers and their decorated horses. This Oneonta Department Store postcard shows women dressed in long gowns and wearing large hats.

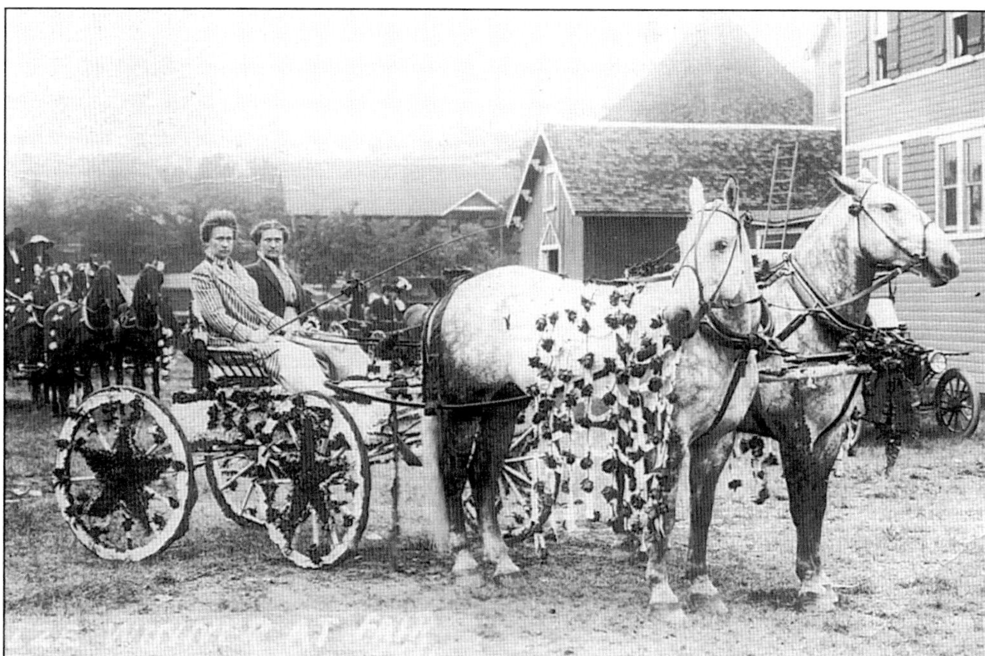

The Fair of 1913. The Oneonta Fair of 1913 was another successful September event. The fair usually took place the week after the New York State Fair. These horses and the rig the women are riding in are adorned with paper carnations.

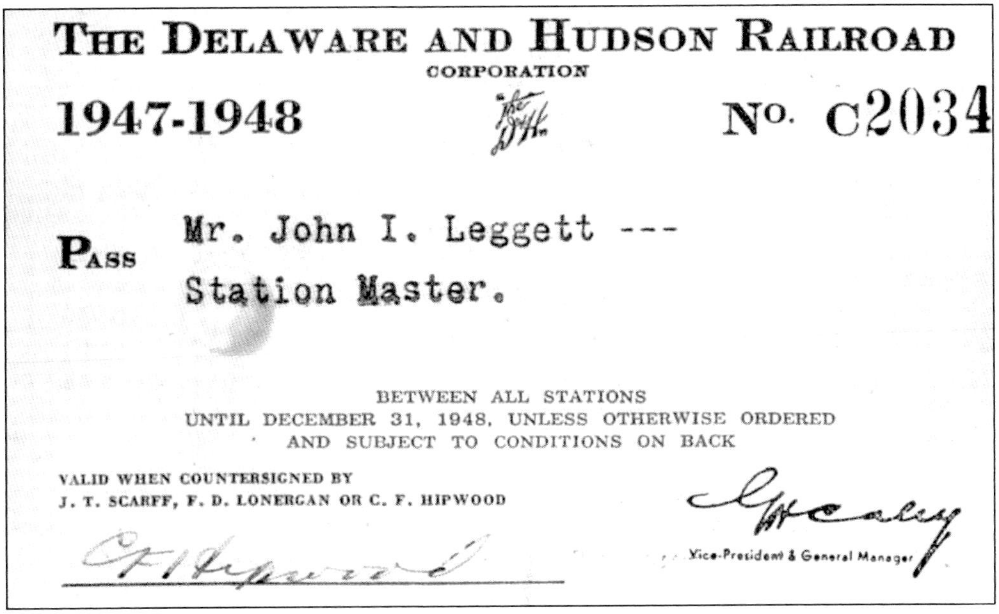
THE DELAWARE AND HUDSON RAILROAD

CORPORATION

1947-1948 No. C2034

PASS Mr. John I. Leggett ---

Station Master.

BETWEEN ALL STATIONS
UNTIL DECEMBER 31, 1948, UNLESS OTHERWISE ORDERED
AND SUBJECT TO CONDITIONS ON BACK

VALID WHEN COUNTERSIGNED BY
J. T. SCARFF, F. D. LONERGAN OR C. F. HIPWOOD

Vice-President & General Manager

A RAILROAD PASS. This 1947–1948 Delaware & Hudson pass was issued to stationmaster John I. Leggett. The reverse side of the pass states that it is not transferable and not good on trains 9 and 10.

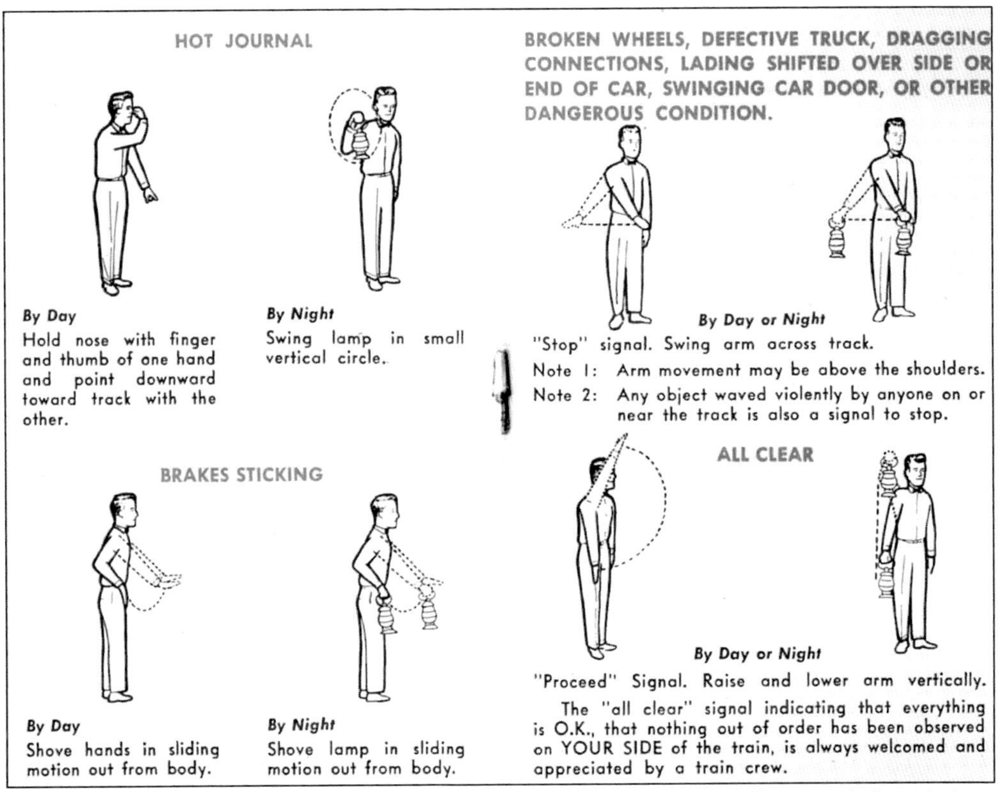

HAND SIGNALS. The Delaware & Hudson printed a small booklet titled "A Knowledge of These Railroad Hand Signals May Help You to Prevent an Accident."

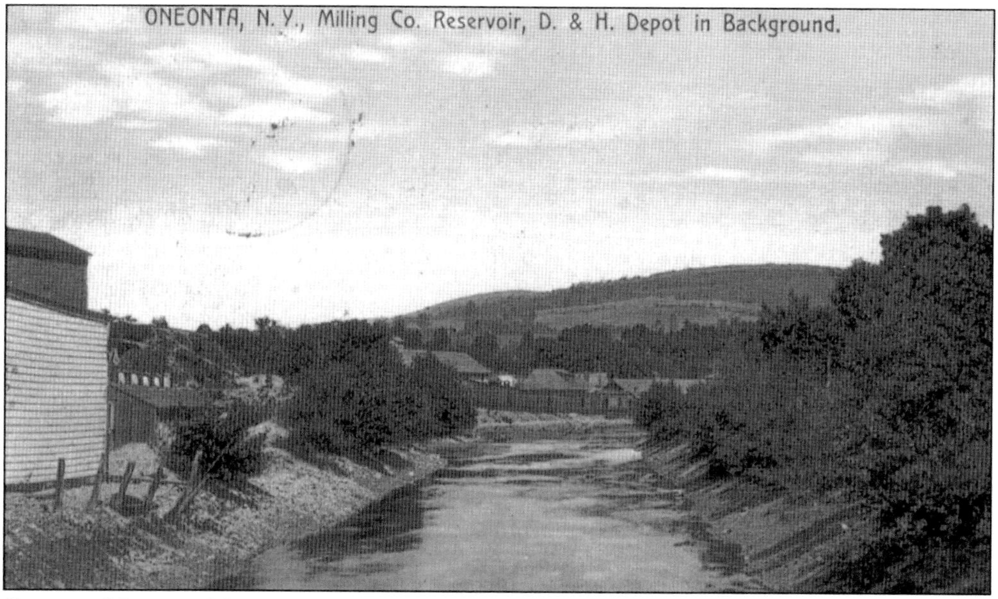

ONEONTA MILLING. Sabotage in Oneonta in 1918 was uncovered when three German spies were caught and sent to jail. A milling company employee found a loaded shotgun shell in the grinding machine hopper after a German immigrant had gone home early. A man working in the Delaware & Hudson yards gained information on troop movement and war supply shipments. He was later discovered to be a lieutenant in the kaiser's army. A third man, later found to be a German major and the paymaster, also worked locally.

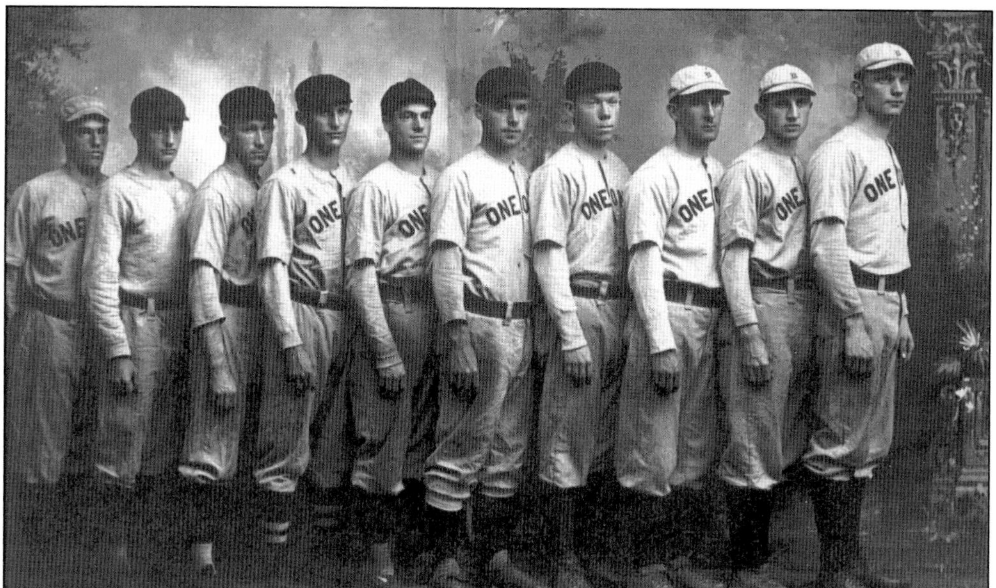

OLD-TIME BASEBALL. Most of the communities surrounding Oneonta had baseball teams composed of college boys. Oneonta's team featured Brown University students. In 1915, team members rode the Delaware & Hudson to get to neighboring towns to play ball. From left to right are Reggie Nash, ? Ayres, ? McGurty, Chic Raymond, Ken Nash, ? Orcutt, ? Raleigh, ? Bliss, ? Snell, and Art Staff.

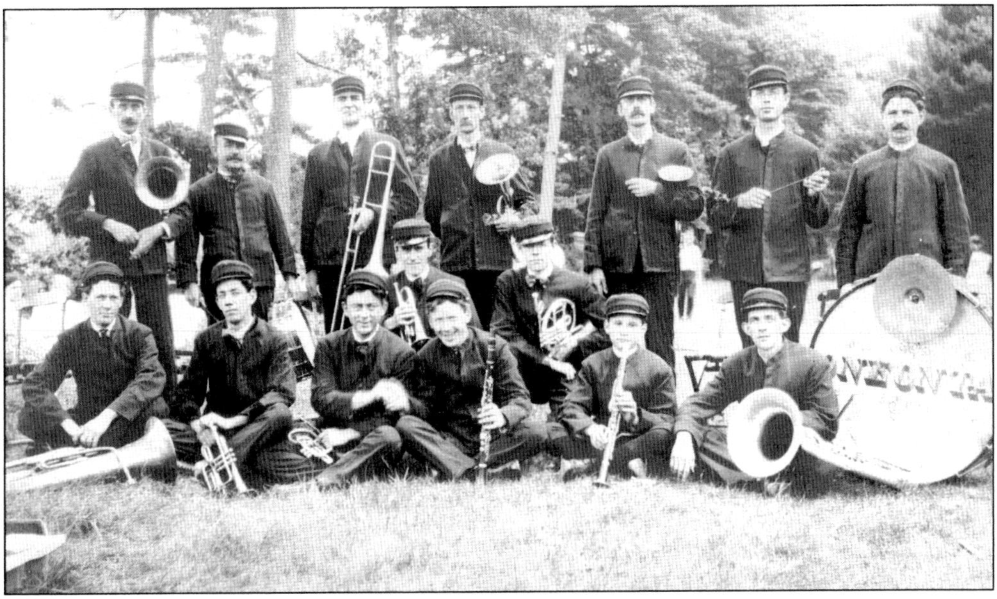

THE ONEONTA CITY BAND. Members of the band pose with their instruments in one of the local parks. The band played at parades and other functions. On Armistice Day 1918, the Oneonta City Band was on the streets early and played in dozens of impromptu concerts.

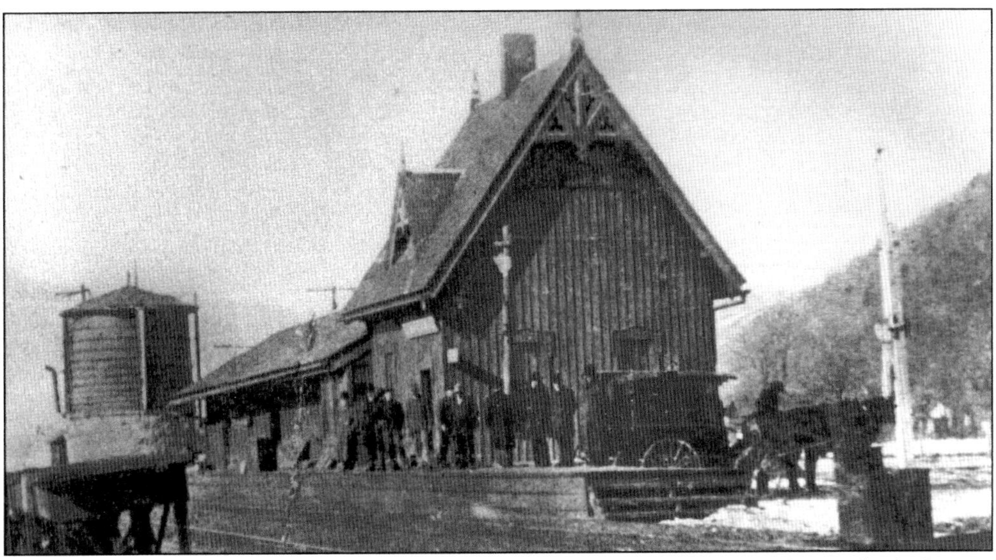

WATER TOWER. The importance of water in the days of steam engines cannot be overlooked. Most stations were equipped with a water tower like this one at the Worcester Station. Water in the tanks had to be treated to minimize foaming and to remove impurities.

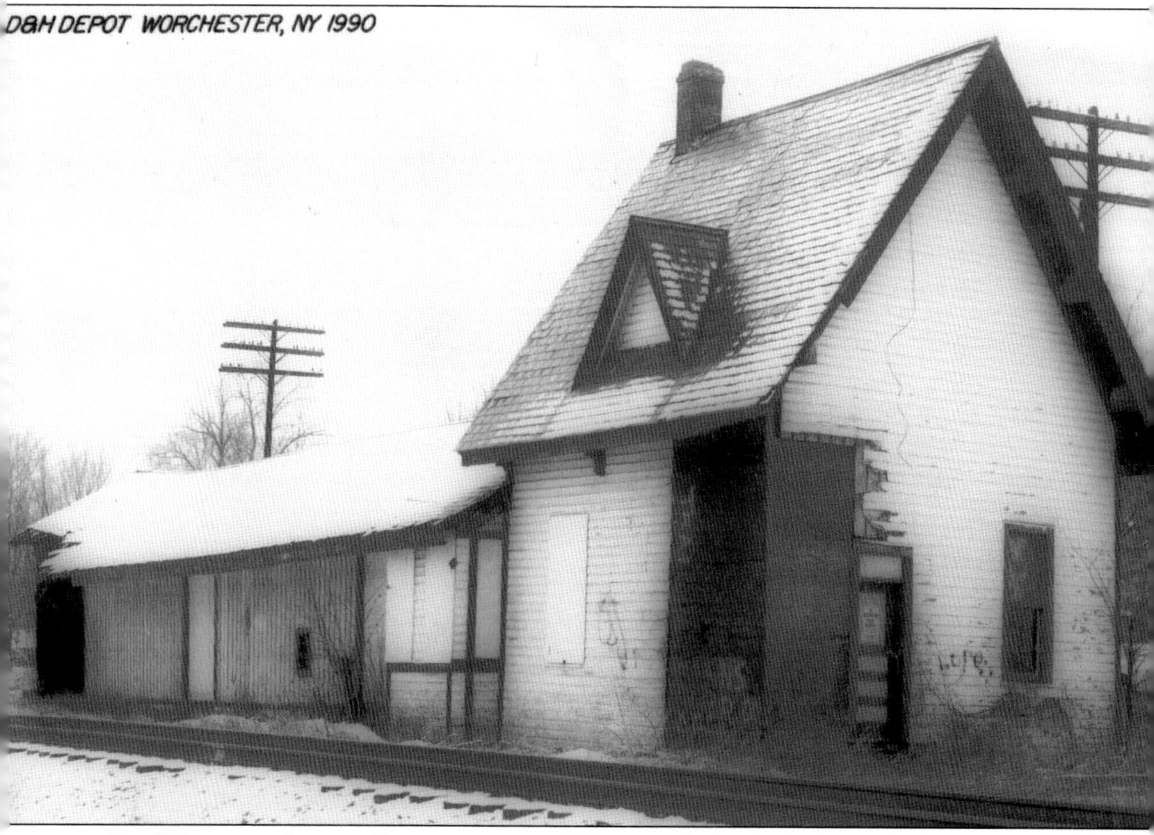

THE WORCESTER STATION. Born into an era of change and growth, the Worcester Station grew and developed from the last few decades of the 19th century into the first half of the 20th century. Built in a Victorian style—embellished with gingerbread, brackets, and slate roof—the station was useful and necessary. When local passenger service ceased, the station began to age, lose its usefulness, and its beauty slowly faded. Derailments took their toll; the roof had to be patched, and a front corner was boarded up. Slowly the station deteriorated beyond repair. Could it have been preserved as a historical landmark? Yes. However, the wheels were already in motion and the decision was made to tear it down. The Worcester Station died in the summer of 1999. Sadly, all that remains is a vacant lot next to the tracks.